THE HANDY SUPREME COURT ANSWER BOOK

The History and Issues Explained

About the Author

David L. Hudson, Jr., J.D., teaches Constitutional Law, First Amendment, and Bar Exam Workshop Classes at Belmont Law School. He has also previously taught classes at the Nashville School of Law and Vanderbilt Law School. In June 2018, the Nashville School of Law awarded him its Distinguished Faculty Award. He speaks widely on Constitutional Law and school law issues around the country. For 17 years, he was an attorney and scholar at the First Amendment Center in Nashville, Tennessee, and he served as a senior law clerk for the Tennessee Supreme Court. He earned his undergraduate degree from Duke University and his law degree from Vanderbilt Law School. He is an author, co-author, or co-editor of more than 50 books, including Visible Ink Press's *The Constitution Explained, The Handy American History Answer Book, The Handy Law Answer Book,* and *The Handy Presidents Answer Book,* 2nd edition.

THE HANDY SUPREME COURT ANSWER BOOK

SECOND EDITION

THE HISTORY AND ISSUES EXPLAINED

David L. Hudson, Jr., J.D.

Detroit

Visible Ink Press®
43311 Joy Rd., #414
Canton, MI 48187-2075

Visible Ink Press is a registered trademark of Visible Ink Press LLC.

Most Visible Ink Press books are available at special quantity discounts when purchased in bulk by corporations, organizations, or groups. Customized printings, special imprints, messages, and excerpts can be produced to meet your needs. For more information, contact Special Markets Director, Visible Ink Press, www.visibleink.com, or 734-667-3211.

Managing Editor: Kevin S. Hile
Cover Design: Mary Claire Krzewinski
Page Design: Alessandro Cinelli, Cinelli Design
Typesetting: Marco Divita
Proofreaders: Christa Gainor and Shoshana Hurwitz
Indexer: Larry Baker

Cover images: Shutterstock.

ISBN: 978-1-57859-782-6 (paperback)
ISBN: 978-1-57859-824-3 (ebook)
ISBN: 978-1-57859-823-6 (hardbound)

Cataloging-in-Publication Data is on file at the Library of Congress.

Printed in the United States of America.

10 9 8 7 6 5 4 3 2 1

Dedication

To the titans of civic education and my dear friends Sue Leeson, Mike Miles, Joe Stewart, and Lindsey Draper.

Also from Visible Ink Press

The Handy Accounting Answer Book
by Amber Gray, Ph.D.
ISBN: 978-1-57859-675-1

The Handy African American History Answer Book
by Jessie Carnie Smith
ISBN: 978-1-57859-452-8

The Handy American Government Answer Book: How Washington, Politics, and Elections Work
by Gina Misiroglu
ISBN: 978-1-57859-639-3

The Handy American History Answer Book
by David L. Hudson Jr.
ISBN: 978-1-57859-471-9

The Handy Anatomy Answer Book, 2nd edition
by Patricia Barnes-Svarney and Thomas E. Svarney
ISBN: 978-1-57859-542-6

The Handy Answer Book for Kids (and Parents), 2nd edition
by Gina Misiroglu
ISBN: 978-1-57859-219-7

The Handy Armed Forces Answer Book
by Richard Estep
ISBN: 978-1-57859-743-7

The Handy Art History Answer Book
by Madelynn Dickerson
ISBN: 978-1-57859-417-7

The Handy Astronomy Answer Book, 3rd edition
by Charles Liu, Ph.D.
ISBN: 978-1-57859-419-1

The Handy Bible Answer Book
by Jennifer Rebecca Prince
ISBN: 978-1-57859-478-8

The Handy Biology Answer Book, 2nd edition
by Patricia Barnes Svarney and Thomas E. Svarney
ISBN: 978-1-57859-490-0

The Handy Boston Answer Book
by Samuel Willard Crompton
ISBN: 978-1-57859-593-8

The Handy California Answer Book
by Kevin S. Hile
ISBN: 978-1-57859-591-4

The Handy Chemistry Answer Book
by Ian C. Stewart and Justin P. Lamont
ISBN: 978-1-57859-374-3

The Handy Christianity Answer Book
by Steve Werner
ISBN: 978-1-57859-686-7

The Handy Civil War Answer Book
by Samuel Willard Crompton
ISBN: 978-1-57859-476-4

The Handy Communication Answer Book
by Lauren Sergy
ISBN: 978-1-57859-587-7

The Handy Diabetes Answer Book
by Patricia Barnes-Svarney and Thomas E. Svarney
ISBN: 978-1-57859-597-6

The Handy Dinosaur Answer Book, 2nd edition
by Patricia Barnes-Svarney and Thomas E. Svarney
ISBN: 978-1-57859-218-0

The Handy Engineering Answer Book
by DeLean Tolbert Smith, Ph.D.; Aishwary Pawar; Nicole P Pitterson, Ph.D.; and Debra-Ann C Butler, Ph.D.
ISBN: 978-1-57859-770-3

The Handy English Grammar Answer Book
by Christine A. Hult, Ph.D.
ISBN: 978-1-57859-520-4

The Handy Forensic Science Answer Book: Reading Clues at the Crime Scene, Crime Lab, and in Court
by Patricia Barnes-Svarney and Thomas E. Svarney
ISBN: 978-1-57859-621-8

The Handy Geography Answer Book, 3rd edition
by Paul A. Tucci
ISBN: 978-1-57859-576-1

The Handy Geology Answer Book
by Patricia Barnes-Svarney and Thomas E. Svarney
ISBN: 978-1-57859-156-5

The Handy History Answer Book: From the Stone Age to the Digital Age, 4th edition
by Stephen A. Werner, Ph.D.
ISBN: 978-1-57859-680-5

The Handy Hockey Answer Book
by Stan Fischler
ISBN: 978-1-57859-513-6

The Handy Investing Answer Book
by Paul A. Tucci
ISBN: 978-1-57859-486-3

The Handy Islam Answer Book
by John Renard, Ph.D.
ISBN: 978-1-57859-510-5

The Handy Law Answer Book
by David L. Hudson, Jr., J.D.
ISBN: 978-1-57859-217-3

The Handy Literature Answer Book
by Daniel S. Burt and Deborah G. Felder
ISBN: 978-1-57859-635-5

The Handy Math Answer Book, 2nd edition
by Patricia Barnes-Svarney and Thomas E. Svarney
ISBN: 978-1-57859-373-6

The Handy Military History Answer Book
by Samuel Willard Crompton
ISBN: 978-1-57859-509-9

The Handy Mythology Answer Book
by David A. Leeming, Ph.D.
ISBN: 978-1-57859-475-7

The Handy New York City Answer Book
by Chris Barsanti
ISBN: 978-1-57859-586-0

The Handy Nutrition Answer Book
by Patricia Barnes-Svarney and Thomas E. Svarney
ISBN: 978-1-57859-484-9

The Handy Ocean Answer Book
by Patricia Barnes-Svarney and Thomas E. Svarney
ISBN: 978-1-57859-063-6

The Handy Pennsylvania Answer Book
by Lawrence W. Baker
ISBN: 978-1-57859-610-2

The Handy Personal Finance Answer Book
by Paul A. Tucci
ISBN: 978-1-57859-322-4

The Handy Philosophy Answer Book
by Naomi Zack, Ph.D.
ISBN: 978-1-57859-226-5

The Handy Physics Answer Book, 3rd edition
By Charles Liu, Ph.D.
ISBN: 978-1-57859-695-9

The Handy Presidents Answer Book, 2nd edition
by David L. Hudson
ISB N: 978-1-57859-317-0

The Handy Psychology Answer Book, 2nd edition
by Lisa J. Cohen, Ph.D.
ISBN: 978-1-57859-508-2

The Handy Religion Answer Book, 2nd edition
by John Renard, Ph.D.
ISBN: 978-1-57859-379-8

The Handy Science Answer Book, 5th edition
by The Carnegie Library of Pittsburgh
ISBN: 978-1-57859-691-1

The Handy State-by-State Answer Book: Faces, Places, and Famous Dates for All Fifty States
by Samuel Willard Crompton
ISBN: 978-1-57859-565-5

The Handy Supreme Court Answer Book
by David L Hudson, Jr.
ISBN: 978-1-57859-196-1

The Handy Technology Answer Book
by Naomi E. Balaban and James Bobick
ISBN: 978-1-57859-563-1

The Handy Texas Answer Book
by James L. Haley
ISBN: 978-1-57859-634-8

The Handy Weather Answer Book, 2nd edition
by Kevin S. Hile
ISBN: 978-1-57859-221-0

The Handy Western Philosophy Answer Book: The Ancient Greek Influence on Modern Understanding
by Ed D'Angelo, Ph.D.
ISBN: 978-1-57859-556-3

The Handy Wisconsin Answer Book
by Terri Schlichenmeyer and Mark Meier
ISBN: 978-1-57859-661-4

Please visit the "Handy Answers" series website at www.handyanswers.com.

Photo Sources

APN Photography: p. 310.
John Black: p. 227.
BNP Design Studio: p. 230.
Bonnie (Wikicommons): p. 190.
Brown Alumni Magazine: p. 175.
Darlene Wagner Butler: p. 270.
Cbaile19 (Wikicommons): p. 237.
Chensiyuan (Wikicommons): p. 379.
Couperfield (Shutterstock): p. 272.
Tom DeCicco: p. 244.
Doubleday, Page and Company: p. 59.
Dobrunov Nichita Alex: p. 317.
Everett Collection (Shutterstock): p. 303.
Executive Office of the President of the United States: pp. 129, 162, 166.
Bill Fitz-Patrick, White House Photographer: p. 111.
Florida Memory Project: p. 210.
Frypie (Wikicommons): p. 26.
Lynn Gilbert: p. 122.
Harris & Ewing photography: p. 145.
Henry Salem Hubbell: p. 38.
Infrogmation (Wikicommons): p. 116.
Inner Temple Library, London, England: p. 15.
Ben Jacobson: p. 246.
R. Michael Jenkins: p. 160.
Joint Congressional Committee on Inaugural Ceremonies: p. 42.
Jordanuhl7 (Wikicommons): p. 386.
Greg Kelton: p. 219.
Stephanie Kenner: p. 342.
Patrick Leahy, U.S. Senate staffer: p. 156.

Library of Congress Prints and Photographs Division: pp. 65, 79, 86, 89, 95, 153, 179, 194, 207, 263, 283, 296, 307, 314, 332, 359, 373, 377, 382, 393, 399.
Little, Brown and Company: p. 61.
Missouri History Museum: p. 293.
Monkey Business Images: p. 256.
Yash Mori: p. 133.
Paul Morse, the White House: pp. 141, 346.
National Library of France: p. 277.
National Museum of American History: p. 54.
National Portrait Gallery of Eminent Americans: p. 50.
National Portrait Gallery, Smithsonian Institution: p. 279.
New York World-Telegram and Sun: pp. 72, 105.
Olga Nikonova: p. 187.
Yoichi R. Okamoto: p. 102.
Sean Pavone: p. 351.
Steve Petteway, U.S. Supreme Court: p. 119.
Philosophicalswag (Wikicommons): p. 12.
Stephen Rees: p. 235.
RG72 (Wikicommons): p. 222.
Richard Nixon Presidential Library and Museum: p. 8.
Michael Rivera: p. 225.
Sanfranman59 (Wikicommons): p. 19.
Fred Schilling, Collection of the Supreme Court of the United States: p. 45.
Joel Seidenstein: p. 213.
Shutterstock: p. 317.
Gage Skidmore: p. 354.
TWStock: p. 362.
U.S. Army: p. 35.
U.S. Capitol Collection: p. 368.
U.S. Department of Justice: p. 312.
U.S. National Archives and Records Administration: pp. 82, 98, 125, 201, 397.
U.S. News & World Report: p. 322.
U.S. Senate Committee on the Judiciary: p. 32.
U.S. Supreme Court: pp. 29, 184, 252, 338.
Ben Von Klemperer: p. 335.
Julia von Siebenthal: p. 197.
White House Historical Association: p. 4.
White House Photographic Collection: pp. 240, 285.
Zimmytws (Shutterstock): p. 258.
Public Domain: pp. 22, 68, 77, 109, 150, 172, 204, 266, 290, 301, 327, 356, 389.

Table of Contents

Acknowledgments

I would like to thank Roger Jänecke of Visible Ink Press for giving me the opportunity and platform to write the second edition of this book. My association with Visible Ink Press has given me the chance to write about many subjects I love, and the U.S. Supreme Court is at the top of the list. I would also like to thank editor Kevin Hile, who improved the text with his editing prowess.

In my career, I had the privilege of serving as a judicial law clerk for two jurists: former trial court in Davidson County, Tennessee, Judge Marietta Shipley and Tennessee Supreme Court Justice Sharon G. Lee. Judge Shipley gave me my first full-time legal job out of law school, and for that I remain grateful. Justice Lee, a judicial exemplar and a great dissenter, has a great work ethic. I'd also like to thank Tennessee Court of Appeals Judge Jeffrey Usman, Juvenile Court Judge Sheila Calloway (who helped get me through law school), California Judge Rupert Byrdsong, and former criminal court jurist Mark Fishburn. I consider them all close personal friends.

I have had the privilege of teaching at three laws schools: the Nashville School of Law, my alma mater Vanderbilt Law School, and Belmont Law School. Currently, I am a full-time professor at Belmont. I would like to thank Dean Alberto Gonzales for his leadership and support. I also would like to thank all my colleagues at Belmont Law School. I am fortunate to be a member of this fine faculty.

I would like to thank my wife, Carla Hudson, for her unwavering love and support, and my parents, Carol and Dave Hudson, for educating and taking care of me.

I'd also like to thank all of my students through the years at Southeastern Paralegal Institute, Kaplan; Middle Tennessee State University; the Nashville School of Law; Vanderbilt Law School; and of course, Belmont Law School.

I did want to give a special shout out to Zach Lambert, Jacob Glenn, Daniel Horwitz, J. T. Conway, Bill Spaniard, Ken Dyer, Bill "Watauga Compact" Edwards, Div Gopal, Philip Clark, Paul Marsh, Jamie and Jordan Thomason, John Creson, Tim Horne, Chris Rogers, Barrett Rich, Mary Alice Carfi, Robert Dalton, Michael Auffinger, and the incomparable Brian Horowitz.

Introduction

Abortion, affirmative action, capital punishment, medicinal use of marijuana, religious freedom, presidential elections, laws enacted during the War on Terror, expression on social media, and immigration laws. All these pressing societal issues have been examined by a body of nine jurists called the United States Supreme Court. Indeed, the so-called "Court of Last Resort" often has the final say in our legal system. Our fourth (and arguably greatest) chief justice—John Marshall famously declared in *Marbury v. Madison* (1803) that "it is emphatically the province and duty of the judicial department to say what the law is." And in our "judicial department" the U.S. Supreme Court is the highest court.

Like all other public institutions, sometimes the Court has performed poorly, as it did in *Dred Scott v. Sandford* (1857), when it sanctioned slavery, or *Plessy v. Ferguson* (1896), when it approved of segregation, or *Garcetti v. Ceballos* (2006), when it categorically lowered the level of free-speech protections for public employees. Often, however, the Court has led the way to a more just and equitable society, as it did when it unanimously ruled that segregated public schools violated the Equal Protection Clause in *Brown v. Board of Education* (1954) or ruled in *Tinker v. Des Moines Independent Community School District* (1969) that public school students are persons under the Constitution and retain a level of free-speech rights even at school.

Yet, the Court remains shrouded in secrecy at least more so than the other two branches of government. Supreme Court oral arguments are not televised, and some Supreme Court justices are not known by most of the American public.

The second edition of *The Handy Supreme Court Answer Book* seeks to increase reader knowledge on this important public institution. However, it takes a fundamentally different approach than the first edition of this book. In the first edition, I examined the Court chronologically through the different chief justices. This makes sense since many times we refer to the Supreme Court by the last name of the sitting chief justice (e.g., the Warren Court after Chief Justice Earl Warren or the current Roberts Court after Chief Justice John G. Roberts Jr.) The first edition examined all seventeen chief justices and their Courts.

The second edition takes a topical approach to the Court. It first examines the history of the Court and then takes a deeper dive into "Historic Supreme Court Justices"—those justices who had a significant impact on the Court and society. With these justices, many of their most significant opinions are discussed.

This edition then enlightens readers on the confirmation process—one that has become much more contentious in modern times. Consider the controversial hearings involving Justices Clarence Thomas and Brett Kavanaugh, who were both confirmed by the Senate by the slimmest of margins amidst allegations of sexual harassment or misconduct years earlier.

The book then discusses some of the more interesting topics in American law, including freedom of speech, freedom of religion, criminal justice, and race issues. All of these subjects contain a rich tapestry of legal decisions, especially when it comes to how the Court has often changed its positions quite significantly over time. The next topical chapter deals with abortion. Obviously, the Court's recent overruling of *Roe v. Wade* (1973) in *Dobbs v. Jackson Women's Health Organization* (2022) was, to put it mildly, headline news of the first order. The final topical chapter is about gun rights—an area in which the Court has made significant changes since the first edition. In this era of mass shootings, the topic has become even more controversial.

The final chapter is for all you trivia buffs and Court nerds. It might provide you the information for that nagging bonus question for trivia competitions at your nearby favorite restaurant or bar. It provides an interesting array of delicious tidbits of information about various justices through the years.

This project has been a labor of love. I hope the readers enjoy it as much as I enjoyed writing it.

History of the U.S. Supreme Court

How was the U.S. Supreme Court created?

Article III, Section 1 of the U.S. Constitution provided that "the judicial Power of the United States, shall be vested in one supreme Court, and in such inferior Courts the Congress may from time to time ordain and establish." The Constitution was adopted in 1787 and ratified in 1788. However, the Constitution did not create the U.S. Supreme Court.

Instead, the Court was created by Congress through passing the Judiciary Act of 1789, which established the Court's jurisdiction. The Judiciary Act of 1789 called for six justices on the Court: a chief justice and five associate justices.

Why is the Judiciary Act of 1789 so important?

This law is important because it created the federal judicial system in the United States. Justice Sandra Day O'Connor, in her book *The Majesty of the Law: Reflections of a Supreme Court Justice*, writes that the Judiciary Act of 1789 "stands as the single most important legislative enactment of the nation's founding years."

Who was the principal author of the Judiciary Act of 1789?

Oliver Ellsworth of Connecticut was the principal author of the Judiciary Act of 1789. A member of the Philadelphia Convention in 1787, Ellsworth became a U.S. senator when the Senate first convened in 1789. He was elected chair of the committee that was designed to follow the dictates of Article III of the new Constitution in order to create a federal judiciary. William Paterson from New Jersey, another member of the 1787 Convention, also assisted in the drafting of the Judiciary Act of 1789.

Both Ellsworth and Paterson later became justices on the U.S. Supreme Court.

What type of federal court system did Congress create in the Judiciary Act of 1789?

Congress created a three-tiered system of federal courts. At the bottom level were federal district court judges. The next level—the intermediate level—consists of the federal circuit courts of appeals. Finally, the highest court is the U.S. Supreme Court.

DID YOU KNOW?

Does Article III of the Constitution call for a chief justice?

Ironically, Article III of the Constitution does not mention a chief justice at all. It only mentions that "one supreme Court" will exist. However, Article I, Section 3 mentions a "Chief Justice" when talking about the impeachment of a president. It reads: "When the President of the United States is tried, the Chief Justice shall preside."

Today, we still have this three-tiered system of federal courts, consisting of 94 different federal judicial districts, 13 federal courts of appeals, and one U.S. Supreme Court.

Under the Constitution, who appoints U.S. Supreme Court justices?

The Constitution provides that the president has the power to appoint "Judges of the Supreme Court." Article II, Section 2 says that the president has the power to appoint U.S. Supreme Court justices and other federal judges but that it be done "with the Advice and Consent of the Senate." Thus, the president nominates U.S. Supreme Court justices, and the U.S. Senate then confirms or denies the selection.

Which Founding Father first proposed how justices would obtain their positions?

Nathaniel Gorham, one of the two Massachusetts members of the Constitutional Convention of 1787 that created the Constitution, first proposed the idea that the president should nominate the justices and the Senate should confirm them. Gorham never served as a federal judge, but he did serve one term as a judge of the Middlesex County Court of Common Pleas.

Does the Constitution explicitly give the power of judicial review to the judiciary?

No, the U.S. Constitution does not mention the concept of judicial review, which is the concept that the judicial branch has the power to declare acts of the legislative and executive branches of government unconstitutional. It is the power of judicial review that gives the U.S. Supreme Court the power to strike down federal and state laws that violate some aspect of the Constitution.

Many Framers assumed that the Court would have the power to declare laws unconstitutional, but it is not specifically mentioned in the Constitution. Several lower courts asserted the judiciary's power of judicial review, and, most famously, Chief

The actions of James Madison, the secretary of state acting on orders of incoming President Jefferson, led to the Supreme Court's *Marbury v. Madison* ruling and the introduction of the Court's jurisdiction in matters of judicial review.

Justice John Marshall clearly established the power of judicial review when he wrote in *Marbury v. Madison* (1803): "It is emphatically the province of the judicial department to declare what the law is."

What other provision of the Constitution implies a power of judicial review?

The Supremacy Clause of the Constitution, found in Article VI of the Constitution, provides support for the concept of judicial review, at least according to some legal historians and scholars. Chief Justice John Marshall cited the Supremacy Clause in his *Marbury v. Madison* opinion, writing:

"It also is not entirely unworthy of observation that in declaring what shall be the supreme law of the land, the constitution itself is first mentioned; and not the laws of the United States generally, but those only which shall be made in pursuance of the constitution, have that rank. Thus, the particular phraseology of the Constitution of the United States confirms and strengthens the principle, supposed to be essential to all written Constitutions, that a law repugnant to the Constitution is void and that courts, as well as other departments, are bound by that instrument."

What does Article III say about life tenure for federal judges?

Article III, in effect, provides life tenure for federal judges. It does not set a time limit but says that federal judges "shall hold their Offices during good behavior." Article III, Section 4 provides for the removal of "all civil Officers of the United States ... on Impeachment for, and Conviction of, Treason, Bribery, or other high Crimes and Misdemeanors."

DID YOU KNOW?

What does the Supremacy Clause say?

The Supremacy Clause reads: "This Constitution, and the Laws of the United States which shall be made in Pursuance thereof; and all Treaties made, or which shall be under the Authority of the United States, shall be the supreme Law of the Land and the Judges in every State shall be bound thereby, any Thing in the Constitution or Laws of any State to the Contrary Notwithstanding."

It means that federal law is supreme over state law. This concept is often called preemption.

The Framers of the Constitution gave life tenure to federal judges in order to ensure an independent judiciary, a judiciary that would not bow to the political pressures of the day. Federal judges often have had to make difficult decisions that a significant segment of the public may question quite critically. For this very reason, Alexander Hamilton wrote in Federal Paper #78 that "the complete independence of the courts of justice is peculiarly essential in a limited Constitution."

Hamilton added: "If then the courts are to be considered as the bulwarks of a limited constitution against legislative encroachments, this consideration will afford a strong argument for the permanent tenure of judicial officers, since nothing will contribute so much as this to the independent spirit of judges, which must be essential to the faithful performance of so arduous a duty."

Can U.S. Supreme Court justices be impeached?

Yes, federal judges—including U.S. Supreme Court justices—can be impeached. The Constitution provides that federal judges "shall hold their Offices during good behavior." They can be impeached for "Treason, Bribery, or other high Crimes and Misdemeanors." This means that federal judges, and U.S. Supreme Court justices, can be removed from office; they receive lifetime appointments but theoretically can be removed for really bad behavior.

Have any U.S. Supreme Court justices been impeached?

Justice Samuel Chase, who signed the Declaration of Independence and served as the chief judge of Maryland's highest state court, was impeached by the U.S. House of Representatives but not convicted in the Senate.

The U.S. Constitution gives the U.S. House of Representatives the "sole power of Impeachment" and the U.S. Senate "the sole Power to try all impeachments." It takes a two-thirds majority vote in the Senate for someone to be impeached and removed from office.

Justice Chase landed into trouble on the U.S. Supreme Court for his conduct during the sedition trial of James Callendar. Justice Chase apparently conducted himself in a very partisan manner during this trial. Justice Chase also attacked President Thomas Jefferson, saying that the president had engaged in "seditious attacks on the principles of the Constitution." Alfred H. Knight wrote in his book *The Wizards of Washington: Triumphs and Tragedies of the United States Supreme Court*: "As a target for impeachment and removal, the eccentric Federalist Chase was the answer to a partisan Republican's prayer."

The House of Representatives impeached Justice Chase 72–32 on eight charges in March 1804. However, the Senate acquitted Justice Chase with only a 19–15 vote for conviction on the closest count, which was still short of the necessary two-thirds majority, or 24 votes.

Many view the acquittal of Justice Chase as essential to the principle of an independent judiciary.

What justice in modern times faced an impeachment threat?

Justice William O. Douglas, who served on the Court from 1939–1975, faced an impeachment threat in April 1970 when House leader Gerald Ford, a future president, called for the impeachment of Justice Douglas. Ford said that Justice Douglas "was unfit" and "should be removed." He also said that "an impeachable offense is whatever a majority of the House of Representatives considers it to be at a given moment in history."

Several House Democrats responded that such an attempt was "an attack on the integrity and the independence of the United States Supreme Court." Critics charged that Justice Douglas had a connection with the Parvin Foundation. Others criticized his book *Points of Rebellion*, which critics charged fomented youth ac-

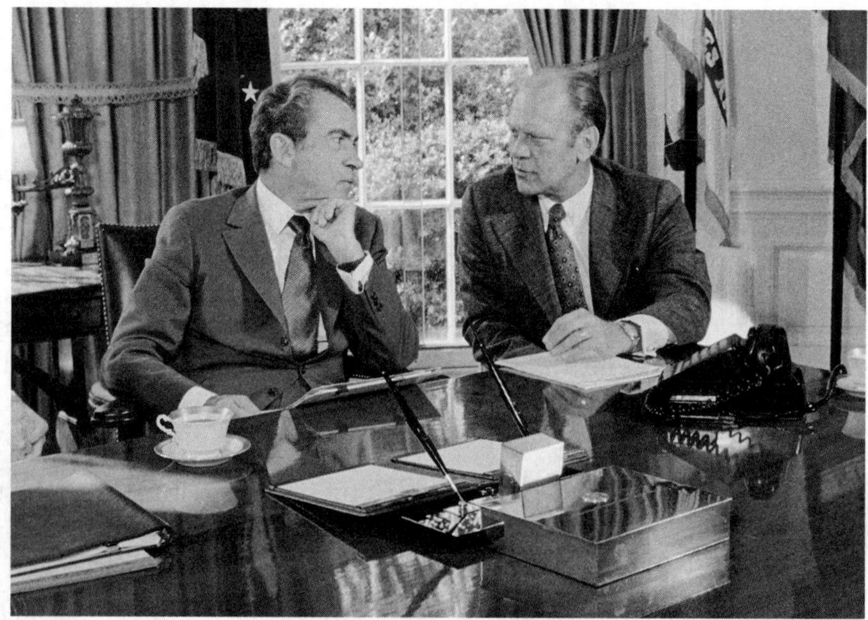

House Minority Leader Gerald Ford, pictured here in 1973 as vice president-designate with President Nixon in the Oval Office, initiated impeachment proceedings against Justice William O. Douglas. Declaring Douglas unfit, Ford cited—perhaps ironically, considering Ford's future pardon of the disgraced Nixon—the justice's perceived conflicts of interest.

tivists at the time. Others mentioned the fact that he had written an article on folk singing that was published by Ralph Ginzburg, who had a pornography case before the U.S. Supreme Court.

Justice Hugo Black was incensed at the attack on his longtime colleague. According to Bruce Murphy in his biography of Justice Douglas, *Wild Bill*, Justice Black told a group of southern congressmen: "I have known Bill Douglas for thirty years. He's never knowingly done any improper, unethical, or corrupt thing. Tell his detractors that in spite of my age, I think I have one trial left in me. Tell them that if they move against Bill Douglas, I'll resign from the Court and represent him. It will be the biggest, most important case I ever tried."

What happened with Justice Douglas's impeachment effort?

After a six-month investigation, on December 15, 1970, the Impeachment Subcommittee of the Judiciary Committee ruled by a 3–1 vote that a substantial ground for impeachment did not exist. Three Democrats voted against impeachment: Emanuel Celler of Brooklyn, Byron G. Rogers of Colorado, and Jack Brooks of Texas. One Republican, Edward Hutchinson from Michigan, dissented. The other Republican on the subcommittee, William M. McCullough of Ohio, declined to vote either way. Justice Douglas told the press after learning of the subcommittee's report: "The Select Committee has now performed its constitutional duties and I will try to continue to perform mine."

Where did the U.S. Supreme Court first meet?

The Court met in the Royal Exchange Building on Broad Street in New York City on February 2, 1790. The Court met on the second floor of the building in the afternoons, as the New York State Legis-

DID YOU KNOW?

What greeting does the marshal announce when the Court comes into session?

When the Court comes into session, the marshal announces: "Oyez! Oyez! Oyez! All persons having business before the Honorable, the Supreme Court of the United States, are admonished to draw near and give their attention, for the Court is now sitting. God save the United States and this Honorable Court."

lature met in the room during the morning hours. The Court met in New York for only one year, meeting in Philadelphia the next year.

Why did many early U.S. Supreme Court justices quit their jobs?

Many early justices left their jobs after only a short time because they did not enjoy the practice of circuit riding. Under the early system, U.S. Supreme Court justices had to "ride circuit," meaning that they had to travel to hear appeals on circuit courts. These appeals consisted of one U.S. Supreme Court justice and two district court judges. Twice a year, the U.S. Supreme Court justices had to engage in this practice. Justice James Iredell referred to himself as a "traveling postboy." Justice Thomas Johnson went even further in his opposition; he simply quit his job.

When the capital moved to Washington, D.C., where did the U.S. Supreme Court meet?

When the capital moved from New York City to Washington, D.C., so did the U.S. Supreme Court. The problem was that it did not have a permanent home. From 1801 to 1809, the justices met in different rooms in the basement of the Capitol Building. In 1810, the Court also met at a tavern, Long's Tavern. In 1810, the Court met in a specific room in the Capitol Building.

In what rented home did the Court meet after the Capitol Building burned down?

The U.S. Supreme Court met for two years—1815 and 1816—in Bell's Tavern, a rented home. The Court had to meet there because the Capitol Building was burned to the ground by the British during the War of 1812.

When did the Court meet in the old Senate chamber?

The U.S. Supreme Court met in the old Senate chamber, on the first floor of the Capitol Building, from 1860 to 1935, when it moved into its own building—the U.S. Supreme Court Building—where it holds court today.

When did the Court require attorneys to file written briefs?

In 1821, the U.S. Supreme Court began requiring attorneys to file written briefs before the Court. Now the practice is customary. Since 2007, attorneys have been required to file their briefs both electronically and in print.

What famous cases did John Paul Frank argue before the Court?

In addition to being a U.S. Supreme Court scholar, John Paul Frank was a first-rate attorney. He represented Ernesto Miranda

DID YOU KNOW?

What is the nickname of the U.S. Supreme Court Building?

The current building that houses the Supreme Court of the United States was proposed in 1921 by then-President William Howard Taft. Also nicknamed the Marble Palace, the grand edifice was designed by famed architect Cass Gilbert and was completed in 1935.

The nickname of the building is the Marble Palace because white marble represents the primary material used in the building. According to the U.S. Supreme Court's own website, $3 million worth of marble was used in its construction. Famous attorney and scholar John Paul Frank published a book about the U.S. Supreme Court in 1958 entitled *Marble Palace: The Supreme Court in American Life*.

in the famous *Miranda v. Arizona* case that was decided by the Warren Court in 1966. In *Miranda*, the Court declared that police must inform suspects of their rights before placing them under arrest and in custodial interrogation. He also argued for the Arizona State Bar in the attorney advertising case *Bates v. State Bar of Arizona* (1977). In that decision, the Court ruled that Arizona attorneys John Bates and Van O'Steen had a First Amendment right to publish a newspaper ad announcing their prices for routine, low-cost legal services.

Who was the architect of the new U.S. Supreme Court Building?

Cass Gilbert, who also designed the Customs House and the U.S. Chamber of Commerce Building in Washington, D.C., was the architect of the new U.S. Supreme Court Building. Unfortunately, Gilbert died before the completion of the building, which was then handled by his son, Cass Gilbert Jr.

TERMS

When does the U.S. Supreme Court meet?

The U.S. Supreme Court convenes on the first Monday of October for the start of its new term. The Court's term usually ends at the end of June. Federal law 28 U.S.C. §2 provides this: "The Supreme Court shall hold at the seat of government a term of court commencing on the first Monday in October of each year and may hold such adjourned or special terms as may be necessary."

When did the Court first begin its term on the first Monday of October?

The U.S. Supreme Court first began its term on the first Monday of October in the year 1917. Congress had passed a law effectuating such a change in a 1916 statute. In the mid-19th century, the Court was beginning its term in December and meeting through March. However, the Court's docket exploded in growth, as the Court was hearing many more cases. To accommodate this expanding docket, Congress allowed the Court in 1866 to set its own starting point for its terms. The Court moved its starting time to October. In 1873, Congress formalized this development by passing a law that moved the Court's term from the first Monday in December to the second Monday in October. It remained there until 1917.

When did the Court originally begin its new term?

The Judiciary Act of 1789 provided that the Court's term shall begin on the first Monday of February and the first Monday of August. The first meeting of the Court occurred on February 2, 1790.

When does the Court generally conclude its term?

The U.S. Supreme Court usually finishes all of its opinions by the end of June. It is quite rare for a U.S. Supreme Court opinion to be released after June 30.

Does the Court ever meet outside of its traditional term time?

Yes, the Court sometimes holds special sessions in important cases. For example, the Court held a special session on July 19, 1942, to hear the case of *Ex parte Quirin* in order to determine whether alleged German saboteurs were entitled to a federal habeas corpus review of their military commission convictions. More recently, the Court called a special session to hear the case of

McConnell v. Federal Election Commission in September 2003. The case involved a major First Amendment challenge to the Bipartisan Campaign Reform Act, a federal law restricting soft-money spending and other funding restrictions in political elections.

PROCESSES

How is a case brought to the U.S. Supreme Court?

The U.S. Supreme Court has discretionary jurisdiction over the vast majority of cases, at least since 1925, when Congress passed the Judiciary Act of 1925. This means that most cases originate in the lower courts, and the U.S. Supreme Court does not have to review the lower court's decision unless it decides to grant certiorari, or review.

Seeking a writ of certiorari is a process that dates back to the earliest days of English common law, an accumulation of precedents that underlies much of our modern concept of justice.

In more than 90 percent of the Court's cases, the party asking the Court to hear the case, the petitioner, petitions the Court for review in a document called a petition for writ of certiorari. The opposing party, called the respondent, then responds in a document asking the Court not to accept the case for review. The Court then decides whether the case is "certworthy," or acceptable for review.

The briefs filed during the certiorari phase are sometimes called "the cert briefs." If the Court grants review, then each side files another brief. These are briefs on the merits, or "merit briefs."

The term "brief" is a bit of a misnomer. These legal documents are not short. Oftentimes, they are around 50 pages long, or even much longer if you count the pages in the appendix.

What determines whether or not the U.S. Supreme Court will hear a case?

The U.S. Supreme Court has discretionary jurisdiction, which means that in the vast majority of cases, the Court has discretion on whether or not it will hear a particular case. The Court only hears 70 out of 8,000 cases each term, so the chances for review in any particular case are extremely small.

However, the Court has provided "consideration" for cases that it might take in Rule 10 of its U.S. Supreme Court Rules.

Rule 10 provides this:

> Considerations governing review on writ of certiorari: Review on a writ of certiorari is not a matter of right, but of judicial discretion. A petition for a writ of certiorari will be granted only for compelling reasons. The following, although neither controlling nor fully measuring the Court's discretion, indicate the character of the reasons the Court considers:

(a) a United States court of appeals has entered a decision in conflict with the decision of another United States court of appeals on the same important matter; has decided an important federal question in a way that conflicts with a decision by a state court of last resort; or has so far departed from the accepted and usual course of judicial proceedings, or sanctioned such a departure by a lower court, as to call for an exercise of this Court's supervisory power;

(b) a state court of last resort has decided an important federal question in a way that conflicts with the decision of another state court of last resort or of a United States court of appeals;

(c) a state court or a United States court of appeals has decided an important question of federal law that has not been, but should be, settled by this Court, or has decided an important federal question in a way that conflicts with relevant decisions of this Court.

What is the importance of circuit splits?

Even experienced Court observers warn that it is impossible to predict with great accuracy when the U.S. Supreme Court will agree to hear a case. However, one of the best predictors is when a case presents an issue that divides the lower federal appeals courts. This is called a circuit split. Rule 10(a) of the U.S. Supreme Court Rules identifies as an important consideration when a federal appeals court decision conflicts with another federal appeals court decision.

A circuit split means that different interpretations or rulings occur by different circuit courts of appeals. For example, let's say that on a key Fourth Amendment issue, the Sixth Circuit and the

Ninth Circuit disagree. Because the Sixth Circuit and the Ninth Circuit have ruled differently on this issue, a classic circuit split has occurred.

What are circuit assignments?

Sometimes, litigants will seek an immediate stay of a lower-court ruling before a particular U.S. Supreme Court justice. The circuits are divided among the nine justices for them to consider these emergency applications. As of September 28, 2022, the U.S. Supreme Court's own website identifies the circuit assignments as follows:

- **For the District of Columbia Circuit: John G. Roberts Jr., Chief Justice**
- **For the First Circuit: Ketanji Brown Jackson, Associate Justice** (Maine, Massachusetts, New Hampshire, Puerto Rico, Rhode Island)
- **For the Second Circuit: Sonia Sotomayor, Associate Justice** (Connecticut, New York, Vermont)
- **For the Third Circuit: Samuel A. Alito Jr., Associate Justice** (Delaware, New Jersey, Pennsylvania, Virgin Islands)
- **For the Fourth Circuit: John G. Roberts Jr., Chief Justice** (Maryland, North Carolina, South Carolina, West Virginia, Virginia)
- **For the Fifth Circuit: Samuel A. Alito Jr., Associate Justice** (Louisiana, Mississippi, Texas)
- **For the Sixth Circuit: Brett M. Kavanaugh, Associate Justice** (Kentucky, Michigan, Ohio, Tennessee)
- **For the Seventh Circuit: Amy Coney Barrett, Associate Justice** (Illinois, Indiana, Wisconsin)
- **For the Eighth Circuit: Brett M. Kavanaugh, Associate Justice** (Arkansas, Iowa, Minnesota, Missouri, Nebraska, North Dakota, South Dakota)

The Ninth Circuit is headquartered at San Francisco's James R. Browning U.S. Court of Appeals Building, with additional regular meeting places in Seattle, Washington; Portland, Oregon; and Pasadena, California.

- **For the Ninth Circuit: Elena Kagan, Associate Justice** (Alaska, Arizona, California, Guam, Hawaii, Idaho, Oregon, Montana, Nevada, Northern Mariana Islands, Washington)
- **For the 10th Circuit: Neil M. Gorsuch, Associate Justice** (Colorado, Kansas, New Mexico, Oklahoma, Utah, Wyoming)
- **For the 11th Circuit: Clarence Thomas, Associate Justice** (Alabama, Florida, Georgia)
- **For the Federal Circuit: John G. Roberts Jr., Chief Justice**

What is the discuss list?

The discuss list refers to a group of cases that the justices, primarily the chief justice, determine are cases worthy of discussion in the Court's focus at conference meetings. If a case makes the discuss list, it has a far better chance of being accepted for review.

On September 27, 2001, in a lecture at the University of Guanajuato in Mexico, Chief Justice William H. Rehnquist spoke about the Court's discuss list, stating: "Shortly before each conference, I send out a list of the petitions to be decided during that conference

DID YOU KNOW?

What is the rule of four?

The rule of four refers to a U.S. Supreme Court practice that the Court will hear a case if four justices agree the case is certworthy, or worthy of being reviewed. The practice has been in existence since at least 1924.

that I want to discuss. Each of the other Justices may ask to have additional cases put on the discuss list. If at any particular conference there are 100 petitions to be decided, there may be anywhere from 15 to 30 that are on the discuss list. The petitions for certiorari that are not discussed are denied without any recorded vote."

Where do the justices decide whether to accept a case for review?

The justices decide which cases they will review in their weekly meetings in conference. These meetings take place in the Conference Room in the U.S. Supreme Court Building. Only the nine justices attend these conference meetings; law clerks and other personnel are not allowed to attend. If someone knocks on the door, the most junior justice must answer the door.

The chief justice normally begins the meetings by bringing up the cases on the discuss list. The chief justice then speaks about particular cases and whether he or she believes each case should be reviewed. The customary practice is that each of the justices speaks in order of seniority. Each justice briefly states their position on the case and which way they are leaning in terms of voting.

When the Court decides to hear a case, what happens next?

The Court informs the clerk of the Court, who must then schedule oral argument. Under Rule 25, the petitioner then must draft a written document called a brief (a bit of a misnomer because briefs can be up to 50 pages long) within 45 days of the Court's order that it has accepted the case. The respondent then has 30 days from the date of the petitioner's filing to file its response brief. The petitioner may then file a reply brief as long as it is filed more than one week before the oral argument.

What is an oral argument?

An oral argument is the process by which attorneys come before the U.S. Supreme Court and present their case. The attorneys face questioning about the case from individual justices. Rule 28 provides that generally, each side is given 30 minutes for arguments. The petitioner presents first, and then the respondent follows. The petitioner can reserve some time for rebuttal after the respondent's argument. The oral argument is important because it offers the advocates the only time with which to interact with the justices and persuade them to their points of view.

The justices vary in how much they question the attorney's advocates. Justice Antonin Scalia was known for being quite vocal at oral arguments, firing many questions at the attorneys. On the current Court, Justice Sonia Sotomayor also is a very active questioner. On the other hand, Justice Clarence Thomas is normally quite reticent at oral arguments. In most cases, he does not ask a single question.

What does Rule 28 say about oral arguments?

Rule 28 provides this:

Oral Argument should emphasize and clarify the written arguments in the briefs on the merits. Counsel should assume that all Justices have read the briefs before oral argument. Oral argument read from a prepared text is not favored. Unless the Court directs otherwise, each side is allowed one-half hour for argument. Counsel is not required to use all the allotted time. Regardless of the number of counsel participating in oral argument, counsel making the opening argument shall present the case fairly and completely and not reserve points of substance for rebuttal.

What types of attorneys argue cases before the U.S. Supreme Court?

Most lawyers never argue a case before the U.S. Supreme Court. Some attorneys practice regularly before the U.S. Supreme Court as members of the U.S. Supreme Court Bar. The great Daniel Webster (1782–1852), a U.S. congressman and attorney from Massachusetts, argued nearly 250 cases before the U.S. Supreme Court. He was involved in many landmark decisions, such

This portrait of Daniel Webster was commissioned in honor of his victory in 1819's landmark *Dartmouth College v. Woodward* case before the Supreme Court.

as *Dartmouth College v. Woodward* (1819), *Gibbons v. Ogden* (1824), and *Charles River Bridge v. Warren Bridge* (1837). John William Davis (1873–1955) argued 140 cases before the U.S. Supreme Court, including *Youngstown Sheet and Tube Co. v. Sawyer* (1952) and *Brown v. Board of Education* (1954).

At the present time, Tom Goldstein of Goldstein & Russell, P.C. has argued 44 cases before the U.S. Supreme Court. His practice consists nearly entirely of U.S. Supreme Court cases. Other lawyers may argue one case before the U.S. Supreme Court, having represented the litigant from the beginning of the case.

Those who serve as solicitor general, a position appointed by the president to argue for the United States, naturally argue many more cases than even those members of the U.S. Supreme Court Bar who regularly argue cases.

When does the Court hear oral arguments?

The Court generally hears oral arguments two weeks out of every month from October through April. During the weeks of oral arguments, the Court hears cases from 10:00 A.M. to 12:00 P.M. Eastern Standard Time on Monday, Tuesday, and Wednesday.

After the oral argument, when does the Court decide the case?

The Court meets in conference to discuss the justices' initial votes in the case. The Court discusses the cases argued on Monday in its Wednesday afternoon conference meeting. For the cases argued on Tuesday and Wednesday, the Court discusses them in its Friday conference meeting.

The chief justice opens the discussions, outlining the applicable laws and facts and his or her views of the case. This practice extends to all the justices in order of seniority. The justices also discuss how they plan to decide the case. The chief justice announces the vote. If the chief justice is in the majority, he or she assigns who will write the majority opinion for the Court. If the chief justice is in the minority, the most senior justice in the majority makes the opinion assignments.

No specific timetable exists for when the Court will issue its opinions, though in nearly all cases, the Court will issue a decision by the end of June. In a few cases, however, the Court will not issue an opinion and will ask for a re-argument. For example, the Roberts Court ordered a re-argument in 2006 in the case of *Garcetti v. Ceballos*, a highly watched case involving the free-speech rights of public employees.

Has the oral argument rule always provided for 30 minutes to each side?

No, the oral argument has not always been 30 minutes. In fact, oral arguments used to take several days in some cases. Many of the justices chafed under the process of hearing lawyers give speeches hour upon hour. In 1849, the Court adopted Rule 53, which set the time limit for each attorney at two hours each. If attorneys wished to argue longer than two hours, they had to petition for special permission. In 1925, the Court limited the argument time to one hour on each side. The Court said that this change was "due to the crowded calendar of the Court." In 1970, the Court changed its rules again, limiting each side to the present-day requirement of 30 minutes each.

What are the different types of opinions?

Several different types of opinions exist, including majority, plurality, concurring, and dissenting opinions, plus so-called per curiam opinions:

- A majority opinion is one that must have a majority of the Court sign on to it, namely five out of nine justices. This opinion is the ruling of the Court. It stands as precedent for future cases. If all justices vote with the majority, the opinion is said to be a unanimous opinion.

- A plurality opinion is the main opinion of the Court but one that fails to command a majority of the justices. For instance, a case may have four justices agreeing with one opinion, two justices who file concurring opinions but do not join the other four, and three justices in dissent. In this 4–2–3 split, no majority opinion exists. However, the opinion of four, the plurality opinion, is the one that stands as the ruling of the Court.

- A concurring opinion is an opinion that agrees with the result but not the reasoning of the majority or main opinion of the Court. A justice who writes a concurring opinion may want to emphasize particular points of the law or simply indicate that the main opinion reached the right result by taking the wrong path.

- A dissenting opinion is an opinion that disagrees with the result of the majority opinion.

- A per curiam opinion is an opinion rendered by the Court, or a majority of the Court, collectively instead of a single justice.

If the majority opinion becomes the law of the land, are concurring and dissenting opinions important?

Yes, concurring and even dissenting opinions can be important. Sometimes, the law will develop such that a concurring opinion will actually become the guidepost for future decisions in the area. A classic example was Justice John Marshall Harlan II's concurring opinion in the Fourth Amendment case *Katz v. United States* (1967). While Justice Potter Stewart wrote the Court's majority opinion, Justice Harlan's concurring opinion created the "reasonable expectation of privacy" test that has become the opinion now relied on by the majority of lower courts.

Similarly, dissenting opinions can be important, particularly if the U.S. Supreme Court overrules itself in a particular area of the law. A classic example of a dissenting opinion that became the law of the land was Justice Black's dissenting opinion in the Sixth Amendment right to counsel in the case of *Betts v. Brady* (1942). The majority in *Betts* ruled that state courts did not have to provide an attorney to all indigent defendants charged with felonies in cases other than ones involving the death penalty. However, the Court overruled that decision 21 years later in *Gideon v. Wainwright* (1963), and in a remarkable irony, Justice Black had the honor of writing the unanimous opinion for the Court, taking the same position that he took in dissent in *Betts*.

What are amicus briefs?

Amicus, or friend of the Court, briefs are briefs filed by interested outside parties who wish to emphasize particular aspects of a case and stress its importance to the Court. Amicus briefs are a regular staple of U.S. Supreme Court practice, particularly in

Cases that attract high public attention and passion, such as 2022's *Dobbs v. Jackson Women's Health Organization* (which reversed the federal protection of abortion rights conferred by 1973's *Roe v. Wade*), are also likely to attract higher numbers of amicus briefs than those with an interest in swaying the court's opinion.

DID YOU KNOW?

What rule speaks of amicus briefs?

Rule 37 of the U.S. Supreme Court Rules addresses amicus briefs. It states that "an amicus curiae brief that brings to the attention of the Court relevant matter not already brought to its attention by the parties may be of considerable help to the Court. An amicus curiae brief that does not serve this purpose burdens the Court, and its filing is not favored. An amicus curiae brief may be filed only by an attorney admitted to practice before this Court as provided in Rule 5."

important, high-profile decisions. For example, approximately 90 amicus briefs were filed before the Court in the affirmative action in education cases of *Grutter v. Bollinger* and *Gratz v. Bollinger.*

However, even that pales in comparison to the recent abortion decision, *Dobbs v. Jackson Women's Health Organization* (2022), as more than 140 amicus briefs were filed in that decision.

Sometimes, justices seem to consider certain amicus briefs as very significant and persuasive. For example, Chief Justice Rehnquist cited the amicus brief of the Association of American Editorial Cartoonists, written by attorney Rosalyn Mazer, in his unanimous opinion for the Court in the celebrated First Amendment decision in *Hustler Magazine v. Falwell* (1988).

PERSONNEL

What is the reporter of the U.S. Supreme Court?

The reporter of decisions is the individual responsible for compiling the U.S. Supreme Court decisions into the United States

Reports, the official compilation of U.S. Supreme Court opinions. The history of the Court has had 17 reporters. They are:

Alexander Dallas	1790–1800
William Cranch	1801–1815
Henry Wheaton	1816–1827
Richard Peters	1828–1842
Benjamin Howard	1843–1860
Jeremiah Black	1861–1862
John Wallace	1863–1874
William Otto	1875–1883
John Davis	1883–1902
Charles Butler	1902–1916
Ernest Knaebel	1916–1944
Walter Wyatt	1946–1963
Henry Putzel Jr.	1964–1979
Henry Curtis Lind	1979–1989
Frank D. Wagner	1989–2010
Christine Luchok Fallon	2011–2020
Rebecca Anne Womeldorf	2021-present

What is the background of the reporter?

The reporter is an attorney with an impressive background. For example, the current reporter, Rebecca Anne Womeldorf, graduated from law school summa cum laude and clerked for Justice Lewis F. Powell Jr. and Justice Anthony Kennedy on the U.S. Supreme Court. She worked for the litigation firm Hollingsworth LLP in Washington, D.C., for many years before serving as secretary and chief counsel to the Committee on Rules of Practice and Procedure of the Judicial Conference of the United States.

Who is the clerk of the Court?

The clerk of the Court is the person who oversees the administration of the Court's docket and caseload. The position of clerk is established by federal law 28 U.S.C. §671, which provides in part: "The Supreme Court may appoint and fix the compensation of a clerk and one or more deputy clerks. The clerk shall be subject to removal by the Court. Deputy clerks shall be subject to removal by the clerk with the approval of the Court or the Chief Justice of the United States."

The U.S. Supreme Court has had 20 clerks in its history:

John Tucker	1790–1791
Samuel Bayard	1791–1800
Elias B. Caldwell	1800–1825
William Griffith	1826–1827
William T. Carroll	1827–1863
D. W. Middleton	1863–1880
James H. McKenney	1880–1913
James Maher	1913–1921
William R. Stansbury	1921–1927
Charles Elmore Copley	1927–1952
Harold B. Willey	1952–1956
John T. Fey	1956–1958
James Browning	1958–1961
John F. Davis	1961–1970
E. Robert Seaver	1970–1972
Michael Rodak	1972–1981

The current clerk of the Supreme Court of the United States is Scott S. Harris, who was appointed in 2013 after 11 years as legal counsel to the court.

Alexander Stevas	1981–1985
Joseph F. Spaniol Jr.	1986–1991
William K. Suter	1991–2013
Scott S. Harris	2013–present

What is the background of the clerk of the U.S. Supreme Court?

The clerk of the U.S. Supreme Court is a well-respected attorney. The current clerk, Scott S. Harris, graduated from the University of Virginia School of Law and worked at the law firm Wiley Rein & Felding in Washington, D.C., before becoming an assistant U.S. attorney general. In 2002, he became legal counsel to the U.S. Supreme Court and then assumed the title of clerk in 2013 upon the retirement of his predecessor, William K. Suter.

LAW CLERKS

What are law clerks?

Each U.S. Supreme Court hires several law clerks to assist in the screening of cases in the certiorari pool, writing of memoranda on legal issues, drafting of opinions, and other legal matters. Most justices hire four law clerks. Many law clerks are recent graduates of prestigious law schools such as Harvard or Yale. Many law clerks serve for a U.S. Supreme Court justice after having clerked for a federal circuit court of appeals judge. Most clerks work for a justice for one year, though some will work on two-year terms.

What U.S. Supreme Court justice started the practice of hiring a law clerk?

Justice Horace Gray instituted the practice of law clerks in 1882 when he joined the Court. When he was a member of the

DID YOU KNOW?

What law clerk leaked the *Roe v. Wade* decision?

Larry Hammond, a law clerk to Justice Powell, leaked the *Roe v. Wade* ruling in 1973, or the basis of it, to an acquaintance of his from law school, who was a reporter for *Time* magazine. Chief Justice Warren E. Burger forgave Hammond for his indiscretion, and he was allowed to stay for another term with Justice Powell.

Supreme Judicial Court of Massachusetts, Justice Gray had started the practice there as well, hiring future U.S. Supreme Court justice Louis Brandeis. Justice Gray paid for the clerk out of his own pocket. The clerks were selected by Justice Gray's half brother, Harvard Law professor John Chipman Gray. The practice became formalized when Congress passed a 1922 law that allowed each justice to hire one law clerk for a salary of $3,600.

What U.S. Supreme Court clerk was indicted in 1919?

Ashton Fox Embry, a law clerk to Justice Joseph McKenna, was indicted for providing secret, insider information about Court rulings to Wall Street traders. Embry had left his clerk position ostensibly to work on his banking business. However, a few weeks later, the U.S. Department of Justice charged Embry with conspiring "to deprive the United States of its lawful right and duty of promulgating information in the way and at the time required by law and at departmental regulation."

However, the case against Embry never went to trial and eventually was dismissed in 1929.

What law clerk wrote a book about his experiences called *Closed Chambers*?

Edward Lazarus, who clerked for Justice Harry A. Blackmun during the 1988–1989 term, later wrote a book entitled *Closed Chambers*. The book relayed many internal Court discussions and, to some, represented a breach of secrecy that clerks are supposed to maintain. Lazarus has had a successful post-clerk career, including serving as the chief of staff at the Federal Communications Commission and as general counsel to Sonos, Inc.

What functions do law clerks serve?

Law clerks often serve as initial screeners of the thousands of cases that are appealed to the U.S. Supreme Court. They will often write memos explaining to the justices which cases are "certworthy," or worthy of their attention. Nearly all of the justices pool their clerks together in a "cert pool" to examine the thousands of petitions that come to the Court each year. Justice Powell proposed the idea of the cert pool in 1972 in order to save time and increase

Edward Lazarus published his court insider book, *Closed Chambers*, after serving as clerk for Justice Harry A. Blackmun.

efficiency. Critics charge that it gives too much power to the law clerks. Seven of the nine current justices participate in the cert pool. The two exceptions are Justice Samuel A. Alito Jr. and Justice Neil M. Gorsuch.

The law clerks also write research memoranda and draft opinions for the justices. The responsibility of law clerks obviously depends upon each particular justice. Some justices delegate more responsibility to the clerks for opinion drafting than others.

Who are some of the more famous law clerks?

Many U.S. Supreme Court law clerks have achieved great prominence in the legal profession. Here are just a few:

- **Ken Starr:** Former federal appeals court and independent counsel who investigated President Bill Clinton (leading to his impeachment) and clerked for Chief Justice Warren E. Burger.
- **Richard Posner:** Longtime judge on the U.S. Court of Appeals for the Seventh Circuit, author of more than 40 books, and clerked for Justice William J. Brennan Jr. Justice Brennan once said that in his life, he met two geniuses: Justice William O. Douglas and Judge Richard Posner.
- **Robert O'Neil:** Former president of the University of Virginia, founder of the Thomas Jefferson Center for the Protection of Free Expression, and clerked for Justice William J. Brennan Jr. He was a co-clerk with Richard Posner.
- **Alan Dershowitz:** Harvard Law professor, well-known author and legal commentator, and clerked for Justice Arthur Goldberg.
- **Laura Ingraham:** Fox television news commentator with her own show on the same network called *The Ingraham Angle* and clerked for Justice Clarence Thomas.

What is the Supreme Court Fellows Program?

In 1973, Chief Justice Burger established the Supreme Court Fellows Program to provide assistance to the Court, the Federal Judicial Center, the Administrative Office of the United States Courts, and the U.S. Sentencing Commission. The fellows help with the Court's workload, write research memoranda, and do other work at the behest largely of the chief justice.

Since the 2000–2001 term, the chief justice has selected four individuals to serve as U.S. Supreme Court fellows. One goes with the U.S. Supreme Court, one with the Federal Judicial Center, one with the Administrative Office of the United States Courts, and one with the U.S. Sentencing Commission.

Who were among the inaugural U.S. Supreme Court fellows Class of 1973–1974?

The inaugural U.S. Supreme Court fellows Class of 1973–1974 consisted of three individuals: Gordon Gee, who is now the president of the University of West Virginia; Russell Wheeler, a visiting fellow with the Brookings Institution, who for many years directed the Federal Judicial Center in Washington, D.C.; and Howard R. Whitcomb, who for many years taught political science at Lehigh University in Pennsylvania.

What is the marshal of the U.S. Supreme Court?

The marshal of the U.S. Supreme Court is the person who oversees the security, maintenance, and operation of the U.S. Su-

Prior to her appointment as the 11th marshal of the United States Supreme Court, Gail Anne Curley was an attorney in the U.S. Army.

preme Court Building. Federal law 28 U.S.C. §672 has provided for this position since 1867. The U.S. Supreme Court has had 11 marshals:

Richard C. Parsons	1867–1872
John Nicolay	1872–1887
John M. Wright	1888–1915
Frank Key Green	1915–1938
Thomas E. Waggaman	1938–1952
T. Perry Lippitt	1952–1972
Frank M. Hepler	1972–1976
Alfred M. Wong	1976–1994
Dale E. Bosley	1994–2001
Pamela Talkin	2001–2021
Gail A. Curley	2021–present

What is the Office of Legal Counsel?

The Office of Legal Counsel is an administrative unit under the control of the chief justice of the U.S. Supreme Court. It consists of two attorneys who help the Court in cases involving petitions for extraordinary writs and cases in which the Court's original jurisdiction is invoked.

What was the original oath that federal judges had to take?

Section 8 of the Judiciary Act of 1789 provides that U.S. Supreme Court and district judges had to take the following oath: "I, [justice's name], do solemnly swear or affirm, that I will administer justice without respect to persons, and do equal right to the poor and to the rich, and that I will faithfully and impartially discharge and perform all the duties incumbent on me as [type of judge] according to the best of my abilities and understanding, agreeable to the constitution and laws of the United States. So help me God."

The oath was amended in 1990 by replacing "according to the best of my abilities and understanding, agreeable to the Constitution" with the words "under the Constitution."

REFORMS

What president introduced an infamous court-packing plan in 1937?

President Franklin D. Roosevelt, upset over the U.S. Supreme Court's invalidating many key pieces of his New Deal legislative agenda, proposed a Judicial Reorganization Plan that would call for another justice to be added to the U.S. Supreme Court when a sitting member reached 70 years of age.

Roosevelt was primarily upset at the rulings of the so-called "Four Horsemen" of the Court, who were generally judicial conservatives who were resistant to the expansive nature of Roosevelt's New Deal agenda. Those "Four Horsemen" were Justice Pierce Butler, Justice George Sutherland, Justice James Clark McReynolds, and Justice Willis Van Devanter.

Roosevelt introduced his Judicial Reorganization Plan in one of his "Fireside Chats," where he spoke directly to the American public. Roosevelt stated in part:

I want to talk with you very simply about the need for present action in this crisis—the need to meet the unanswered challenge of one-third of a Nation ill-nourished, ill-clad, ill-housed.

Last Thursday I described the American form of Government as a three-horse team provided by the Constitution to the American people so that their field might be plowed. The three horses are, of course, the three branches of government—the Congress, the Executive and the Courts. Two of the horses are pulling in unison today; the third is not. Those who have intimated that the President of the United States is trying to drive that team, overlook the simple fact that the President, as Chief Executive, is himself one of the three horses.

It is the American people themselves who are in the driver's seat.

It is the American people themselves who want the furrow plowed.

It is the American people themselves who expect the third horse to pull in unison with the other two.

I hope that you have re-read the Constitution of the United States in these past few weeks. Like the Bible, it ought to be read again and again.

It is an easy document to understand when you remember that it was called into being because the Articles of Confederation under which the original thirteen States tried to operate after the Revolution showed the need of a National Government with power enough to handle national problems. In its Preamble, the Constitution states that it was intended to form a more perfect Union and promote the general welfare; and the powers given to the Congress to carry out those purposes can be best described by saying that they were all the powers needed to meet each and every problem which then had a national character and which could not be met by merely local action.

But the framers went further. Having in mind that in succeeding generations many other problems then undreamed of would become national problems, they gave to the Congress the ample broad powers "to levy taxes … and provide for the common defense and general welfare of the United States."

That, my friends, is what I honestly believe to have been the clear and underlying purpose of the patriots who wrote a Federal Constitution to create a National Government with national power, intended as they said, "to form a more perfect union … for ourselves and our posterity."

For nearly twenty years there was no conflict between the Congress and the Court. Then Congress passed a statute which, in 1803, the Court said violated an express provision of the Constitution. The Court claimed the power to declare it unconstitutional and did so declare it. But a little later the Court itself admitted that it was an extraordinary power to exercise and through Mr. Justice Washington laid down this limitation upon it: "It is but a decent respect due to the wisdom, the integrity and the patriot-

In response to rulings that were unfavorable to much of his New Deal agenda, President Franklin D. Roosevelt proposed court packing as a means to dilute the power of more conservative holdovers.

ism of the legislative body, by which any law is passed, to presume in favor of its validity until its violation of the Constitution is proved beyond all reasonable doubt."

But since the rise of the modern movement for social and economic progress through legislation, the Court has more and more often and more and more boldly asserted a power to veto laws passed by the Congress and State Legislatures in complete disregard of this original limitation.

In the last four years the sound rule of giving statutes the benefit of all reasonable doubt has been cast aside. The Court has been acting not as a judicial body, but as a policy-making body.

When the Congress has sought to stabilize national agriculture, to improve the conditions of labor, to safeguard business against unfair competition, to protect our national resources, and in many other ways, to serve our clearly national needs, the majority of the Court has been assuming the power to pass on the wisdom of these Acts of the Congress—and to approve or disapprove the public policy written into these laws....

We have, therefore, reached the point as a Nation where we must take action to save the Constitution from the Court and the Court from itself. We must find a way to take an appeal from the Supreme Court to the Constitution itself. We want a Supreme Court which will do justice under the Constitution—not over it. In our Courts we want a government of laws and not of men.

I want—as all Americans want—an independent judiciary as proposed by the framers of the Constitution. That means a Supreme Court that will enforce the Constitution as written—that will refuse to amend the Constitution by the arbitrary exercise of judicial power—amendment by judicial say-so. It does not mean a judiciary so independent that it can deny the existence of facts universally recognized.

DID YOU KNOW?

Did Congress ever try to permanently set the number of justices at nine?

Yes. Senator John Butler, a Republican senator from Maryland, introduced a constitutional amendment in the 1950s to keep the U.S. Supreme Court membership at nine. Butler said that the purpose of the proposed amendment was to "forestall future attempts to undermine the integrity and independence of the Supreme Court." Butler's proposal cleared the Senate but did not pass the House.

In 2021, U.S. Rep. Mark Green from Tennessee introduced a House Joint Resolution that would set the number of justices at nine.

The Senate Judiciary Committee recommended against Roosevelt's court-packing plan, calling it "a needless, futile, and utterly dangerous abandonment of constitutional principle."

What various New Deal legislations did the U.S. Supreme Court invalidate?

Here is a listing of the New Deal legislations that were invalidated by the U.S. Supreme Court:

- Agricultural Adjustment Act of 1933: *U.S. v. Butler* (1936)
- Agricultural Adjustment Act of 1933 (later amendments): *Rickert Rice Mills v. Founteno* (1936)
- Economy Act of 1933 (one clause): *Lynch v. U.S.* (1934)
- National Industrial Recovery Act: *Schecter Poultry Co. v. U.S.* (1935)

- Another part of the National Industrial Recovery Act: *Panama Refining Co. v. Ryan* (1935)
- Home Owners Loan Act of 1933: *Hopkins Savings Assn. v. Cleary* (1935)
- Railroad Retirement Act: *Railroad Retirement Board v. Alton R. Co.* (1935)
- Bituminous Coal Conservation Act: *Carter v. Carter Coal Co.* (1936)
- Frazier-Lemke Act of 1934: *Louisville Bank v. Radford* (1935)

Which justice changed his vote from one minimum wage case to the other?

Justice Owen Roberts switched his vote from striking down a minimum-wage law in *Morehead v. New York Ex. Rel. Tipaldo* (1936) to upholding a similar Washington state law in *West Coast Hotel Co. v. Parrish* (1937). It was said that Justice Roberts's change of mind was the "switch in time that saved nine," a reference to President Franklin D. Roosevelt's sharp criticism of the Court and proposal in 1937 to "pack" the Court with additional justices. In reality, Justice Roberts had indicated his support for the minimum-wage law in a Court conference in December 1936 before President Roosevelt's court-packing plan was announced.

What president issued an executive order ordering a commission to study various reform proposals to the U.S. Supreme Court?

President Joseph Biden signed Executive Order 14023, which created a commission to study the U.S. Supreme Court and various reform proposals. The functions of the Commission are listed in the order as follows:

FUNCTIONS OF COMMISSION

(a) The Commission shall produce a report for the President that includes the following:

(i) An account of the contemporary commentary and debate about the role and operation of the Supreme Court in our constitutional system and about the functioning of the constitutional process by which the President nominates and, by and with the advice and consent of the Senate, appoints Justices to the Supreme Court;

(ii) The historical background of other periods in the Nation's history when the Supreme Court's role and the nominations and advice-and-consent process were subject to critical assessment and prompted proposals for reform; and

(iii) An analysis of the principal arguments in the contemporary public debate for and against Supreme Court reform, including an appraisal of the merits and legality of particular reform proposals.

(b) The Commission shall solicit public comment, including other expert views, to ensure that its work is informed by a broad spectrum of ideas.

(c) The Commission shall submit its report to the President within 180 days of the date of the Commission's first public meeting.

Mere months after taking the presidential oath administered by Chief Justice John Roberts, President Biden issued Executive Order 14023 with the intent of reforming the Supreme Court.

What were some of the reform proposals considered by this Commission?

The Commission studied proposals that it grouped into four categories of reforms: (1) the size and composition of the Court; (2) the tenure of the justices; (3) the powers of the Court and its role in the constitutional system; and (4) the Court's transparency and internal processes.

What were the arguments for and against expanding the size of the Court?

The Commission, in its draft report issued in December 2021, did not take a position on whether the Court's size and composition should be changed. Rather, it presented arguments both for and against expanding the number of justices. Proponents of such measures contend that the current U.S. Supreme Court has issued a series of rulings that undermine democracy and could serve to delegitimize the Court. Others contend that expanding the Court's size could allow more diversity on the Court and give its members the opportunity to hear more cases.

"Expanded diversity could enrich the Court's decision making, and a Court that was drawn from a broader cross-section of society would be well received by the public," the report reads. "A larger Supreme Court might also be able to decide more cases and to spend more time on emergency applications—an element of the Court's work that has attracted considerable attention as is discussed in Chapter 5 of this Report."

The report also noted that most other courts had more justices or judges on their high courts. Consider the following:

7 Judges	Australia
9 Judges	Canada, United States

10 Judges	Chile
11 Judges	France, South Africa
12 Judges	Belgium, Ireland, Spain, United Kingdom
14 Judges	Austria, South Korea
15 Judges	Italy, Japan
16 Judges	Germany, Sweden
18 Judges	Denmark

However, opponents of changing the size of the U.S. Supreme Court emphasize that changing the size of the Court simply because many do not agree with certain rulings of the Court would threaten judicial independence.

"Critics of Court expansion worry that such efforts would pose considerable risk to our constitutional system, including by spurring parties able to take control of the White House and Congress at the same time to routinely add Justices to bring the Court more into line with their ideological stances or partisan political aims," the report reads. "Court packing, in the critics' view, would compromise the Court's long-term capacity to perform its essential role of policing the excesses of the other branches and protecting individual rights."

A primary argument against Court expansion is that having nine U.S. Supreme Court justices has become something of a "constitutional norm" and that changing it would undermine the independence of the Court. Another argument is that attempts to expand the Court would never stop: "Opponents of Court packing in this moment warn that it would also almost certainly generate a continuous cycle of future expansions. Expanding the Court would be on the agenda of every administration under unified government."

What other structural reforms did the Commission consider?

The Commission considered various proposals where U.S. Supreme Court justices would rotate on panels to decide cases, much as judges at courts of appeals normally hear cases with different panels. These rotation and panel systems may run into a constitutional hurdle, according to the Commission, which cited the language from Article III of the Constitution that "[t]he judicial Power of the United States, shall be vested in one supreme Court, and in such inferior Courts as the Congress may from time to time ordain and establish."

Another type of proposal was one that seeks to provide for some partisan or ideological balance to the Court. One proposal was that each president would get to appoint two members to the Court each term. A related proposal was that the Court must consist of an equal, or closely equal, number of members from each of the two main political parties. This is what the Commission called a "balanced bench" proposal. However, the Commission noted that "it is far from clear that ideological balance is in and of itself a desirable goal. If there is no such balance in the political branches, requiring such balance on the Court could make the Court insufficiently reflective of or connected to electoral outcomes."

What proposals did the Commission consider regarding term limits?

The Court considered the proposal that justices serve one nonrenewable, 18-year term. The Commission noted that a group

The 2020 Roberts Court (Front row, left to right: Associate Justice Samuel A. Alito, Jr., Associate Justice Clarence Thomas, Chief Justice John G. Roberts, Jr., Associate Justice Stephen G. Breyer, and Associate Justice Sonia Sotomayor. Back row, left to right: Associate Justice Brett M. Kavanaugh, Associate Justice Elena Kagan, Associate Justice Neil M. Gorsuch, and Associate Justice Amy Coney Barrett).

of scholars had proposed such a system and that similar proposals have been endorsed by think tanks along the ideological spectrum.

The Commission noted that the United States is an outlier in providing life tenure for its high judges. "The United States is the only major constitutional democracy in the world that has neither a retirement age nor a fixed term limit for its high court Justices," the report reads. "Among the world's democracies, at least 27 have term limits for their constitutional courts. And those that do not have term limits, such as the Supreme Court of the United Kingdom, typically impose age limits."

The argument for term limits devolves into the idea that justices wield too much power, as many serve more than 30 years on the Court. The report notes that "life tenure arguably arrogates too much power to single individuals."

However, the Commission also presented the arguments of those who are in favor of retaining life tenure for justices. "In the main, the opponents argue that the current system of appointing and protecting the independence and neutrality of federal judges and Justices, through life tenure, has worked well for over 230 years," the report reads. "The independent federal judiciary, protected by lifetime tenure, is one of the most signal accomplishments of our constitutional system."

Ultimately, opponents of altering life tenure emphasize that the "federal system of life tenure is the gold standard for judicial independence."

Did any of the Commission members introduce separate statements?

Yes, two Commission members, former federal judges Thomas Griffith and David Levi, submitted a joint statement in which they emphasize the importance of an independent federal judiciary. They wrote in part: "In our view, most of the proposed reforms discussed in the Commission report—including 'court packing' and term limits—are without substantial merit; they are not related to any defect or deficiency in the Court or its procedures and they threaten judicial independence. We must not permit the Supreme Court to become collateral damage in the divisiveness that marks the current age."

Commissioner Adam White, senior fellow at the American Enterprise Institute, also issued a separate statement in which he decried proposals to pack the Court:

> Court-packing is anathema to constitutional government. While Congress is empowered by the Constitution to add seats to the Court, the history of Court expansion is one of admirable self-restraint by Congress. Over the nation's first century, Congress largely set the Court's size by reference to the judiciary's genuine needs, particularly in terms of the justices' old circuit-riding duties in a fast-growing continental republic. Since 1869, the Court's size has remained stable, and for one and a half centuries the nine-justice bench has proved conducive to the justices' work of deliberation, decision, and explanation.
>
> To pack the Court would impair the Court, not improve it: destabilizing it, further politicizing it, and complicating its basic work of hearing and deciding cases under the rule of law. And one needs a willing suspension of disbelief not to see that Court packing would inaugurate an era of re-packing, destroying the Court's function and character as a court of law.

Historic Justices on the Court, Part I

CHIEF JUSTICE JOHN MARSHALL

Why is Chief Justice John Marshall considered the greatest chief justice in Court history by many historians and others?

In his 1996 biography of Chief Justice Marshall, author Jean Edward Smith referred to Chief Justice Marshall as "the Definer of the Nation." Chief Justice Marshall's opinions gave the U.S. Supreme Court and the judicial branch the power and respect they deserved and placed the judicial branch on a closer level to Congress and the president. William Winslow Crosskey, in his essay on Chief Justice Marshall for the book *Mr. Justice* (eds. Allison Dunham and Philip B. Kurland), writes: "Some very distinguished and able men have been Chief Justice; but by universal consent, Marshall is recognized to stand pre-eminent—indeed, unrivaled—among them. The appellation, 'the Great Chief Justice,' is still, as it long has been, a completely unambiguous reference to John Marshall."

Chief Justice Marshall did this in many ways. He persuaded his colleagues to drop the practice of seriatim opinions, where each justice would speak and issue an individual opinion. Under Chief Justice Marshall, the Court often spoke in one unified voice, many times through the chief justice. He also established the principle of judicial review in *Marbury v. Madison* (1803), which gave the judiciary the power to review the constitutionality of legislative and executive acts. U.S. Supreme Court justice Sandra Day O'Connor wrote in her book *The Majesty of the Law*: "It is no overstatement to claim that Chief Justice Marshall fulfilled the Constitution's promise of an independent federal judiciary."

Another factor contributing to Chief Justice Marshall's greatness was the fact that he was the first chief justice, John Jay, to serve for a significant period of time. Chief Justice Marshall served on the Court for 34 years. Meanwhile, the first chief justice served six years; the second, Chief Justice John Rutledge, served less than one year; and the third, Chief Justice Oliver Ellsworth, served about five years. Chief Justice Marshall was also on the Court during the formative

John Marshall, the fourth Chief Justice of the U.S. Supreme Court, presided over the landmark *Marbury v. Madison* (1803) case, which firmly established the principle of judicial review.

years of the nation and the Court and possessed great leadership abilities that enabled him to guide the Court during his long tenure.

What government positions did Chief Justice John Marshall hold before serving as chief justice?

Chief Justice Marshall served many terms in the Virginia House of Delegates, beginning in 1782. He also served as a delegate to the Virginia state convention for the ratification of the U.S. Constitution, the minister to France from 1797 to 1798, a U.S. representative in Congress from 1799 to 1800, and the secretary of state under President John Adams from 1800 to 1801.

Was Chief Justice John Marshall President Adams's first choice as chief justice?

No, President John Adams first offered the chief justice position to former chief justice John Jay, who declined. Adams also considered sitting justices William Cushing and William Paterson. However, ultimately, Adams picked his sitting secretary of state, Chief Justice Marshall.

Ironically, Adams had offered Chief Justice Marshall a seat on the U.S. Supreme Court back in 1798, but Chief Justice Marshall declined because he sought a position in Congress. Adams then appointed Bushrod Washington, the nephew of George Washington.

Who did Chief Justice John Marshall believe should be chief justice?

Chief Justice Marshall advised President Adams that the appointment of chief justice should go to Justice Paterson, one of the drafters of the Judiciary Act of 1789 and a leading Framer at the 1787 Philadelphia Convention that created the Constitution.

Over what impeachment trial did Chief Justice John Marshall preside?

Chief Justice Marshall presided over the impeachment trial of former vice president Aaron Burr in 1807 in his capacity as a circuit judge (U.S. Supreme Court justices had the detestable duty of riding circuit for much of the 19th century). Chief Justice Marshall's rulings in the case effectively nullified the prosecution's treason charges against Burr. His rulings also inspired the antagonism of President Thomas Jefferson, not an ally of Chief Justice Marshall.

In what case did Chief Justice John Marshall lay out the power of judicial review?

Chief Justice Marshall established the power of judicial review in the famous case of *Marbury v. Madison* (1803). He proclaimed that "it is emphatically the province and duty of the judicial department to say what the law is."

The case involved a power struggle between the two major political parties of the time: the Federalists and the Democratic-Republicans. President John Adams, a Federalist, was leaving office, having lost to his political rival and former vice president Thomas Jefferson, a Democratic-Republican. The Federalist Congress quickly passed a new judiciary act that created many new judgeships, including 45 justice of the peace positions. Adams's secretary of state—none other than Marshall himself—then had to sign the commissions for these "midnight justices" in order for them to take office.

Whose attacks in the press caused Chief Justice John Marshall to write anonymous replies under the name "a friend to the Constitution"?

Spencer Roane, a jurist on the Virginia Supreme Court, attacked the Marshall Court for several of its rulings. His attacks intensified in 1819 after the Court's decision in *McCullough v. Maryland,* which Roane viewed as yet another attack on state sovereignty. Roane and his friend William Brockenbrough wrote essays in the *Richmond Enquirer* heavily criticizing the Court's decision. Chief Justice Marshall responded with a series of newspaper editorials signed as either "a friend to the Union" or "a friend to the Constitution."

DID YOU KNOW?

Unfortunately, Marshall did not have time to deliver all of the commissions before the new Jefferson administration took over the White House. Seventeen justices of the peace, including William Marbury, did not receive their commissions before the new president took office. Marbury then sued Jefferson's secretary of state, James Madison, asking the Court to issue a writ of mandamus, forcing Madison to deliver Marbury his commission.

Marshall, now chief justice, noted that Marbury was entitled to his commission, as he had been appointed by the president and was otherwise qualified for the position. Chief Justice Marshall also determined, in his opinion, that Madison had wrongfully withheld Marbury's commission from him.

However, Chief Justice Marshall also ruled that Marbury's suit must fail because Section 13 of the Judiciary Act of 1789, which authorized the Court to issue a writ of mandamus, was unconstitutional. Chief Justice Marshall reasoned that Section 13 of the law conflicted with Article III of the U.S. Constitution, which provided that the U.S. Supreme Court did not have original jurisdiction over Marbury's case, only appellate jurisdiction. In other words, Chief Justice Marshall reasoned that Section 13 was unconstitutional because it attempted to confer original jurisdiction to litigants like William Marbury, but the Constitution only had appellate jurisdiction, meaning that Marbury first had to sue in a lower court. Chief Justice Marshall wrote that "the jurisdiction had to be appellate, not original."

In what decision did Chief Justice John Marshall write that Congress had the power to create a national bank?

The Marshall Court unanimously ruled in *McCullough v. Maryland* (1819) that Congress had the power to create a national bank and that the state of Maryland could not tax a branch of the National Bank located within its borders. Maryland had levied a tax on all banks not chartered by the state. James McCullough, the cashier of the National Bank, refused to pay the Maryland state tax, leading to the legal dispute.

In his opinion for the Court, Chief Justice Marshall reasoned that Congress had the power to create the National Bank based on its powers under the Necessary and Proper Clause of the Constitution. This clause, sometimes called the "Elastic Clause," pro-

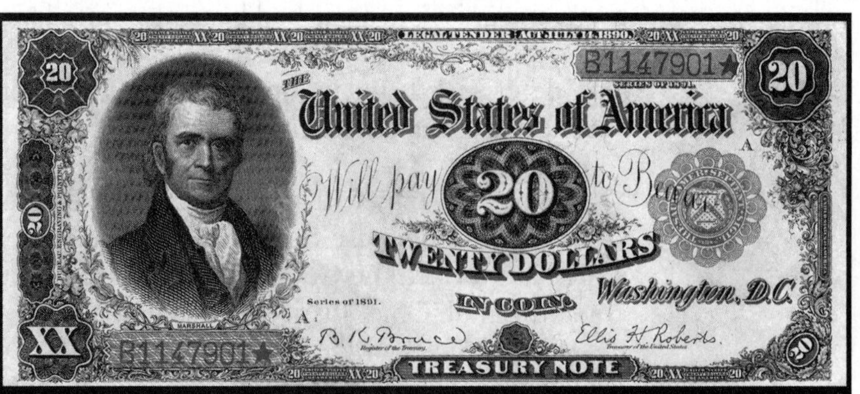

Justice Marshall's service—which included affirming Congress's right to establish a national bank—would be commemorated by the inclusion of his portrait on a $20 treasury note.

vides this: "To make all Laws which shall be necessary and proper for carrying into Execution the foregoing Powers, and all other Powers vested by this Constitution in the Government of the United States, or in any Department or Officer thereof."

Chief Justice Marshall interpreted this clause and the powers of Congress broadly. In oft-cited language, he wrote:

> We admit, as all must admit, that the powers of the government are limited, and that its limits are not to be transcended. But we think the sound construction of the constitution must allow to the national legislature that discretion, with respect to the means by which the powers it confers are to be carried into execution, which will enable that body to perform the high duties assigned to it, in the manner most beneficial to the people. Let the end be legitimate, let it be within the scope of the constitution, and all means which are appropriate, which are plainly adapted to that end, which are not prohibited, but consist with the letter and spirit of the constitution, are constitutional.

The Marshall Court struck down a state law for the first time in what decision?

The Marshall Court invalidated a state law for the first time in *Fletcher v. Peck* (1810) in a case that involved questionable land deals. In 1795, the state of Georgia sold more than 30 million acres of land (located in present-day Alabama and Mississippi) to several northern land companies. These companies, in turn, sold the Yazoo land (so called for the Yazoo nation) to third parties at much higher prices. It was revealed that many Georgia legislators received bribes for their votes in approving the land sales. In the next round of elections, these legislators were voted out of office, and the new legislature passed a law in 1796 that annulled the original sale contracts.

This presented a problem for innocent third parties who purchased the land without knowledge of the shady origins of how the land was first acquired. In a planned lawsuit, Robert Fletcher of New Hampshire sued John Peck of Massachusetts in 1803 to "quiet" his title in order to ensure that he had a valid claim to the land.

The Court ruled that the Georgia law invalidating the Yazoo land sales was unconstitutional because it violated the Constitution's Contract Clause, preventing states from impairing the obligations of contracts. Chief Justice Marshall reasoned that the new law could negatively impact innocent third-party purchasers such as Robert Fletcher. "If the original transaction was infected with fraud, these purchasers did not participate in it, and had no notice of it," he wrote. "They were innocent." Chief Justice Marshall ruled that Fletcher had "vested rights" in the land that he had innocently purchased.

In what decision did Chief Justice John Marshall broadly define Congress's interstate commerce powers?

The Marshall Court broadly defined commerce in *Gibbons v. Ogden* (1824), a case that featured a battle of steamboat entrepreneurs. The state of New York had granted an exclusive license to Robert Livingston and Robert Fulton, the inventor of the steamboat, to operate steamboats in the New York Harbor and the Hudson River. Livingston and Fulton then licensed Aaron Ogden.

Ogden's former business partner, Thomas Gibbons, wanted to break up this monopoly. He had acquired a federal permit to operate steamboats between New York and New Jersey. Ogden sued Gibbons, arguing that Gibbons's activities were infringing on Ogden's exclusive monopoly. Ogden sought an injunction, ordering Gibbons to cease infringing on his exclusive privilege.

Gibbons, backed by the wealthy Cornelius Vanderbilt, fought back in court by hiring perhaps the best lawyer in America: Daniel

Webster. The U.S. Supreme Court ruled that Ogden's exclusive monopoly was invalid because it infringed on Congress's Commerce Clause powers. Chief Justice Marshall broadly defined the powers of Congress's commerce powers, writing: "Commerce, undoubtedly, is traffic, but it is something more: it is intercourse. It describes the commercial intercourse between nations, and parts of nations, in all its branches, and is regulated by prescribing rules for carrying on that intercourse."

JUSTICE OLIVER WENDELL HOLMES JR.

Why is Justice Oliver Wendell Holmes Jr. considered such a great justice?

Justice Holmes is considered perhaps the foremost legal thinker and developer of law (perhaps aside from Chief Justice John Marshall) in U.S. Supreme Court history. He had a scholarly bent, knowledge of philosophy, and a mind that could absorb different kinds of information easily. For example, Judge Richard A. Posner of the U.S. Court of Appeals for the Seventh Circuit once called Justice Holmes "the most influential figure in the history of American law." Legal historian Richard MacGregor Burns writes of Justice Holmes: "Holmes was a kind of Enlightenment philosopher, son of an eminent man of letters, acquainted with such literati as Emerson and Longfellow, one of the few Americans who could converse on easy terms in London with John Stuart Mill and Prime Minister William Gladstone."

Where do scholars rate Justice Holmes in terms of the quality of his writing?

Most Court historians believe that Justice Holmes was one of the finest, if not the finest, writer to sit on the High Court, though

Justice Benjamin N. Cardozo and Justice Robert H. Jackson also are considered first-rate linguists.

Characteristic of this assessment is one from famous lawyer Francis Biddle, who contributed an essay on Justice Holmes to *Mr. Justice* (eds. Allison Dunham and Philip Kurland). Biddle explained: "One cannot describe Holmes without recording the quality of his wit as in writing, words, and thought indistinguishable, so that his clarity, his freshness, and his poet's touch clothed his ideas in a style that made them sound inevitable."

Was Justice Holmes a veteran?

Yes; Justice Holmes served honorably with the Massachusetts 20th Volunteers during the U.S. Civil War. He fought on the side of the Union and was wounded three different times in battle. Biographers Anthony Murray and Edwin G. Quattlebaum II write in their book *Justice Holmes: The Measure of His Thought*: "Holmes believed that his wartime experiences molded his thought and character in significant ways." Justice Holmes was wounded severely in both the Battle of Ball's Bluff in Virginia and the Battle of Antietam.

In what oft-criticized decision did Justice Holmes offer a powerful dissent?

The Fuller Court ruled 5–4 in *Lochner v. New York* (1905) that a state law limiting employers to a 10-hour workday and a 60-hour work week for their employees violated an employer's liberty of contract rights under the 14th Amendment. The dispute arose after Utica bakery owner Joseph Lochner allegedly worked employee Aman Schmitter longer than 60 hours a week.

This violated an 1897 New York law that imposed the work-hour limitations in order to protect the health and safety of

Oliver Wendell Holmes Jr., one of the most influential American judges, was appointed by President Theodore Roosevelt in 1902 and served until his retirement at age 90.

workers, many of whom toiled in less than savory conditions. A sharply divided Court struck down the law, finding it to be a violation of the employer's liberty of contract.

Justice Holmes criticized the majority for reading its own economic theories into the Constitution. He said that the law should not be struck down unless it could be shown that it was irrational and did not further the state's legitimate interest in health. Justice Holmes famously wrote:

> The Fourteenth Amendment does not enact Mr. Herbert Spencer's Social Statics.... Some of these laws embody convictions or prejudices which judges are likely to share. Some may not. But a constitution is not intended to embody a particular economic theory, whether of paternalism and the organic relation of the citizen to the state or of laissez faire. It is made for people of fundamentally different views, and the accident of our finding certain opinions natural and familiar, or novel, and even shocking, ought not to conclude our judgment upon the question whether statutes embodying them conflict with the Constitution of the United States.

DID YOU KNOW?

In what decision did Justice Holmes advocate the "stream of commerce" theory?

Justice Holmes advocated the "stream of commerce" theory in the Court's unanimous decision in *Swift & Co. v. United States* (1905). The Court ruled that a group of meatpacking houses engaged in a variety of activities, including fixing and bidding up prices, that violated the Sherman Antitrust Act. The meatpacking houses contended that their activities were intrastate in nature, but the Court noted that the sale of cattle resembled a "current of commerce" that was interstate in nature.

In what decision did the Holmes Court uphold a contempt citation for a newspaper publishing unfavorable cartoons?

The Court ruled 7–2 in *Patterson v. Colorado* (1907) that Thomas Patterson, owner of both the *Rocky Mountain News* and *The Denver Times*, could be punished for contempt for published articles and cartoons highly critical of the Colorado Supreme Court. The Court, in an opinion by Justice Holmes, did not extend the First Amendment protections of freedom of the press to the states via the 14th Amendment. Justice Holmes also noted that the primary purpose of the Free Press Clause was to prevent prior restraints on speech rather than subsequent punishments for expression.

Justice Holmes wrote:

> A publication likely to reach the eyes of a jury, declaring a witness in a pending cause a perjurer, would be none the less a contempt that it was true. It would tend to obstruct the administration of justice, because even a cor-

> rect conclusion is not to be reached or helped in that way, if our system of trials is to be maintained. The theory of our system is that the conclusions to be reached in a case will be induced only by evidence and argument in open court, and not by any outside influence, whether of private talk or public print.

Why is Justice Holmes considered so important for First Amendment jurisprudence?

Justice Holmes is sometimes called "the Father of the First Amendment" because he wrote some of the seminal free-speech decisions back in 1919. Justice Holmes created the so-called "clear

Known as a gifted communicator and legal scholar well before his appointment to the highest bench, Holmes published his still-relevant book *The Common Law* in 1881, and since then it has never been out of print.

and present danger" test in order to identify when political speech is protected and when it is not. In other words, the speech of a political dissident, such as a socialist or an anarchist, is protected under the First Amendment unless it creates a "clear and present danger" to the government or established order.

Initially, Justice Holmes's articulation of the "clear and present danger" test was not very protective of free speech in *Schenck v. United States* (1919). In fact, Justice Holmes applied that test quite broadly in order to cover the relatively harmless speech disseminated by Charles Schenck and Elizabeth Baer. His initial articulation of the "clear and present danger" test was this:

> The question in every case is whether the words used are used in such circumstances and are of such a nature as to create a clear and present danger that they will bring about the substantive evils that Congress has a right to prevent. It is a question of proximity and degree. When a nation is at war many things that might be said in time of peace are such a hindrance to its effort that their utterance will not be endured so long as men fight and that no Court could regard them as protected by any constitutional right.

To Justice Holmes, freedom of speech was not as protected during times of war as it was during times of peace. Thus, he affirmed the convictions of Schenck and Baer. Much criticism of this opinion occurred in scholarly circles.

However, over the summer of 1919, Justice Holmes came back with a dissenting opinion in the fall—*Abrams v. United States* (1919)—that was very protective of freedom of speech. In fact, many refer to Justice Holmes's dissent as "the Great Dissent." In his dissenting opinion, Justice Holmes introduced what is sometimes known as "the marketplace of ideas" metaphor. He wrote:

> Persecution for the expression of opinions seems to me perfectly logical. If you have no doubt of your premises or your power and want a certain result with all your heart you naturally express your wishes in law and sweep away all opposition. To allow opposition by speech seems

to indicate that you think the speech impotent, as when a man says that he has squared the circle, or that you do not care whole heartedly for the result, or that you doubt either your power or your premises. But when men have realized that time has upset many fighting faiths, they may come to believe even more than they believe the very foundations of their own conduct that the ultimate good desired is better reached by free trade in ideas—that the best test of truth is the power of the thought to get itself accepted in the competition of the market, and that truth is the only ground upon which their wishes safely can be carried out. That at any rate is the theory of our Constitution. It is an experiment, as all life is an experiment. Every year if not every day we have to wager our salvation upon some prophecy based upon imperfect knowledge. While that experiment is part of our system I think that we should be eternally vigilant against attempts to check the expression of opinions that we loathe and believe to be fraught with death, unless they so imminently threaten immediate interference with the lawful and pressing purposes of the law that an immediate check is required to save the country. I wholly disagree with the argument of the Government that the First Amendment left the common law as to seditious libel in force.

JUSTICE LOUIS BRANDEIS

How did Justice Louis Brandeis contribute to the development of the right to privacy as a lawyer?

Justice Brandeis co-authored a seminal article in the *Harvard Law Review* with his law partner, Samuel Warren, titled "The Right to Privacy." Justice Brandeis and Warren argued that threats to privacy were endemic in society: "The press is overstepping in every direction the obvious bounds of propriety and decency. Gossip is

DID YOU KNOW?

In what case as a lawyer did Justice Brandeis write what became known as a "Brandeis brief"?

Justice Brandeis wrote his first so-called "Brandeis brief" in *Muller v. Oregon* (1908), a case involving a challenge to an Oregon law limiting the number of hours women could work. Justice Brandeis submitted a brief in support of the law that contained much social science, medical, and other materials rather than legal precedent. The brief was more than 100 pages long. It had an impact on the Court, which upheld the Oregon law.

no longer the resource of the idle and the vicious, but has become a trade, which is pursued with industry as well as effrontery."

Justice Brandeis and Warren identified two grave threats to privacy: (1) new technology and (2) conduct of the press. With regard to new technologies, they worried about instantaneous photographs and numerous mechanical devices that invade personal privacy. They also felt that the press was invading the private lives of people.

They explained that "the common law secures to each individual the right of determining, ordinarily, to what extent his thoughts, sentiments, and emotions shall be communicated to others." However, the justices did explain that information was not private if it related to "public or general interest."

In what famous dissent did Justice Brandeis talk about the importance of privacy?

Justice Brandeis issued the most comprehensive dissenting opinion on privacy in *Olmstead v. United States* (1928), though Justice Holmes, Justice Pierce Butler, and Chief Justice Harlan Fiske Stone also wrote dissenting opinions.

Justice Brandeis recognized that individual privacy can be invaded in different ways through technological advancements. In a moment of prescience, he wrote: "Ways may someday be developed by which the government, without removing papers from secret drawers, can reproduce them in court, and by which it will be enabled to expose to a jury the most intimate occurrences of the home." He explained that invading privacy by listening to telephone conversations was as great as, if not greater than, opening an individual's mail. He also questioned the government's culpability in sanctioning what he termed "unlawful wiretapping." He warned that the government itself would become a lawbreaker.

He explained in potent language: "The makers of our Constitution undertook to secure conditions favorable to the pursuit of happiness. They sought to protect Americans in their beliefs, their thoughts, their emotions and their sensations. They conferred, as against the government, the right to be let alone the most comprehensive of rights and the right most valued by civilized men. To protect that right, every unjustifiable intrusion by the government, whatever the means employed, must be deemed a violation of the Fourth Amendment."

Justice Louis Brandeis was described admiringly by his successor William O. Douglas as "a militant crusader for social justice ... [who is] dangerous because of his brilliance, his arithmetic, his courage ... [and] dangerous because he was incorruptible."

In what famous concurring opinion did Justice Brandeis lay out his theory of the First Amendment?

Justice Brandeis wrote one of the most consequential opinions in a concurrence in *Whitney v. California* (1927), a case involving a First Amendment challenge to California's criminal syndicalism law. Such a law was used to target dissident political groups, including communists and socialists. Charlotte Anita Whitney was convicted of violating the law for a speech she gave in Oakland, California, on behalf of the Communist Labor Party of California, which supported the International Workers of the World. The California law prohibited people from organizing, assisting, and assembling people together to advocate, teach, aid, and abet criminal syndicalism. Whitney was arrested during the height of the Red Scare, a time period when government officials were concerned about a communist uprising similar to the Bolshevik Revolution in Russia led by Vladimir Lenin.

The majority affirmed Whitney's conviction and upheld the statute, finding that it did not violate First Amendment freedoms. Writing for the majority, Justice Edward Terry Sanford concluded that the law is not "an unreasonable or arbitrary exercise of the police power of the State; unwarrantably infringing upon any right of free speech, assembly or association, or that those persons are protected from punishment by the due process clause who abuse such rights by joining and furthering an organization thus menacing the peace and welfare of the State."

The decision is better known for the concurring opinion of Justice Brandeis, which was joined by Justice Holmes. Justice Brandeis's concurrence, which reads more like a dissent, became a blueprint for the justification of free speech. He wrote that even advocacy of illegal conduct could not justify restricting speech unless the speech incites immediate lawless action, a test that the U.S. Supreme Court would eventually adopt in the 1969 decision *Brandenburg v. Ohio*. However, Justice Brandeis concurred with the majority because "there was other testimony which tended to establish the existence of a conspiracy, on the part of members of the International Workers of the World, to commit present serious crimes, and likewise to show that such a conspiracy would be furthered by the activity of the society of which Miss Whitney was a member."

In his opinion, Justice Brandeis advocated for support of what has come to be known as the counter-speech doctrine: that when confronted by hostile or offensive speech, the response should be to counter it with positive speech rather than engage in outright censorship. Justice Brandeis famously wrote: "If there be time to expose through discussion the falsehood and fallacies, to aver the evil by the processes of education, the remedy to be applied is more speech, not enforced silence."

Justice Brandeis's concurrence was filled with other oft-cited passages that formed the basis of modern First Amendment jurisprudence. Here are a couple more gems from his pen:

> They believed that freedom to think as you will and to speak as you think are means indispensable to the discovery and spread of political truth; that without free speech and assembly discussion would be futile; that with them, discussion affords ordinarily adequate protection against the dissemination of noxious doctrine; that the greatest menace to freedom is an inert people; that public discussion is a political duty; and that this should be a fundamental principle of the American government.

> Fear of serious injury cannot alone justify suppression of free speech and assembly. Men feared witches and burnt women. It is the function of speech to free men from the bondage of irrational fears. To justify suppression of free speech there must be reasonable ground to fear that serious evil will result if free speech is practiced.

After the verdict, what happened to Charlotte Anita Whitney?

California governor Clement Calhoun Young pardoned Whitney in June 1927. Named national party chairman of the Communist Party in 1936, she unsuccessfully ran for a U.S. Senate seat in 1950. She died in San Francisco in 1955.

CHIEF JUSTICE EARL WARREN

Why is Chief Justice Earl Warren considered a great jurist?

Chief Justice Warren is considered a great jurist because he was considered a persuasive leader of the Court. Henry Abraham writes:

> Earl Warren—who involved his clerks heavily in the production of his opinions—was not a great lawyer in the mold of a Taney or a Hughes; not a great legal scholar in the tradition of a Brandeis or Frankfurter; not a supreme stylist like a Cardozo or a Jackson; not a judicial philosopher like a Holmes or a Black; not a resourceful, efficient administrator like a Taft or a Warren Earl Burger, his successor. But he was the chief justice par excellence—second in institutional-leadership greatness to John Marshall himself in the eyes of most impartial students of the Court as well as the Warren Court's legion

Appointed in 1953 by President Eisenhower, Chief Justice Earl Warren left his third term as governor of California to head up a Supreme Court that has been called the most liberal in U.S. history.

> of critics. Like Marshall he understood and utilized the tools of pervasive and persuasive power leadership available to him; a genuine statesman, he knew how to bring men together, how to set a tone, and how to fashion a mood. He was a wise man and a warm, kind human being. He was his Court, the judicial activist Court: he viewed law as an instrument to get the right result.

Chief Justice Warren's U.S. Supreme Court colleague, Justice William J. Brennan Jr., said of the man he called "Super Chief": "He had everything. He was hard-working. He knew how to work with people. He was marvelous with people. He would take approaches that would often escape my eye. He was just extraordinary."

What were Chief Justice Warren's positions before becoming a U.S. Supreme Court justice?

Chief Justice Warren served in public office from 1919 until his resignation from the U.S. Supreme Court in 1969. From 1919 to 1920, he served as deputy city attorney for Oakland, California. From 1920 to 1925, he served as district attorney for Alameda County. From 1939 to 1943, he served as California attorney general. From 1943 to 1953, he served as governor of California. In 1948, Chief Justice Warren ran for vice president with Republican presidential candidate Thomas E. Dewey. In 1952, Chief Justice Warren sought the Republican nomination for president, but he later withdrew and supported General Dwight D. Eisenhower. Eisenhower returned the favor the next year by nominating Chief Justice Warren as chief justice.

What was Chief Justice Warren's military experience?

Chief Justice Warren served his country during World War I, rising to the rank of captain.

What was the historical irony of the Warren Court being the great liberal court?

Chief Justice Warren was not considered a great liberal during his tenure as a California public official as a state attorney general and governor. He supported the internment of thousands of Japanese American citizens during the time of World War II. Nearly 120,000 people of Japanese ancestry were removed from the West Coast of the United States and placed in "war relocation camps." Chief Justice Warren publicly stated his support for the relocation: "If the Japs are released, no one will be able to tell a saboteur from any other Jap." Chief Justice Warren later acknowledged his regret for this, writing in his memoirs: "I have since deeply regretted the removal order and my own testimony advocating it, because it was not in keeping with our American concept of freedom and the rights of citizens."

In fact, Bernard Schwartz, in his biography of Chief Justice Warren, *Super Chief*, writes: "There was no hint of greatness in the first phase of Warren's career. An honest, hard-working, and vigorous law enforcement officer, there was little to distinguish Warren from his peers. Even in his later role as Governor of California, nothing foreshadowed his performance as Chief Justice."

What other positions did President Eisenhower consider appointing Chief Justice Warren to before the U.S. Supreme Court?

President Eisenhower had discussed with Governor Warren the possibility of serving as secretary of labor and secretary of the interior. However, he declined those cabinet posts. Then, Eisenhower offered him the position of solicitor general. He was prepared to accept that position, but then Chief Justice Fred M. Vinson died unexpectedly, and an opening for chief justice occurred.

What was *Brown v. Board of Education*?

Brown v. Board of Education of Topeka was one of the most important U.S. Supreme Court decisions ever. On May 17, 1954, the Court's opinion invalidated segregated public schools as violative of the Equal Protection Clause. The decision was a consolidation of challenges to segregated public schools in the states of Kansas, Delaware, South Carolina, and Virginia. The other cases were *Briggs v. Elliott* (South Carolina), *Davis v. County School Board of Prince Edward County* (Virginia), and *Gebhart v. Belton* (Delaware). A group of African Americans, represented by the NAACP, mounted a challenge to the segregated school systems. They not only alleged that the schools their children attended were inferior to schools attended by white children, but they also alleged that separating schools based on race was unconstitutional on its face.

The Court ruled that segregated public schools were "inherently unequal." The Court wrote: "We conclude that, in the field of public education, the doctrine of 'separate but equal' has no place. Separate educational facilities are inherently unequal. Therefore, we hold that the plaintiffs and others similarly situated for whom the actions have been brought are, by reason of the segregation complained of, deprived of the equal protection of the laws guaranteed by the Fourteenth Amendment."

Chief Justice Warren also emphasized the importance of education in his unanimous opinion, writing:

> Today, education is perhaps the most important function of state and local governments. Compulsory school attendance laws and the great expenditures for education both demonstrate our recognition of the importance of education to our democratic society. It is required in the performance of our most basic public responsibilities, even service in the armed forces. It is the very foundation of good citizenship. Today it is a principal instrument in

awakening the child to cultural values, in preparing him for later professional training, and in helping him to adjust normally to his environment. In these days, it is doubtful that any child may reasonably be expected to succeed in life if he is denied the opportunity of an education. Such an opportunity, where the state has undertaken to provide it, is a right which must be made available to all on equal terms.

We come then to the question presented: does segregation of children in public schools solely on the basis of race, even though the physical facilities and other "tangible" factors may be equal, deprive the children of the minority group of equal educational opportunities? We believe that it does.

What decision did *Brown v. Board of Education* overrule?

The Court overruled its 1896 decision *Plessy v. Ferguson*, which had established the separate but equal doctrine. The Court

Under Chief Justice Earl Warren, the Supreme Court ruled unanimously in *Brown v. Board of Education* that racial segregation in schools violated the Equal Protections clause and was therefore unconstitutional.

DID YOU KNOW?

How was Chief Justice Warren crucial to the *Brown* decision?

Brown v. Board of Education originally came before the U.S. Supreme Court for argument in 1952. The justices were divided on the question and ordered a re-argument. Then, in September 1953, Chief Justice Vinson died. Chief Justice Warren assumed the mantle of chief justice and persuaded his colleagues that the importance of their decision required a unanimous voice from the Court. Chief Justice Warren wrote a short, 10-page opinion for the lawyer and layperson alike to understand. Historians say that without the leadership of Chief Justice Warren, the U.S. Supreme Court may not have been able to speak with such a single voice. Justice Felix Frankfurter allegedly told two law clerks upon hearing of the death of Chief Justice Vinson: "This is the first indication that I have ever had that there is a God."

ruled that the separate but equal doctrine had "no place" in public education. The *Brown* decision led to the invalidation of a whole host of segregation laws across the country.

What decision in criminal justice did Chief Justice Warren write that caused great controversy?

Chief Justice Warren authored the Court's decision in *Miranda v. Arizona* (1966), a decision that required police officers to read suspects their rights when placing such individuals in custodial interrogation and arrest. Chief Justice Warren explained the essence of the ruling as follows in the first part of his opinion:

> The prosecution may not use statements, whether exculpatory or inculpatory, stemming from custodial in-

> terrogation of the defendant unless it demonstrates the use of procedural safeguards effective to secure the privilege against self-incrimination. By custodial interrogation, we mean questioning initiated by law enforcement officers after a person has been taken into custody or otherwise deprived of his freedom of action in any significant way. As for the procedural safeguards to be employed, unless other fully effective means are devised to inform accused persons of their right of silence and to assure a continuous opportunity to exercise it, the following measures are required. Prior to any questioning, the person must be warned that he has a right to remain silent, that any statement he does make may be used as evidence against him, and that he has a right to the presence of an attorney, either retained or appointed.

Chief Justice Warren emphasized that it was the standard practice of the Federal Bureau of Investigation to give such warnings to suspects before questioning.

Chief Justice Warren's opinion caused great controversy both inside and outside the Court. Legal historian Bernard Schwartz, in his book *Super Chief*, explains: "The bitterness about *Miranda* was not confined to the Court's critics. The *Miranda* dissenters also thought that the decision was a disservice to both Court and country."

What decision did Chief Justice Warren write that upheld the police practice of stop and frisk?

Chief Justice Warren wrote the Court's decision in *Terry v. Ohio* (1968), which upheld the practice of police officers stopping a suspect based on reasonable suspicion and then frisking that suspect if the officer reasonably believes that the suspect might have a weapon. The case involved a veteran detective with the Cleveland police department, Martin McFadden, who felt that

John Terry and another man were casing a jewelry store for a pending robbery.

McFadden approached the men, patted them down, and found a pistol on Terry, who contended that his conviction for carrying a concealed weapon should be reversed because McFadden had engaged in an unlawful search and seizure.

However, the Court ruled 8–1 (with only Justice William O. Douglas dissenting) that Officer McFadden's actions were justified as a legitimate stop and frisk. During oral arguments, Chief Justice Warren seemed to hint that he was concerned about police officers having the ability to protect themselves. Chief Justice Warren asked: "How far do you want us to go? I suppose you will agree that a police officer has a right to protect himself. Does the officer have the right to frisk a man to see if he has a weapon?"

Chief Justice Warren reflected these concerns in his majority opinion, writing: "When an officer is justified in believing that the individual whose suspicious behavior he is investigating at close range is armed and presently dangerous to the officer or to others, it would appear to be clearly unreasonable to deny the officer the power to take necessary measures to determine whether the person is in fact carrying a weapon and to neutralize the threat of physical harm."

Chief Justice Warren emphasized the need for the frisk in order to ensure officer safety:

> The crux of this case, however, is not the propriety of Officer McFadden's taking steps to investigate petitioner's suspicious behavior, but, rather, whether there was justification for McFadden's invasion of Terry's personal security by searching him for weapons in the course of that investigation. We are now concerned with more than the governmental interest in investigating crime; in addition, there is the more immediate interest of the police officer in taking steps to assure himself that the person with whom he is dealing is not armed with a weapon that could unexpectedly and fatally be used

against him. Certainly it would be unreasonable to require that police officers take unnecessary risks in the performance of their duties. American criminals have a long tradition of armed violence, and every year in this country many law enforcement officers are killed in the line of duty, and thousands more are wounded.

In what famous decision did Chief Justice Warren uphold a conviction for burning draft cards?

Chief Justice Warren reasoned in *United States v. O'Brien* (1968) that the government could prosecute David Paul O'Brien for burning his draft card and that the federal law prohibiting the burning of such cards did not violate the First Amendment. O'Brien, who burned his card along with three others on the Boston courthouse steps, argued that his act of burning the draft card was a form of protected protest, a form of symbolic speech.

Chief Justice Warren questioned this at the oral argument, asking O'Brien's lawyer: "What cases do you have that equate the burning of the draft card to symbolic speech?" A federal district court had upheld O'Brien's conviction, but the U.S. Court of Appeals for the First Circuit had reversed its decision, finding that O'Brien had engaged in a form of symbolic speech. "In singling out persons engaging in protest for special treatment the amendment strikes at the very core of what the First Amendment protects," the appeals court explained. "It has long been beyond doubt that symbolic action may be protected speech."

However, the U.S. government appealed to the U.S. Supreme Court and prevailed with Chief Justice Warren, writing the majority opinion. "We cannot accept the view that an apparently limitless variety of conduct can be labeled 'speech' whenever the person engaging in the conduct intends thereby to express an idea," Chief Justice Warren wrote. "However, even on the assumption that the alleged communicative element in O'Brien's conduct is sufficient

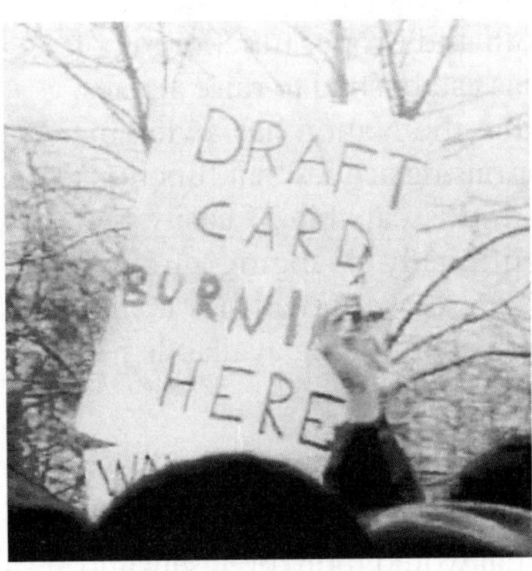

During the late 1960s, the burning of draft cards became a common form of protest against U.S. participation in the war in Vietnam.

to bring into play the First Amendment, it does not necessarily follow that the destruction of a registration certificate is constitutionally protected activity."

Chief Justice Warren created what is known in First Amendment law as the "O'Brien test" for evaluating restrictions that involve both speech and conduct. He explained: "Whatever imprecision inheres in these terms, we think it clear that a government regulation is sufficiently justified if it is within the constitutional power of the Government; if it furthers an important or substantial governmental interest; if the governmental interest is unrelated to the suppression of free expression; and if the incidental restriction on alleged First Amendment freedoms is no greater than is essential to the furtherance of that interest."

Chief Justice Warren reasoned that the federal government surely had the power to enforce the draft and to ensure the orderly administration of the draft. It followed, according to Chief Justice Warren, that the draft cards were an important part of this process. Furthermore, the protection of the draft cards from intentional mutilation was designed to ensure the orderly flow of the draft system, not to target antiwar protesters.

Chief Justice Warren explained:

> We think it apparent that the continuing availability to each registrant of his Selective Service certificates sub-

stantially furthers the smooth and proper functioning of the system that Congress has established to raise armies. We think it also apparent that the Nation has a vital interest in having a system for raising armies that functions with maximum efficiency and is capable of easily and quickly responding to continually changing circumstances. For these reasons, the Government has a substantial interest in assuring the continuing availability of issued Selective Service certificates.

It is equally clear that the 1965 Amendment specifically protects this substantial governmental interest. We perceive no alternative means that would more precisely and narrowly assure the continuing availability of issued Selective Service certificates than a law which prohibits their willful mutilation or destruction. The 1965 Amendment prohibits such conduct and does nothing more. In other words, both the governmental interest and the operation of the 1965 Amendment are limited to the noncommunicative aspect of O'Brien's conduct. The governmental interest and the scope of the 1965 Amendment are limited to preventing harm to the smooth and efficient functioning of the Selective Service System. When O'Brien deliberately rendered unavailable his registration certificate, he willfully frustrated this governmental interest. For this noncommunicative impact of his conduct, and for nothing else, he was convicted.

JUSTICE HUGO BLACK

What was Justice Hugo Black's experience before being appointed to the U.S. Supreme Court?

Justice Black engaged in the private practice of law in both Ashland and then Birmingham after earning a law degree from the University of Alabama. He also served as a police court judge in Birmingham for a time. His legal practice was interrupted when he went to serve his country in the U.S. Army during World War I, rising to the rank of captain during his service. After returning home, he resumed his law practice until he ran for a seat in the U.S. Senate. He became a U.S. senator in 1926, where he served as a loyal supporter of President Franklin D. Roosevelt's New Deal program. In 1937, Roosevelt picked Justice Black to replace the retiring justice Willis Van Devanter.

What case did Justice Black argue before the U.S. Supreme Court as a lawyer?

Justice Black argued the case of *Lewis v. Roberts* (1925) before the U.S. Supreme Court. Justice Black represented Henry Lewis, an African American convict, who was injured while working underground in a coal mine for Montevallo Mining Company. Lewis and other inmates had been "leased" to the mining company. Lewis was seriously injured and had obtained a judgment against Montevallo. However, the company declared bankruptcy and

Hugo Black was appointed by President Franklin Delano Roosevelt in 1937. He served until 1971, retiring from the Court mere days before suffering a fatal stroke.

claimed that it did not have to pay Lewis because the debt owed to Lewis was not based on a contract.

The U.S. Supreme Court unanimously reversed the decision in *Lewis v. Roberts*, reasoning that a tort suit could not so easily be discharged in bankruptcy. Justice Black had taken the case because he thought the treatment of Henry Lewis was a travesty of justice.

Why is Justice Black considered such a significant justice?

Justice Black was one of the most consequential justices ever to serve on the Court, where he enjoyed a nearly 34-year tenure. His impact was felt because he contributed opinions that changed and impacted many different areas of American law. Irving Dilliard wrote of Justice Black's impact in his piece "The Individual and the Bill of Absolute Rights" in the book *Hugo Black and the Supreme Court: A Symposium*: "But, Mr. Justice Black's unquestioned place in history stands on far more solid substance than three decades of Supreme Court service with almost as many colleagues in the span as years. His importance is secured in accomplishment, not in mere endurance. He has left his own clear impress on many vital aspects of our law and life, and has made significant contributions in still other areas."

What was Justice Black's position on freedom of the press and the criticism of public officials?

Justice Black believed that the First Amendment's Press Clause provided carte blanche to the press to criticize public officials free from defamation laws. The U.S. Supreme Court provided significant—but certainly not absolute—protection to the press from defamation suits in *New York Times Co. v. Sullivan* (1964), reasoning that public officials could only recover for defamation claims if they could show that the press acted knowing the information it printed was false or acting in reckless disregard as to the truth or falsity of the statement.

This ruling did not go far enough for Justice Black, who wrote a separate concurring opinion. "We would, I think, more faithfully interpret the First Amendment by holding that at the very least it leaves the people and the press free to criticize officials and discuss public affairs with impunity." Justice Black added that "an unconditional right to say what one pleases about public affairs is what I consider to be the minimum guarantee of the First Amendment."

In what famous decision did Justice Black get vindication 21 years later?

Justice Black wrote the Court's majority opinion in *Gideon v. Wainwright* (1963), ruling that the Sixth Amendment's right to assistance of counsel also applied to state and local governments through the Due Process Clause of the 14th Amendment. The decision meant that Clarence Earl Gideon, a Florida inmate convicted of theft for breaking into a pool room, had his rights violated when a Florida state judge refused his request for an appointed lawyer.

The decision was sweet vindication for Justice Black, who had dissented on the exact same issue 21 years prior in *Betts v. Brady* (1942). In that decision, the Court ruled that Smith Betts, a Maryland farmhand convicted of robbery, did not have his rights violated when a Maryland judge refused to appoint him a lawyer. Maryland law at that time provided that indigent or poor defendants were entitled to an appointed lawyer only when they were charged with murder or rape.

Betts had argued that the Sixth Amendment's right to assistance of counsel was part of the essential "liberty" protected by the Due Process Clause of the 14th Amendment, which provides that no state shall deprive an individual of "life, liberty, or property without due process of law."

But the U.S. Supreme Court ruled against Smith Betts. The majority reasoned that "in the great majority of the States, it has been the considered judgment of the people, their representatives, and their courts that appointment of counsel is not a fundamental right, essential to a fair trial. On the contrary, the matter has generally been deemed one of legislative policy."

Justice Black vigorously dissented in *Betts*. "Denial to the poor of the request for counsel in proceedings based on charges of serious crime has long been regarded as shocking to the 'universal sense of justice' throughout this country," he wrote.

Though Justice Black was in the dissent in 1942, he was assigned the majority opinion in *Gideon v. Wainwright* and did not miss the opportunity to criticize and overrule *Betts v. Brady*. He emphasized the importance of having an attorney in memorable language:

DIVISION OF CORRECTIONS
CORRESPONDENCE REGULATIONS

MAIL WILL NOT BE DELIVERED WHICH DOES NOT CONFORM WITH THESE RULES

No. 1 -- Only 2 letters each week, not to exceed 2 sheets letter-size 8 1/2 x 11" and written *on one side only*, and if ruled paper, do not write between lines. *Your complete name* must be signed at the close of your letter. *Clippings, stamps, letters* from other people, *stationery* or *cash must not be enclosed* in your letters.

No. 2 -- All *letters* must be addressed in the *complete prison name* of the inmate. *Cell number*, where applicable, and *prison number* must be placed in lower left corner of envelope, with your complete name and address in the upper left corner.

No. 3 -- *Do not send any packages without a Package Permit*. Unauthorized *packages* will be destroyed.

No. 4 -- *Letters* must be written in English only.

No. 5 -- *Books, magazines, pamphlets*, and *newspapers* of reputable character will be delivered *only if* mailed direct from the publisher.

No. 6 -- *Money* must be sent in the form of *Postal Money Orders* only, in the inmate's complete prison name and prison number.

INSTITUTION ____ CELL NUMBER ____

NAME ____ NUMBER ____

In The Supreme Court of The United States
Washington D.C.

Clarence Earl Gideon
Petitioner
vs.
H.G. Cochran, Jr, as Director, Divisions of corrections State of Florida

Petition for a writ of Certiorari Directed to The Supreme Court State of Florida.

No. 890 Misc.
OCT. TERM 1961
U. S. Supreme Court

To: The Honorable Earl Warren, Chief Justice of the United States

Comes now the petitioner, Clarence Earl Gideon, a citizen of The United States of America, in proper person, and appearing as his own counsel. Who petitions this Honorable Court for a Writ of Certiorari directed to The Supreme Court of The State of Florida, To review the order and Judgement of the court below denying The petitioner a writ of Habeus Corpus.

Petitioner submits That The Supreme Court of The United States has The authority and jurisdiction to review The final Judgement of The Supreme Court of The State of Florida The highest court of The State Under sec. 344(B) Title 28 U.S.C.A. and Because The "Due process clause" of The

Gideon v. Wainwright was brought to the Supreme Court's attention by the handwritten petition for certiorari from prisoner Clarence Earl Gideon, a poor man who had unsuccessfully represented himself in his own defense after being denied counsel.

> That government hires lawyers to prosecute and defendants who have the money hire lawyers to defend are the strongest indications of the widespread belief that lawyers in criminal courts are necessities, not luxuries. The right of one charged with crime to counsel may not be deemed fundamental and essential to fair trials in some countries, but it is in ours. From the very beginning, our state and national constitutions and laws have laid great emphasis on procedural and substantive safeguards designed to assure fair trials before impartial tribunals in which every defendant stands equal before the law. This noble ideal cannot be realized if the poor man charged with crime has to face his accusers without a lawyer to assist him.

Anthony Lewis, in his famous book on the *Gideon v. Wainwright* case entitled *Gideon's Trumpet,* writes that Justice Black told a friend shortly after the release of his decision in 1963: "When *Betts v. Brady* was decided, I never thought I'd live to see it overruled."

JUSTICE WILLIAM O. DOUGLAS

What are some highlights of Justice William O. Douglas's tenure on the Court?

First of all, Justice Douglas holds the record for the longest tenure on the Court at more than 36 years, spanning from 1939 to 1975. Second, Justice Douglas holds the record for the most opinions total and the most dissenting opinions. He was a progressive who had a very strong capacity for protecting freedom of expression values in his opinions. He also had a highly independent streak, as his nickname "Wild Bill" indicates. His personal life was different from the other justices on the Court, as he had four marriages with progressively younger spouses.

What positions did Justice Douglas hold before ascending to the High Court?

After graduating from Columbia Law School, Justice Douglas briefly worked in private practice at the New York law firm Cravath, DeGersdorff, Swaine, and Wood. He then transitioned into academia, teaching first at Columbia and then at Yale Law School. President Franklin D. Roosevelt then appointed him to the Securities and Exchange Commission in 1934. Five years later, Roosevelt tapped him for the U.S. Supreme Court.

What famous decision regarding prosecutorial failure to turn over exculpatory evidence did Justice Douglas write?

Justice Douglas wrote the Court's opinion in *Brady v. Maryland* (1963), which generally stands for the principle that prosecutors must turn over exculpatory evidence to criminal defendants and their counsel. The case involved the death penalty prosecution of John Leo Brady, who, along with Donald Boblit, had committed armed robbery, which led to the death of an older friend of Brady's named William Brooks. Brady and Boblit had planned to rob Brooks and steal his car for a bank robbery. However, Boblit shot and killed Brooks, something Brady did not want to happen. Brady was prosecuted for the death penalty and convicted. However, his counsel learned that prosecutors had failed to turn over evidence of Boblit's confession, in which he had said that he (Boblit) was the shooter, not Brady.

Justice Douglas reasoned that the failure of the prosecution to turn over this evidence denied Brady his due-process rights and that he was entitled to a new trial with regard to punishment. Justice Douglas explained that "the suppression by the prosecution of evidence favorable to an accused on request violates due process where the evidence is material either to guilt or to punishment."

DID YOU KNOW?

What was the "Black Fear of Silence"?

This was an article that Justice Douglas wrote in 1952 for the *New York Times Magazine*. In the piece, Justice Douglas warned of an increasing orthodoxy of thought and fear of anything different. Justice Douglas wrote this piece as the United States of America was gripped in an anticommunism fervor that, to many historians, went overboard and threatened freedom of speech and conscience. Justice Douglas warns in his article about an "ominous trend" toward orthodoxy and a fear of different ideas. Justice Douglas advocated for wide protection of freedom of expression, even for controversial or dissident ideas.

In part because of this ruling, Brady was spared the death penalty. Additionally, the state of Maryland and Brady's lawyers never agreed on when his new trial on punishment would start. In 1973, Brady's lawyers argued that his rights to a speedy trial were violated. Brady was paroled in 1974. He lived until the age of 76 and passed away in 2009. He never got into criminal trouble again.

In what dissent did Justice Douglas warn about suppressing speech simply because the speakers were communists?

Justice Douglas dissented in *Dennis v. United States* (1951), a case in which the majority of the Court upheld convictions of a dozen members of the American Communist Party allegedly for plotting the overthrow of the United States and other seditious activities.

But in his dissenting opinion, Justice Douglas said that the evidence at the trial did not show evidence of sedition or terror.

Defendants Robert Thompson and Benjamin Davis, seen surrounded by pickets as they leave the Federal Courthouse in New York City, were convicted alongside nine other leaders of the Communist Party of conspiring to overthrow the U.S. government. The Supreme Court did not overturn the conviction, but Justice Douglas's dissent still serves as a memorable defense of free speech.

Instead, according to Justice Douglas, the evidence showed that the defendants preached the tenets of the Marxist–Leninist doctrine without resorting to sedition or terror.

He explained:

So far as the present record is concerned, what petitioners did was to organize people to teach and themselves teach the Marxist–Leninist doctrine contained chiefly in four books: Stalin, *Foundations of Leninism* (1924); Marx and Engels, *Manifesto of the Communist Party* (1848); Lenin, *The State and Revolution* (1917); *History of the Communist Party of the Soviet Union* (B.) (1939).

Those books are to Soviet Communism what *Mein Kampf* was to Nazism. If they are understood, the ugliness of Communism is revealed, its deceit and cunning are exposed, the nature of its activities becomes apparent, and the chances of its success less likely. That is not, of

> course, the reason why petitioners chose these books for their classrooms. They are fervent Communists to whom these volumes are gospel. They preached the creed with the hope that some day it would be acted upon.
>
> The opinion of the Court does not outlaw these texts nor condemn them to the fire, as the Communists do literature offensive to their creed. But if the books themselves are not outlawed, if they can lawfully remain on library shelves, by what reasoning does their use in a classroom become a crime? It would not be a crime under the Act to introduce these books to a class, though that would be teaching what the creed of violent overthrow of the Government is. The Act, as construed, requires the element of intent—that those who teach the creed believe in it. The crime then depends not on what is taught but on who the teacher is. That is to make freedom of speech turn not on what is said, but on the intent with which it is said. Once we start down that road we enter territory dangerous to the liberties of every citizen.

In what opinion did Justice Douglas explain that the purpose of speech was to invite dispute?

Justice Douglas wrote these words in *Terminiello v. City of Chicago* (1949), a case involving the prosecution of Arthur Terminiello for giving a fiery speech in a Chicago auditorium. Terminiello, a Catholic priest, gave a speech at a meeting of the Christian Veterans group. He made some anti-Semitic comments as well as negative comments about President Franklin D. Roosevelt and First Lady Eleanor Roosevelt.

He was arrested and charged with disorderly conduct. However, the U.S. Supreme Court reversed his conviction, with Justice Douglas writing the majority opinion. Justice Douglas reasoned that a "function of free speech under our system of government is to invite dispute." He added that speech "may indeed best serve its high purpose when it induces a condition of unrest, creates dissatisfaction with conditions as they are, or even stirs people to anger."

In what decision did Justice Douglas say that obscenity law was a "hodge-podge"?

Justice Douglas called obscenity law a "hodge-podge" in his dissenting opinion in *Miller v. California* (1973). Under consideration was the conviction of California-based pornographer Marvin Miller for mailing brochures advertising books of a sexual nature. The majority upheld his conviction and, in the process, created a new test for obscenity now known as the "Miller Test," which examines whether a work appeals predominantly to someone who has a prurient (morbid or shameful) interest in sex; is patently offensive; or lacks serious literary, artistic, political, or scientific value.

Justice Douglas wrote a dissenting opinion in which he criticized obscenity law. He also famously wrote that "obscenity—which even we cannot define with precision—is a hodge-podge. To send men to jail for violating standards they cannot understand, construe, and apply is a monstrous thing to do in a Nation dedicated to fair trials and due process."

He added:

> We deal with highly emotional, not rational, questions. To many the Song of Solomon is obscene. I do not think we, the judges, were ever given the constitutional power to make definitions of obscenity. If it is to be defined, let the people debate and decide by a constitutional amendment what they want to ban as obscene and what standards they want the legislatures and the courts to apply. Perhaps the people will decide that the path towards a mature, integrated society require that all ideas compet-

William O. Douglas, the longest-serving associate justice, was appointed by President Franklin D. Roosevelt in 1939 and retired in 1975.

ing for acceptance must have no censor. Perhaps they will decide otherwise. Whatever the choice, the courts will have some guidelines. Now we have none except our own predilections.

In what decision did Justice Douglas file a lone dissent against the practice of stop and frisk?

Justice Douglas filed a lone dissent in *Terry v. Ohio* (1968), a case in which the Court upheld the practice of "stop and frisk" if a police officer possesses reasonable suspicion that a person may be carrying a weapon. The case involved a veteran police detective named Martin McFadden, who observed three men involved in what he suspected was a potential stick-up job. McFadden went up to the men and frisked them. He found a weapon on defendant John Terry. Terry claimed that the police needed probable cause to frisk him for weapons. The majority of the Court disagreed with Terry and upheld the officer's conduct.

Justice Douglas filed a solitary dissent. He believed that frisking a person required the police to have probable cause. He explained in powerful language:

> The infringement on personal liberty of any "seizure" of a person can only be "reasonable" under the Fourth Amendment if we require the police to possess "probable cause" before they seize him. Only that line draws a meaningful distinction between an officer's mere inkling and the presence of facts within the officer's personal knowledge which would convince a reasonable man that the person seized has committed, is committing, or is about to commit a particular crime. "In dealing with probable cause, … as the very name implies, we deal with probabilities. These are not technical; they are the factual and practical considerations of everyday life on which reasonable and prudent men, not legal technicians, act."
>
> To give the police greater power than a magistrate is to take a long step down the totalitarian path. Perhaps such a step is desirable to cope with modern forms of lawlessness. But if it is taken, it should be the deliberate choice of the people through a constitutional amendment. Until the Fourth Amendment, which is closely allied with the Fifth, is rewritten, the person and the effects of the individual are beyond the reach of all government agencies until there are reasonable grounds to believe (probable cause) that a criminal venture has been launched or is about to be launched.
>
> There have been powerful hydraulic pressures throughout our history that bear heavily on the Court to water down constitutional guarantees and give the police the upper hand. That hydraulic pressure has probably never been greater than it is today.
>
> Yet if the individual is no longer to be sovereign, if the police can pick him up whenever they do not like the cut of his jib, if they can "seize" and "search" him in their

discretion, we enter a new regime. The decision to enter it should be made only after a full debate by the people of this country.

Historic Justices on the Court, Part II

JUSTICE WILLIAM J. BRENNAN JR.

Why is Justice William J. Brennan Jr. considered such a great justice?

Justice Brennan is considered a great justice because he wrote so many influential opinions and shaped many different areas of the law. He was a driving force in his first 10 years or so on the Court when he served as Chief Justice Earl Warren's key ally. He served more than 33 years on the Court and was able to persuade colleagues not only because of his keen intellect but because of his classy and personable nature.

Justice Byron White wrote of Justice Brennan in a tribute published in the *Yale Law Journal*: "William J. Brennan will surely be remembered as among the greatest Justices who have ever sat on the Supreme Court. And well he should be." Justice Thurgood Marshall wrote of Justice Brennan in a tribute piece published in the *Harvard Law Review*: "To my mind, what so distinguished Justice Brennan was his faithfulness to a consistent legal vision of how the Constitution should be interpreted. That vision was based on an unwavering commitment to certain core principles, especially first amendment freedoms and basic principles of civil rights and civil liberties."

What was Justice Brennan's prior judicial experience?

Justice Brennan served on the New Jersey state courts. He was initially appointed to the New Jersey Superior Court by Republican New Jersey governor Alfred E. Driscoll in 1949. One year later, he was elevated to the Appellate Division of the New Jersey Superior Court. Then, in 1951, he was appointed to the New Jersey Supreme Court by Driscoll.

Who nominated him to the U.S. Supreme Court?

Republican president Dwight D. Eisenhower made a recess appointment of Justice Brennan to the U.S. Supreme Court on October 15, 1956. Later, the U.S. Senate formally approved of Justice Brennan in 1957. The only U.S. senator to oppose Justice Brennan's confirmation was Republican senator Joseph McCarthy, known for his excessive anticommunist zeal. The unusual fact of Justice Brennan's nomination was that Eisenhower was a Republican and Justice Brennan was a Democrat.

What was Justice Brennan's view of the death penalty?

Like his longtime colleague and friend Justice Thurgood Marshall, Justice Brennan was a consistent opponent of the death penalty. In a lecture at Harvard, Justice Brennan stated: "The calculated killing of a human being by the state involves, by its very

William J. Brennan Jr. was appointed by President Eisenhower in 1956, serving until his retirement in 1990.

nature, an absolute denial of the executed person's humanity and thus violates the command of the Eighth Amendment."

Justice Brennan was one of the justices who ruled in *Furman v. Georgia* (1972) that the death penalty is unconstitutional, a position he retained for the rest of his life. In his concurring opinion, Justice Brennan explained: "In sum, the punishment of death is inconsistent with all four principles: death is an unusually severe and degrading punishment; there is a strong probability that it is inflicted arbitrarily; its rejection by contemporary society is virtually total; and there is no reason to believe that it serves any penal purpose more effectively than the less severe punishment of imprisonment. The function of these principles is to enable a court to determine whether a punishment comports with human dignity. Death, quite simply, does not."

What important contribution did Justice Brennan make to state constitutional law?

It is no exaggeration to say that Justice Brennan revitalized interest and passion for state constitutional law. Justice Brennan became concerned with a series of rulings by the U.S. Supreme

Court during the Burger Court era and realized that if the U.S. Supreme Court will not provide proper protection for individual rights, state high courts could provide such protection under their state constitutions.

The U.S. Constitution sets a floor on the protection of individual liberties but not a ceiling. This means that a state high court cannot provide less protection than the U.S. Supreme Court has done when it comes to interpreting the U.S. Bill of Rights, but a state high court can provide greater protection under its state bill of rights.

In a 1986 lecture published in the *New York University Law Review* entitled "The Bill of Rights and the States: The Revival of State Constitutions as Guardians of Individual Rights," he wrote: "This rebirth of interest in state constitutional law should be greeted with equal enthusiasm by all those who support our federal system, liberals and conservatives alike. The development and protection of individual rights pursuant to state constitutions presents no threat to enforcement of national standards; state courts may not provide a level of protection less than that offered by the federal Constitution. Nor should these developments be greeted with dismay by conservatives; the state laboratories are once again open for business."

Why is Justice Brennan considered such an important justice in freedom of expression jurisprudence?

Justice Brennan authored numerous landmark opinions in the area of freedom of expression. For example, he wrote the Court's decision in *New York Times Co. v. Sullivan* (1964), which many regard as the most important free-speech opinion in American jurisprudence. Before *Sullivan*, state defamation laws were immune from First Amendment scrutiny. This left not enough protection for those who criticized government officials.

The *Sullivan* case involved an editorial advertisement published in the *New York Times* that criticized civil rights abuses occurring in Montgomery, Alabama. L. B. Sullivan, the police commissioner in Montgomery, sued for libel. An Alabama state jury awarded him $500,000 in damages. Though some factually inaccurate statements were included, the U.S. Supreme Court reversed its decision. Justice Brennan explained that libel can claim no "talismanic immunity" from the First Amendment. He also explained that individuals must have the ability to criticize the government and government officials, writing of the importance of a "profound national commitment to the principle that debate on public issues should be uninhibited, robust, and wide-open" and "may well include vehement, caustic and sometimes unpleasantly sharp attacks on government and public officials."

Justice Brennan also created a new standard for those suing public officials for defamation: that the plaintiff must show, by clear and convincing evidence, actual malice, defined as knowing the information was false or acting in "reckless disregard" as far as whether the statement was true or false.

Justice Brennan added:

> What a State may not constitutionally bring about by means of a criminal statute is likewise beyond the reach of its civil law of libel. The fear of damage awards under a rule such as that invoked by the Alabama courts here may be markedly more inhibiting than the fear of prosecution under a criminal statute....
>
> A rule compelling the critic of official conduct to guarantee the truth of all his factual assertions—and to do so on pain of libel judgments virtually unlimited in amount—leads to a comparable "self-censorship." Allowance of the defense of truth, with the burden of proving it on the defendant, does not mean that only false speech will be deterred....
>
> The rule thus dampens the vigor and limits the variety of public debate. It is inconsistent with the First and Fourteenth Amendments. The constitutional guarantees require, we think, a federal rule that prohibits a public official from recovering damages for a defamatory false-

The sole exception in Justice Brennan's near-unanimous confirmation, Senator Joseph McCarthy (pictured) had been stung by Brennan's prior remarks about anti-communist "witch-hunts."

hood relating to his official conduct unless he proves that the statement was made with "actual malice"—that is, with knowledge that it was false or with reckless disregard of whether it was false or not.

What other decisions did Justice Brennan write that ensured his First Amendment legacy?

A few years later, he wrote an opinion that was very important for freedom of expression on college campuses. The decision *Keyishian v. New York Board of Regents* (1967) involved a New York law that required public employees to sign an oath that they were not members of the Communist Party. The law was designed to rid college campuses of so-called "subversives." Justice Brennan invalidated the provision, writing: "Our Nation is deeply committed to safeguarding academic freedom, which is of transcendent value to all of us, and not merely to the teachers concerned. That freedom is therefore a special concern of the First Amendment, which does not tolerate laws that cast a pall of orthodoxy over the classroom."

Justice Brennan authored a powerful dissenting opinion in *Hazelwood School District v. Kuhlmeier* (1988), a case involving the censorship of a high school newspaper by the principal. The majority reasoned that the principal could engage in such censorship as long as he had a legitimate educational reason. But Justice Brennan, in dissent, wrote passionately: "Unthinking contempt for individual rights is intolerable for any state official. It is particularly insidious from one to whom the public entrusts the task of inculcating in its youth an appreciation for the cherished democratic liberties that our Constitution guarantees."

The next year, in 1989, Justice Brennan wrote the Court's majority opinion in the flag-burning case of *Texas v. Johnson* (1989). Gregory Lee Johnson was charged with violating a Texas flag desecration law after burning an American flag outside of the Republican National Convention in Dallas, Texas. Justice Brennan, however, explained that Johnson's act, however distasteful, was a form of political dissent. He famously explained: "If there is bedrock principle underlying the First Amendment, it is that the government may not prohibit the expression of an idea simply because society finds the idea itself offensive or disagreeable."

How did Justice Brennan change his position with regard to obscenity?

Justice Brennan wrote the Court's seminal obscenity opinion in *Roth v. United States* (1957), reasoning that obscenity was not a form of protected speech and could be outlawed by federal and state authorities. Justice Brennan reasoned that "obscenity is not within the area of constitutionally protected speech or press." He noted that for years, many states had passed laws outlawing obscene material. However, the difficult task was fashioning a test that judges could use to distinguish unprotected obscenity from sexual expression deserving of protection. In *Roth*, Justice Brennan fashioned the following test: "whether to the average person, applying contemporary community standards, the dominant theme of the material taken as a whole appeals to the prurient interest."

However, 16 years later in a dissenting opinion in *Paris Adult Theatre I v. Slaton* (1973), Justice Brennan changed positions and

DID YOU KNOW?

How did Justice Brennan protect due process rights?

Justice Brennan authored the Court's decision in *Goldberg v. Kelly* (1971), holding that an individual could not be deprived of state welfare benefits without having a hearing and a chance to contest the evidence for why the benefits should be ended. He explained that "important governmental interests are promoted by affording recipients a pre-termination evidentiary hearing." He explained that "forces not within the control of the poor contribute to their poverty." The stakes were simply too high for welfare recipients to allow state officials to deprive individuals of these needed benefits.

ruled that obscenity laws were too vague and subjective and posed too great a threat to freedom of expression. "As a result of our failure to define standards with predictable application to any given piece of material, there is no probability of regularity in obscenity decisions in state and lower federal courts," he wrote. "I would hold, therefore, that at least in the absence of distribution to juveniles or obtrusive exposure to unconsenting adults, the First and Fourteenth Amendments prohibit the State and Federal Governments from attempting wholly to suppress sexually oriented materials on the basis of their allegedly 'obscene' content."

How did Justice Brennan protect the free exercise rights of individuals?

Justice Brennan wrote the Court's opinion in *Sherbert v.Verner* (1963), reasoning that the state of South Carolina violated the Free Exercise Clause of the First Amendment when it denied unemployment compensation benefits to a Seventh-day Adventist named Adele Sherbert after she was fired from her job for refusing to work on Saturdays, her Sabbath day. Justice Brennan reasoned that Seventh-day Adventists should be treated the same as other workers, that the state should be neutral when it comes to matters of religion.

What decision did Justice Brennan write that led to a litany of reapportionment decisions?

Baker v. Carr (1962) allowed litigants to sue state officials in federal courts to reapportion or reorganize legislative districts to reflect a fairer balance of power between urban and rural areas. The case arose in Tennessee because state officials had refused to redraw legislative district boundaries, giving rural voters a much greater proportional share of voting power. The state argued that it did not have the authority to consider this political question. However, the Court ruled 6–2 that it did have such authority: "We conclude that the complaint's allegations of a denial of equal protection present a justiciable constitutional cause of action upon which appellants are entitled to a trial and a decision." In his opinion, Justice Brennan concluded that "the right asserted is within the reach of judicial protection under the Fourteenth Amendment." Chief Justice Warren later called the decision "the most vital" of any during his tenure. He wrote in his memoirs: "The reason I am of the opinion that *Baker v. Carr* is so important is because I believe so devoutly that, to paraphrase Abraham Lincoln's famous epigram, ours is a government of all the people, by all the people, and for all the people." The decision directly led to a series of reapportionment cases.

JUSTICE THURGOOD MARSHALL

Why is Justice Thurgood Marshall considered so great?

Justice Marshall is considered great because of his historic significance in advocating on behalf of civil rights and for being the most consistent defender of individual rights on the U.S. Supreme Court during his 24-year tenure. Juan Williams wrote in 1990 that Justice Marshall was "the most important black man of this century." Others have called him the most important lawyer of the 20th century. Professor Drew Days wrote of Justice Marshall: "He has been a supreme conscience. In the law he remains our supreme conscience."

His longtime colleague and confidant on the Court, Justice Brennan, said of Justice Marshall: "Thurgood is one of our century's legal giants. Before he joined the judiciary, he was probably the most important legal advocate in America and the central figure in our nation's struggle to eliminate institutional racism."

What was Justice Thurgood Marshall's first name at birth?

Justice Marshall was born in 1908 as Thoroughgood Marshall in Baltimore, Maryland. He changed the name to Thurgood in the second grade.

The Supreme Court's first black justice, Thurgood Marshall was appointed by President Lyndon B. Johnson in 1967 and served until his retirement in 1991.

DID YOU KNOW?

Where was Justice Thurgood Marshall nearly lynched?

Justice Marshall nearly faced death in Columbia, Tennessee, on November 28, 1946. Justice Marshall had come to Columbia after the so-called "Columbia Race Riots" to offer counsel for the African American men who were tried in criminal court for a shootout with whites who had forcibly invaded the African American section of town.

Local law-enforcement officials had grabbed Justice Marshall from the vehicle that he drove with Nashville-based African American lawyer Z. Alexander Looby and Chattanooga-based white attorney Maurice Weaver, who had helped defend the African Americans charged after the Columbia Race Riots. After the police grabbed Justice Marshall, they took him down to the Duck River near a big tree. Fortunately, Looby and Weaver followed, and the police drove Justice Marshall back to Columbia, where they tried to charge him with drunk driving, a false charge. A local magistrate let Justice Marshall go.

Who were Justice Thurgood Marshall's mentors in law?

Justice Marshall's mentors were Charles Hamilton Houston (1895–1950) and William Hastie (1904–1976). Houston was the assistant dean of Howard Law School when Justice Marshall was a student there. Houston took Justice Marshall under his wing and later hired him to work for the NAACP in 1936 as a special assistant counsel. Houston urged Justice Marshall and his classmates to not only be lawyers but also social engineers for justice.

Hastie, who was Houston's second cousin, was an instructor at Harvard Law School. He also had a significant impact on

Justice Marshall's development as a law student. Hastie later became the first African American to serve as a federal appeals court judge.

Where was Justice Thurgood Marshall denied admission to law school because of his race?

The University of Maryland denied Justice Marshall admission to law school because of his race. That is why Justice Marshall attended Howard Law School. In a nice twist of justice, Justice Marshall later represented, with Houston, a man named Donald Gaines Murray, who also was denied admission to Maryland's law school because of the color of his skin. Houston successfully argued the case of *Murray v. Pearson* before the Maryland Court of Appeals (Maryland's highest state court).

Howard Ball, in his biography of Justice Marshall, *A Defiant Life*, relates Justice Marshall's comments about this case: "I filed it the first year I left law school to get even with the bastards … to get even with the whole segregated system."

What was Justice Thurgood Marshall's record as a U.S. Supreme Court litigator before he became a judge?

Before he became a judge, Justice Marshall was the leading civil rights lawyer in the United States. In that capacity as "Mr. Civil Rights," he argued many civil rights cases before the U.S. Supreme Court, including *Brown v. Board of Education.* He also argued many cases before the U.S. Supreme Court when he served as the U.S. solicitor general. In his career, he argued 32 cases before the U.S. Supreme Court, winning 29 of them.

EQUAL JUSTICE UNDER LAW

As the NAACP's chief counsel, Thurgood Marshall (center) argued successfully for the desegregation of schools in *Brown v. Board* (1954).

What were some of Justice Thurgood Marshall's most notable First Amendment opinions?

Justice Marshall was known as one of the most consistent defenders of the First Amendment in the history of the U.S. Supreme Court. One of his most influential opinions was his opinion for the Court in *Chicago Police Dept. v. Mosley* (1972). The case involved a postal worker who, outside of a Chicago high school, protested what he deemed to be racially discriminatory hiring practices by the school. Chicago had an ordinance that prohibited picketing within 150 feet of the schools. However, the ordinance also had an exemption for labor picketing. Thus, under this ordinance, a labor picketer did not violate the First Amendment, but someone like Earl Mosley protesting racial discrimination did violate the ordinance.

To Justice Marshall, this meant that the ordinance discriminated against speech based on content; this is now known as content discrimination. Justice Marshall explained the principle against content discrimination in memorable terms: "Above all else, the First Amendment means that the government may not restrict expression because of its message, its ideas, its subject matter, or its content."

Another one of Justice Marshall's memorable opinions was the case of *Stanley v. Georgia* (1969). The case involved government agents searching the home of Robert E. Stanley for alleged bookmaking activities. They found little to no evidence of bookmaking but did find some films that they deemed obscene. Thus, they charged Stanley under a Georgia obscenity law. However, Justice Marshall reasoned that the agents could not convict Stanley for material that he merely possessed in his home. Justice Marshall famously wrote: "If the First Amendment means anything, it means that a State has no business telling a man, sitting alone in his own house, what books he may read or what films he may watch. Our whole constitutional heritage rebels at the thought of giving government the power to control men's minds."

Justice Marshall also wrote the Court's landmark opinion in *Pickering v. Board of Education* (1968) which, for the first time, recognized explicitly that public employees do not forfeit all of their free-speech protections simply for taking public employment. The case involved a high school science teacher named Marvin Pickering, who was upset that the school board was spending money on a new football field instead of finishing the refurbishment of classrooms. He wrote a letter to the editor of the local newspaper criticizing the school board. His letter read in part: "To sod football fields on borrowed money and then not be able to pay teachers' salaries is getting the cart before the horse." He was fired after the letter was published.

Justice Marshall wrote the Court's majority opinion and explained that "the problem in any case is to arrive at a balance between the interests of the teacher, as a citizen, in commenting upon matters of public concern and the interest of the State, as an employer, in promoting the efficiency of the public services it performs through its employees." In this case, he explained that Marvin Pickering did not criticize people he worked with on a daily basis, such as fellow teachers, students, or his principal. Instead, he criticized the school board.

Justice Marshall also wrote opinions that respected the free-speech rights of prisoners. For example, he eloquently explained why prisoners should possess such rights in his concurring opinion in *Procunier v. Martinez* (1974), a case involving a challenge to the California Department of Corrections's policy of censoring inmate mail. Justice Marshall wrote: "The mails are one of the few vehicles prisoners have for informing the community about their existence and, in these days of strife in our correctional institutions, the plight of prisoners is a matter of urgent public concern. To sustain a policy which chills the communication necessary to inform the public on this issue is at odds with the most basic tenets of the guarantee of freedom of speech."

What were Justice Thurgood Marshall's views on the death penalty?

Justice Marshall consistently viewed the death penalty as a violation of the Eighth Amendment's ban on "cruel and unusual punishment." Justice Marshall explained his view in a comprehensive separate opinion in *Furman v. Georgia* (1972) when a majority of the Court invalidated Georgia's death penalty law. Justice Marshall explained:

> I believe that the following facts would serve to convince even the most hesitant of citizens to condemn death as a sanction: capital punishment is imposed discriminatorily against certain identifiable classes of people; there is evidence that innocent people have been executed before their innocence can be proved; and the death penalty wreaks havoc with our entire criminal justice system....
>
> It also is evident that the burden of capital punishment falls upon the poor, the ignorant, and the underprivileged members of society. It is the poor, and the members of minority groups who are least able to voice their com-

> plaints against capital punishment. Their impotence leaves them victims of a sanction that the wealthier, better-represented, just-as-guilty person can escape. So long as the capital sanction is used only against the forlorn, easily forgotten members of society, legislators are content to maintain the status quo, because change would draw attention to the problem and concern might develop. Ignorance is perpetuated and apathy soon becomes its mate, and we have today's situation.

He wrote the Court's majority opinion in *Ford v. Wainwright* (1986), in which the Court prohibited the execution of the insane. He began his opinion with the following language: "For centuries no jurisdiction has countenanced the execution of the insane, yet this Court has never decided whether the Constitution forbids the practice. Today we keep faith with our common-law heritage in holding that it does."

In 1985, Justice Marshall had delivered a speech at a conference of judges of the U.S. Court of Appeals for the Second Circuit in New York. In that speech, he called on the legal profession to provide better legal representation for capital defendants. He warned about the "extraordinary unfairness" in such defendants as far as not having "an adequate opportunity to present their defenses."

CHIEF JUSTICE WILLIAM H. REHNQUIST

Why is Chief Justice William H. Rehnquist considered an important and significant justice in American history?

Chief Justice Rehnquist served as both associate justice and chief justice during his more than 30 years of service on the High

Appointed as an associate justice by President Nixon in 1972, William Rehnquist was elevated to chief justice by President Reagan in 1986, serving until his death in 2005.

Court. He was a forceful advocate for the positions and issues he cared deeply about, such as federalism, but he also was known as an eminently fair and effective administrator of the Court. He was efficient in serving as chief justice and was very fair in the assignment of power: the power of the chief justice to pick the author of an opinion when the chief justice is in the majority.

Upon his death, President George W. Bush stated: "He was extremely well respected for his powerful intellect. He was respected for his deep commitment to the rule of law and his profound devotion to duty. He provided superb leadership for the federal court system, improving the delivery of justice to the American people and earning the admiration of his colleagues throughout the judiciary."

Even some of his ideological opponents praised him upon his death. For example, Senator Edward Kennedy—who voted against Chief Justice Rehnquist's confirmation—said of the former chief justice: "Chief Justice Rehnquist served this country with the greatest distinction, and I respected his leadership of the federal judiciary and his strong commitment to the integrity and independence of the courts."

DID YOU KNOW?

How did his colleagues on the Court consider Chief Justice Rehnquist?

Perhaps to the surprise of his critics, Chief Justice Rehnquist was regarded by his colleagues as an excellent chief justice. He was known to be efficient in his administration and fair in doling out opinion assignments. Even his ideological opponents routinely praised him for his abilities and efforts as chief justice. Justice Thurgood Marshall, a strong liberal voice on the Court, called Chief Justice Rehnquist "a great Chief Justice." Justice Brennan, another liberal stalwart on the Court, also praised Chief Justice Rehnquist's abilities in the role of chief justice.

Why was his confirmation to chief justice so contentious?

Much of the opposition to Chief Justice Rehnquist involved the same charges during his initial confirmation hearings in 1971: that he had participated in denying or harassing minority voters in Arizona, that he was not truthful about a memorandum he had authored about *Plessy v. Ferguson* (1896) when he was a law clerk in 1952, and that his views were too far to the right on issues of civil rights. Some also criticized him for refusing to recuse himself from the case of *Laird v. Tatum*, a case challenging the military's surveillance system.

But Chief Justice Rehnquist ultimately prevailed by a vote of 67–33. He earned a "well-qualified" mark from the American Bar Association. Democratic senator Howard Heflin also came to support Chief Justice Rehnquist, stating: "I know that there are those who question Justice Rehnquist's sensitivity to civil rights of minorities and women. I do not agree with every opinion of Justice Rehnquist. In fact, I find myself in disagreement with many. But I do not believe those opinions are so extreme as to be unreasonable. Every stream has a right bank and a left bank. There is no question that Justice Rehnquist's views are always close to the right boundary of the stream, but they are nonetheless within the mainstream of modern judicial thought."

President Ronald Reagan praised the ultimate confirmation vote, stating: "This vote in the full Senate is a bipartisan rejection of the political posturing that marred the confirmation hearings. It is clear to all now that the extraordinary controversy surrounding the hearings had little to do with Justice Rehnquist's record or character—both are unassailable and unimpeachable. The attacks come from those whose ideology runs contrary to his profound and unshakable belief in the proper constitutional role of the judiciary in this country."

What positions did Chief Justice Rehnquist hold before joining the U.S. Supreme Court?

After graduating from Stanford Law School at the top of his class, Chief Justice Rehnquist clerked for U.S. Supreme Court justice Robert H. Jackson. He then worked in private practice in Phoe-

Despite much contention surrounding his confirmation, the Senate confirmed Rehnquist as chief justice in a 67–33 vote. Sworn in on September 26, 1986, Chief Justice Rehnquist led the Court for 19 years to the acclamation of his peers.

nix, Arizona, from 1953 to 1969. He then took a job in the Nixon administration, serving as an assistant U.S. attorney general in the Office of Legal Counsel. In late 1971, President Nixon nominated him to serve as an associate justice on the U.S. Supreme Court.

Chief Justice Rehnquist had no prior judicial experience prior to serving on the U.S. Supreme Court.

In what opinion did Chief Justice Rehnquist protect a Ten Commandments monument in a Texas public park?

Chief Justice Rehnquist wrote the Court's plurality opinion in *Van Orden v. Perry* (2005), in which the Court ruled 5–4 that a Ten Commandments monument in a Texas public park—which had been there for nearly 40 years—did not violate the Establishment Clause of the First Amendment. Chief Justice Rehnquist noted that 21 historical markers and 17 monuments surrounded the Texas state capital, that the monument was placed there in 1961, and that even the challenger (a disbarred lawyer named Thomas Van Orden) had walked by the monument for many years before filing a lawsuit.

Chief Justice Rehnquist also noted that a large number of government buildings in Washington, D.C., contained religious displays or monuments. "We need only look within our own Courtroom," the chief justice wrote. "Since 1935, Moses has stood, holding two tablets that reveal portions of the Ten Commandments written in Hebrew, among other lawgivers in the south frieze."

In what decision did Chief Justice Rehnquist uphold a school voucher program?

The U.S. Supreme Court narrowly upheld a Cleveland voucher program in *Zelman v. Simmons-Harris* (2002). The case involved a program that provided tuition assistance to low-income parents. The vast majority of the participating schools in the program were private religious schools. In fact, a majority of the students in the program attended Catholic schools. A constitutional challenge was filed, contending that the state of Ohio violated the Establishment Clause by funding a program that gave substantial benefits to private religious schools.

A federal district judge and a federal appeals court ruled that the voucher program violated the Establishment Clause, reasoning that the primary effect of the program was to benefit religion. However, the U.S. Supreme Court reversed its opinion, focusing on private choice and neutrality. Chief Justice Rehnquist wrote that the program was one of "true private choice." He added: "Program benefits are available to participating families on neutral terms, with no reference to religion. The only preference stated anywhere in the program is a preference for low-income families, who receive greater assistance and are given priority for admission at participating schools."

In what decision did Chief Justice Rehnquist defend the *Miranda* ruling?

Chief Justice Rehnquist defended the 1966 *Miranda* ruling in *Dickerson v. United States* (2000), a ruling invalidating a 1968 federal law that seemingly sought to overrule *Miranda*. The law provided that a failure to read a suspect his Miranda rights was just one of many factors determining whether a subsequent confession was voluntary.

Many expected the Court to overrule *Miranda*, as Chief Justice Rehnquist for many years was a vocal critic of the decision from the Warren Court. Many assumed when Chief Justice Rehnquist announced that he was the author of the Dickerson decision that *Miranda* was doomed. To the surprise of many, Chief Justice Rehnquist refused to overrule *Miranda*, writing that "*Miranda* has become embedded in routine police practice to the point where the warnings have become part of our national culture."

DID YOU KNOW?

What did Chief Justice Rehnquist write about the constitutional right to die?

The U.S. Supreme Court, in a majority opinion authored by Chief Justice Rehnquist, found that the due process right to die did not exist in the 14th Amendment in *Washington v. Glucksberg* (1997). The Court determined that terminally ill patients did not possess a constitutional right to physician-assisted suicide. Chief Justice Rehnquist wrote that a "consistent and almost universal tradition" existed of criminalizing the assisting of suicide. "The States' assisted-suicide bans are not innovations," he wrote. "Rather, they are longstanding expressions of the States' commitment to the protections and preservation of human life."

Did the Rehnquist Court strike down laws as exceeding Congress's power under the Commerce Clause?

Yes, the Rehnquist Court ruled on several occasions that Congress exceeded its constitutional authority under the Commerce Clause. Generally speaking, the U.S. Supreme Court historically has been reluctant to strike down legislation that has been passed pursuant to Congress's Commerce Clause powers. The Commerce Clause gives Congress broad power to regulate interstate commerce. For example, in the 1942 decision *Wickard v. Filburn*, the Court ruled that Congress had the Commerce Clause power to regulate the amount of wheat consumption produced by a private farmer.

However, in the landmark 1995 decision *United States v. Lopez*, the Court ruled 5–4 that Congress exceeded its Commerce Clause powers in passing the Gun Free School Zones Act of 1990. The case involved high school student Alphonso Lopez Jr., who brought a gun to school. He was arrested, charged, and convicted of violating the federal gun law that made it a crime "knowingly to possess a firearm at a place that the individual knows, or has reasonable cause to believe, is a school zone." Chief Justice Rehnquist wrote in his majority opinion that the federal gun law "has nothing to do with 'commerce' or any sort of economic enterprise, however broadly one might define those terms."

The *Lopez* decision represented the first time in more than 60 years that the Court had invalidated legislation enacted under Congress's Commerce Clause powers.

The Rehnquist Court reached a similar result in its 2000 decision *U.S. v. Morrison*, a case dealing with the constitutionality of the Violence Against Women Act. Once again, Chief Justice Rehnquist wrote the majority opinion. He reasoned that Congress once again exceeded its powers under the Commerce Clause because gender-based violence against women was not a commercial or economic activity. The majority reasoned that state governments, not the federal government, should pass legislation dealing with such problems. "The regulation and punishment of intrastate violence that is not directed at the instrumentalities, channels, or goods involved in interstate commerce has always been the province of the State," Chief Justice Rehnquist wrote. "If the allegations here are true, no civilized system of justice could fail to provide her a remedy for the conduct of respondent Morrison. But under our federal system that remedy must be provided by the Commonwealth of Virginia, and not by the United States."

What did the Rehnquist Court decide in the 2000 presidential election?

In the tightly contested presidential election of 2000 between Republican nominee George W. Bush and Democratic nominee Al Gore, the result came down to Florida and its 25 electoral votes. Whichever of the two candidates carried the state would win the presidency.

Bush narrowly held the lead in Florida after the initial vote tally. After an automatic machine recount, Bush maintained an

The hotly contested 2000 presidential election revealed weaknesses in both the election process and the judicial system, and may have irreparably damaged the public's trust in the institution's requisite impartiality.

even narrower lead. Gore's legal team then filed legal motions, asking for manual recounts of votes in four counties. They alleged that many voters who intended to vote for Vice President Gore did not mark the ballot properly. The Bush legal team sought to stop the recount process and have Bush declared the winner.

The Florida Supreme Court had ruled 4–3 that a manual recount should proceed. However, in *Bush v. Gore* (2000) the U.S. Supreme Court reversed its decision by a controversial 5–4 vote. The majority reasoned that equal protection problems existed in ensuring fairness in the manual recount process.

"Instead, we are presented with a situation where a state court with the power to assure uniformity has ordered a statewide recount with minimal procedural safeguards," the Court wrote. "When a court orders a statewide remedy, there must be at least some assurance that the rudimentary requirements of equal treatment and fundamental fairness are satisfied."

Three justices in the majority—Chief Justice Rehnquist, Justice Clarence Thomas, and Justice Antonin Scalia—wrote a con-

curring opinion explaining that the Florida Supreme Court decision was invalid because Article II of the U.S. Constitution provides that state legislatures, not state supreme courts, have the exclusive power in such election matters.

Several of the dissenting justices bitterly criticized the ruling. Justice John Paul Stevens wrote that the actual loser in this process was "the Nation's confidence in the judge as an impartial guardian of the rule of law."

In what free-speech decision did Chief Justice Rehnquist surprise the media and rule in favor of a pornographer?

Chief Justice Rehnquist wrote the Court's unanimous opinion in *Hustler Magazine v. Falwell* (1988), a celebrated free-speech opinion that provided great protection for parody and satire. Larry Flynt, the publisher of *Hustler* magazine, had lampooned preacher and televangelist Jerry Falwell in his magazine. Flynt produced a parody of Campari Liquor ads, which had featured celebrities talking about their "first time": the first time they tasted the liquor but with a sexual double entendre.

Flynt wrote that Falwell's first time was a drunken incestuous rendezvous with his mother in an outhouse. Falwell was outraged and sued Flynt for libel, invasion of privacy, and intentional infliction of emotional distress. Flynt countered that the ad was clearly parody and not to be taken seriously.

Falwell lost on the libel and invasion of privacy claims but won $250,000 from a federal jury on the intentional infliction of emotional distress claim. On appeal, Flynt pressed the First Amendment argument. However, the U.S. Court of Appeals for the Fourth Circuit affirmed the jury verdict.

Flynt's last hope was the U.S. Supreme Court. The media and even Flynt were concerned. "I regret I have brought the issue before the Court and that the national press could be affected by this decision."

However, Chief Justice Rehnquist delivered a free-speech surprise. He explained that "in the world of debate about public affairs, many things done with motives that are less than admirable are protected by the First Amendment." He added that if strong protections for satire or parody did not exist, then "there can be little doubt that political cartoonists and satirists would be subjected to damages awards without any showing that their work falsely defamed its subject."

He rejected the idea that outrageous conduct—the lynchpin of an intentional infliction of an emotional distress claim—could comport with First Amendment values, writing: "'Outrageousness' in the area of political and social discourse has an inherent subjectiveness about it which would allow a jury to impose liability on the basis of jurors' tastes or views, or perhaps on the basis of their dislike of a particular expression."

The *New York Times* praised Chief Justice Rehnquist and the Court, calling the decision "a sparkling vindication of free speech."

JUSTICE RUTH BADER GINSBURG

Why is Justice Ruth Bader Ginsburg considered such a historic U.S. Supreme Court jurist?

Justice Ginsburg, like Justice Thurgood Marshall before her, was a famous lawyer far before she ever became a judge. Though she stood barely five feet tall, she was a giant in American jurisprudence. Known as "the Thurgood Marshall for gender equality," she litigated many cases before the U.S. Supreme Court on gender issues.

She served for 13 years on the U.S. Court of Appeals for the D.C. Circuit and then for 27 years on the U.S. Supreme Court.

Appointed by President Clinton in 1993, Ruth Bader Ginsburg served as an associate justice of the Supreme Court until her death in 2020.

During this time, she became quite well known for her commitment, her attention to detail, and, in her later years, her powerful dissenting opinions.

On her death, Chief Justice John G. Roberts Jr. said of his colleague: "Our Nation has lost a jurist of historic stature. We at the Supreme Court have lost a cherished colleague. Today we mourn, but with confidence that future generations will remember Ruth Bader Ginsburg as we knew her—a tireless and resolute champion of justice." Another colleague, Justice Elena Kagan, was equally effusive in her praise: "To me, as to countless others, Ruth Bader Ginsburg was a hero. As an attorney, she led the fight to grant women equal rights under the law. As a judge, she did justice every day—working to ensure that this country's legal system lives up to its ideals and extends its rights and protections to those once excluded. And in both roles, she held to—indeed, exceeded—the highest standards of legal craft. Her work was as careful as it was creative, as disciplined as it was visionary. It will endure for as long as Americans retain their commitment to law."

Where was Justice Ginsburg born, and who were her parents?

Justice Ginsburg was born in Brooklyn, New York, to Nathan Bader and Cecilia Amster. Her father, Nathan, was born in 1896

near Odessa, Ukraine. Nathan's father left for the United States, and Nathan and the rest of the family joined him four years later. Nathan came to America when he was 13 years old and settled in New York's Lower East Side.

Nathan had no formal education other than a little night school. He went into the family business—Samuel Bader and Sons—as a furrier. Nathan married Cecilia Amster, whose parents came from Austria. Cecilia was born in the United States in 1902. She had top grades at Washington Irving High School in Manhattan but was supposed to work while her brother went on to college.

This later forced her to focus on two things with her daughter: education and independence.

What early experience marked Justice Ginsburg as a future writer?

Ruth Bader became the editor of the *Highway Herald*, her middle school newspaper. She wrote an editorial for the school newspaper called "Landmarks of Constitutional Law," including the Ten Commandments, Magna Carta, English Bill of Rights of 1869, Declaration of Independence, and Charter of the United Nations. She wrote: "The Declaration of Independence of our own U.S. may well be considered one of the most important steps in the shaping of the world. It marked the birth of a new nation, a nation that has so grown in strength as to take its place at the top of the list of the world's great powers."

Where did Justice Ginsburg go to law school?

Justice Ginsburg attended both Harvard Law School and Columbia Law School. She started at Harvard one year behind her husband, Marty Ginsburg. However, when he got a job at a New York City law firm, she transferred from Harvard to Columbia.

What tragedy befell Justice Ginsburg just before her high school graduation?

Her mother, Cecilia, died only two days before her high school graduation. Ginsberg had graduated near the top of her class and, as a salutatorian, was scheduled to speak at the graduation ceremony.

On her mother's death, it was learned that her mother had saved $8,000 (a large sum of money in 1950) for her college education. Justice Ginsburg later said of her mother: "She was the strongest and bravest person I have ever known."

DID YOU KNOW?

She performed very well in law school, earning a place on law review at both schools. She was the very first woman to make law review at Harvard.

It was tough in those days for female law students. She was, in fact, one of only nine female law students at Harvard. She attended a reception with then Harvard dean Erwin Griswold, who brazenly asked each woman why they were in law school taking the place of a man.

In her new class at Columbia, she was one of 12 women. "She was extraordinarily intelligent but low-key and reserved," said one classmate. She also made *Columbia Law Review* and ended up graduating at the top of her class.

Where did Ginsburg go after law school?

She initially tried to work at a private law firm but ran into the awful reality of gender discrimination. When graduation came,

After graduating Columbia Law School tied for first in her class, Ginsburg pursued a career in academia and her calling in civil rights advocacy.

she received only two firm interviews: one from Cadwalader, Wickersham & Taft and one from Casey, Lane & Mittendorf. She did not receive a job offer from either firm. "But to be a woman, a Jew and a mother to boot—that combination was a bit too much," she later said.

She then tried to get a judicial clerkship. Harvard Law professor Albert Sachs had recommended her to Justice Felix Frankfurter of the U.S. Supreme Court, who had been the first justice to hire an African American law clerk, but Justice Frankfurter would not hire a female law clerk.

Columbia Law professor Gerald Gunther took on her case for a judicial clerkship. She had wanted to clerk for Judge Learned Hand of the U.S. Court of Appeals for the Second Circuit, arguably the most famous lower-court federal judge in the country, but he, like Justice Frankfurter, did not hire females to be law clerks.

She finally landed a clerkship with Judge Edmund L. Palmieri: a two-year clerkship. She enjoyed working for Judge Palmieri, who spoke fluent French and Italian.

What international experience did Justice Ginsburg next embark upon after her clerkship?

Not receiving any offers from law firms, she received a call from Hans Smit, the founding director of Columbia Law School's Project on International Procedure. He asked if she would like to write a book on the Swedish legal system. Justice Ginsburg accepted the offer and coauthored a book on civil procedure in Sweden with a prominent appellate judge in Lund named Anders Bruzelius.

The experience was beneficial for Justice Ginsburg, who noticed that 20 to 25 percent of law students were female. She also noticed that the University of Lund had an excellent daycare center. After doing her work in Sweden, she returned home and learned that Rutgers Law School was interested in her.

Where did Justice Ginsburg work as a law professor?

Justice Ginsburg taught at Rutgers from 1963 to 1972. When Dean Willard Heckel hired Justice Ginsburg, she was one of the first 20 women to teach at an American law school full time. She also taught for one year as a visiting professor at Harvard and then left Rutgers to teach at her alma mater, Columbia.

At Rutgers, Justice Ginsburg became one of the first professors to teach a course on gender and the law. Female students at New York University Law School had asked for a course on women and the law but were initially rebuffed. The effort then extended to Rutgers Law School, which had two female faculty members. In 1969, several Rutgers students asked if they could give a seminar course at the school on women and the law.

The students asked Justice Ginsburg to put together a course, and she did. Justice Ginsburg proposed the course "Women's

Rights: Sex Discrimination and the Law." Dean Willard Heckel at Rutgers proved receptive to the idea. He already had encouraged faculty members to explore new courses on civil rights, urban poverty, and representation of the poor.

She became more empowered when she read Simone de Beauvoir's book *The Second Sex*. Fellow Rutgers law professor Eva Hanks said: "She sort of caught fire.... She found her goal or passion starting with that book."

In 1972, she joined her alma mater—Columbia—as its first tenured female faculty member. Columbia was excited. The glee came in part because Justice Ginsburg was what the school's dean, Michael Sovern, called "so distinguished a scholar" that her credentials and honors would stand out in any catalog of professors.

She later coauthored a textbook in 1974, *Sex-Based Discrimination: Text, Cases, and Materials*, with professors Herma Hill Kay and Kenneth Davidson.

Who appointed Justice Ginsburg to the U.S. Court of Appeals for the D.C. Circuit?

President Jimmy Carter appointed Professor Ginsburg to the U.S. Court of Appeals for the D.C. Circuit in 1980. There, she served with future colleague Judge Scalia, with whom she shared a great friendship even though they were ideological opponents on many issues.

On her passing, Carter praised the woman judge that he had helped pave the way for on her rise to the U.S. Supreme Court: "Rosalynn and I are saddened by the passing of Justice Ruth Bader Ginsburg," Carter said in a statement. "A powerful legal mind and a staunch advocate for gender equality, she has been a beacon of justice during her long and remarkable career."

Who appointed Justice Ginsburg to the U.S. Supreme Court?

Justice Ginsburg was appointed to the U.S. Supreme Court by President Bill Clinton. She was not his first choice. He had initially considered New York governor Mario Cuomo, who declined the position. He also considered another cabinet member as well as a federal appeals court from the U.S. Court of Appeals for the First Circuit, Stephen Breyer (whom he later appointed in 1994). But upon meeting Judge Ginsburg, Clinton knew he had found the perfect choice.

He stated to the press on her nomination in 1993:

> As I told Judge Ginsburg last night when I called to ask her to accept the nomination, I decided on her for three reasons. First, in her years on the bench she has genuinely distinguished herself as one of our Nation's best judges, progressive in outlook, wise in judgment, balanced and fair in her opinions. Second, over the course

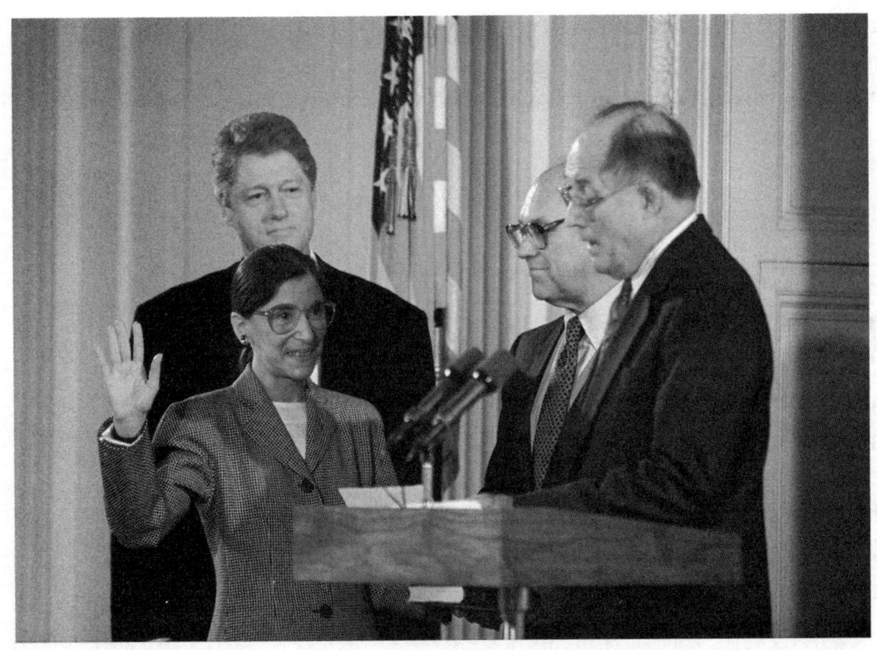

Ginsburg takes her oath on August 10, 1993, sworn in by Chief Justice Rehnquist and flanked by her husband and President Clinton.

of a lifetime, in her pioneering work in behalf of the women of this country, she has compiled a truly historic record of achievement in the finest traditions of American law and citizenship. And finally, I believe that in the years ahead she will be able to be a force for consensus-building on the Supreme Court, just as she has been on the Court of Appeals, so that our judges can become an instrument of our common unity in the expression of their fidelity to the Constitution.

What did Justice Ginsburg say about dissenting opinions?

In her later years on the Court, Justice Ginsburg became quite well known for her powerful dissenting opinions. She viewed dissenting opinions as essential to the judicial process. "My experience teaches that there is nothing better than an impressive dissent to lead the author of the majority opinion to refine and clarify her initial conclusion," she once said.

She also emphasized that dissenting opinions speak to future generations: "Dissents speak to a future age. The greatest dissents do become court opinions and gradually over time their views become the dominant view."

What did Justice Ginsburg write in her dissent in *Bush v. Gore* (2000)?

Justice Ginsburg was one of the justices who dissented in the famous, or infamous, decision of *Bush v. Gore* (2000), the U.S. Supreme Court decision that effectively decided the presidential election that year. The issue involved recounts in Florida, a state that found George W. Bush a mere 537 votes ahead of Al Gore. The Florida result was outcome determinative in the election, as the winner of Florida's electoral votes captured the presidency.

Justice Ginsburg believed that the U.S. Supreme Court should defer to the Florida Supreme Court when it came to interpreting election law in the state of Florida. She explained: "The extraordinary setting of this case has obscured the ordinary principle that dictates its proper resolution: Federal courts defer to state high courts' interpretations of their state's own law. This principle reflects the core of federalism, on which all agree."

She concluded: "In sum, the Court's conclusion that a constitutionally adequate recount is impractical is a prophecy the Court's own judgment will not allow to be tested. Such an untested prophecy should not decide the Presidency of the United States."

Why did Justice Ginsburg dissent in the Lilly Ledbetter case?

Justice Ginsburg dissented in *Ledbetter v. Goodyear* (2007) because she realized that employees may be subject to unlawful pay disparities on the basis of gender but not find out about such disparities until years later. Lilly Ledbetter had worked at a tire factory in Gadsden, Alabama, for nearly 20 years. She was a manager but was paid far less than similarly situated male managers for this time.

However, Ledbetter did not know of these pay disparities until years later. The law at that time provided that an employee must bring such a pay disparity case to the Court within 180 days of the actual discriminatory practice.

The majority of the Court thus ruled that Ledbetter's claims were time-barred. Justice Ginsburg, however, wrote a powerful dissenting opinion:

> The Court's insistence on immediate contest overlooks common characteristics of pay discrimination. Pay disparities often occur, as they did in Ledbetter's case, in small increments; cause to suspect that discrimination is at work develops only over time. Comparative pay information, moreover, is often hidden from the employee's

> view. Employers may keep under wraps the pay differentials maintained among supervisors, no less the reasons for those differentials. Small initial discrepancies may not be seen as meet for a federal case, particularly when the employee, trying to succeed in a nontraditional environment, is averse to making waves....
>
> The realities of the workplace reveal why the discrimination with respect to compensation that Ledbetter suffered does not fit within the category of singular discrete acts "easy to identify." A worker knows immediately if she is denied a promotion or transfer, if she is fired or refused employment. And promotions, transfers, hirings, and firings are generally public events, known to co-workers. When an employer makes a decision of such open and definitive character, an employee can immediately seek out an explanation and evaluate it for pretext. Compensation disparities, in contrast, are often hidden from sight. It is not unusual, decisions in point illustrate, for management to decline to publish employee pay levels, or for employees to keep private their own salaries....
>
> Once again, the ball is in Congress' court. As in 1991, the Legislature may act to correct this Court's parsimonious reading of Title VII.

What did Congress do after the Ledbetter decision?

Congress paid close attention to Justice Ginsburg's historic dissenting opinion and passed the Lilly Ledbetter Fair Pay Act of 2009. The law amends Title VII by providing that the 180-day time period for filing pay discrimination claims starts again each time a new paycheck reflects an act of pay discrimination.

"It is fitting that with the very first bill I sign—the Lilly Ledbetter Fair Pay Restoration Act—we are upholding one of this na-

Ginsburg's dissenting opinion in *Ledbetter v. Goodyear Tire & Rubber Co.* (2007) directly prompted Congress to create the Lilly Ledbetter Fair Pay Act of 2009, amending the Civil Rights Act of 1964. The bill was signed into law by President Obama nine days after he took office in 2009.

tion's first principles: that we are all created equal and each deserve a chance to pursue our own version of happiness," President Barack Obama said upon signing.

What was Justice Ginsburg's dissent in *Vance v. Ball* (2013)?

In *Vance v. Ball* (2013), the U.S. Supreme Court took a very narrow view of who can be a supervisor for the purposes of employment discrimination law. The distinction between a supervisor and a co-employee is very significant in employment law, as the standard for holding an employer liable is much easier if the discriminating employee is a supervisor.

But the majority in *Vance v. Ball* reasoned that a supervisor is only someone who can hire and fire an employee. Justice Ginsburg took a much more pragmatic view of who is considered a supervisor.

"Until today, our decisions have assumed that employees who direct subordinates' work are supervisors," she said. "A supervisor with authority to control subordinates' daily work is no less aided

in his harassment than is a supervisor with authority to fire, demote, or transfer."

She added that "workplace realities fortify my conclusion that harassment by an employee with power to direct subordinates' day-to-day work activities should trigger vicarious employer liability."

Justice Ginsburg added: "Trumpeting the virtues of simplicity and administrability, the Court restricts supervisor status to those with power to take tangible employment actions. In so restricting the definition of supervisor, the Court once again shuts from sight the robust protection against workplace discrimination Congress intended Title VII to secure."

She called on Congress to correct the wrong: "The ball is once again in Congress' court to correct the error into which this Court has fallen, and to restore the robust protections against workplace harassment the Court weakens today."

What did Justice Ginsburg write in her dissent in *Connick v. Thompson* (2011)?

In *Connick v. Thompson* (2011), the U.S. Supreme Court ruled 5–4 to reverse a decision of the U.S. Court of Appeals for the Fifth Circuit that had affirmed a large jury verdict in favor of John Thompson, a man falsely convicted of murder who spent more than a dozen years on death row for a crime he did not commit.

On December 6, 1984, an assailant shot and killed Raymond T. Liuzza Jr., who was the son of a prominent New Orleans business executive. The shooting took place on the street outside the victim's home.

Only one eyewitness was present. That eyewitness said that the shooter was an African American male, 6 feet tall with "close cut hair." At this time, John Thompson was 5 feet, 8 inches tall and wore an Afro. Police reports of the witness identification were not disclosed to Thompson's defense.

About three weeks later, on December 28, 1984, the police linked Thompson to another violent crime: the armed robbery of three siblings. During the incident, the robber's blood was found on the clothing of one of the victims. Testing revealed that the blood type of the perpetrator was Type B. John Thompson had Type O blood.

Prosecutors never disclosed the blood evidence to Thompson's defense team. Police arrested Thompson for the murder; the star witness was Kevin Freeman. Freeman was 6 feet tall and bald. Freeman was the likely actual culprit of the Liuzza murder, but a jury convicted Thompson and sentenced him to death.

The prosecution first tried Thompson for the armed robbery. Then, they tried him on the murder charges. By prosecuting Thompson for armed robbery first—and withholding blood evidence that might have exonerated Thompson of that charge—the district attorney's office disabled Thompson from testifying in his own defense at the murder trial.

Thompson discovered the prosecutors' misconduct through a serendipitous series of events. In 1994, nine years after Thompson's convictions, Gerry Deegan, an assistant prosecutor in the armed robbery trial, learned that he was terminally ill. Soon thereafter, Deegan confessed to his friend and fellow attorney Michael Riehlmann that he had suppressed blood evidence in the armed robbery case.

Deegan did not heed Riehlmann's counsel to reveal what he had done. For five years, Riehlmann, himself a former Orleans Parish prosecutor, kept Deegan's confession to himself.

On April 16, 1999, the state of Louisiana scheduled Thompson's execution. In an eleventh-hour effort to save his life, Thompson's attorneys hired a private investigator. Deep in the crime lab archives, the investigator unearthed a microfiche copy of the lab report identifying the robber's blood type.

The district attorney's office then initiated grand jury proceedings against the prosecutors who had withheld the lab report.

The district attorney, Harry Connick Sr., terminated the grand jury after just one day. He maintained that the lab report would not be Brady material (evidence that could help the defendant) if prosecutors did not know Thompson's blood type.

The unlawfully procured robbery conviction, the Court held, had violated Thompson's right to testify and thus fully present his defense in the murder trial.

Undeterred by his assistants' disregard of Thompson's rights, Connick retried Thompson for the Liuzza murder. Thompson's defense was bolstered by evidence earlier unavailable to him. The jury found Thompson not guilty after only 35 minutes of deliberation. On May 9, 2003, having served more than 18 years in prison for crimes he did not commit, Thompson was released.

On July 16, 2003, Thompson commenced a civil action under federal law 42 U.S.C. §1983 alleging that Connick, other officials of the Orleans Parish District Attorney's office, and the office itself had violated his constitutional rights by wrongfully withholding Brady evidence. A federal jury awarded him $14 million, finding that the district attorney's office was deliberately indifferent to his rights. The U.S. Court of Appeals for the Fifth Circuit affirmed this.

The U.S. Supreme Court reversed its decision 5–4. Justice Thomas wrote the majority opinion. Justice Thomas reasoned that Thompson failed to prove that the violation was "so predictable that failing to train the prosecutors amounted to conscious disregard for defendants' Brady rights."

Justice Ginsburg dissented and read her dissent from the bench. The dissent found that the evidence supports the jury's finding in three ways: (1) Connick failed to ensure that the prosecutors under his direct control knew their constitutional Brady obligations; (2) an obvious need for Brady training existed; and (3) Connick's approach amounted to a "culture of inattention" to Brady material.

Justice Ginsburg explained: "John Thompson spent 18 years in prison, 14 of them isolated on death row, before the truth came to light: He was innocent of the charge of attempted armed robbery, and his subsequent trial on a murder charge, by prosecutorial design, was fundamentally unfair." She added: "From the top down, the evidence showed, members of the District Attorney's Office, including the District Attorney himself, misperceived Brady's compass and therefore inadequately attended to their disclosure obligations."

She concluded: "In sum, the evidence permitted the jury to reach the following conclusions. First, Connick did not ensure that prosecutors in his Office knew their Brady obligations; he neither confirmed their familiarity with Brady when he hired them, nor saw to it that training took place on his watch. Second, the need for Brady training and monitoring was obvious to Connick. Indeed he so testified. Third, Connick's cavalier approach to his staff's knowledge and observation of Brady requirements contributed to a culture of inattention to Brady in Orleans Parish."

In what voting rights decision did Justice Ginsburg dissent?

Justice Ginsburg authored a powerful dissenting opinion in *Shelby County v. Holder* (2013), a case involving a challenge to the

After her death from pancreatic cancer, spontaneous vigils sprang up at the Supreme Court and around the country for the cultural icon sometimes nicknamed The Notorious R.B.G.

so-called preclearance provision of the Voting Rights Act of 1965. That act generally prohibited racially discriminatory practices regarding voting. The preclearance provision required those jurisdictions with a history of discriminatory practices to preclear any changes to their voting laws with the U.S. Department of Justice.

The majority of the U.S. Supreme Court reasoned that the preclearance provision was outdated and no longer needed, as no pervasive evidence existed of an intent to discriminate in Shelby County, Alabama.

However, Justice Ginsburg authored a moving tribute to the underlying purposes of the Voting Rights Act of 1965 and explained why the preclearance provision was still needed:

> Voting discrimination still exists; no one doubts that. But the Court today terminates the remedy that proved to be best suited to block that discrimination. The Voting Rights Act of 1965 (VRA) has worked to combat voting discrimination where other remedies had been tried and failed. Particularly effective is the VRA's requirement of federal preclearance for all changes to voting laws in the regions of the country with the most aggravated records of rank discrimination against minority voting rights....
>
> Answering that need, the Voting Rights Act became one of the most consequential, efficacious, and amply justified exercises of federal legislative power in our Nation's history. Requiring federal preclearance of changes in voting laws in the covered jurisdictions—those States and localities where opposition to the Constitution's commands were most virulent—the VRA provided a fit solution for minority voters as well as for States. Under the preclearance regime established by §5 of the VRA, covered jurisdictions must submit proposed changes in voting laws or procedures to the Department of Justice (DOJ), which has 60 days to respond to the changes.

In one of the most epic lines ever in a U.S. Supreme Court opinion, Justice Ginsburg added: "Throwing out preclearance when it has worked and is continuing to work to stop discriminatory changes is like throwing away your umbrella in a rainstorm because you are not getting wet."

Confirmation Process

How are U.S. Supreme Court justices appointed to the High Court?

Article II, Section 2 provides that the president of the United States shall have the power to nominate "Judges of the Supreme Court." In fact, Article II provides that the president has the power to nominate all federal judges.

The Constitution also provides that the U.S. Senate shall provide "Advice and Consent." This means that the president's judicial nominees must be confirmed by the Senate.

What factors go into the selection of a U.S. Supreme Court justice?

Ideology and politics play key roles, as generally, a president selects a justice who is from his or her own political party. Age also plays a key role, as oftentimes, a president wants to select someone who is not too old and will be able to potentially serve on the Court for a significant amount of time.

David M. O'Brien, in his book *Storm Center: The Supreme Court in American Politics*, explained: "The reality is that every appointment is political. Merit competes with other political considerations like personal and ideological compatibility, with the forces of support or opposition in Congress and the White House, and with demands for representative appointments on the basis of geography, religion, race, gender, and ethnicity."

What is the confirmation process?

After the president nominates a candidate to the U.S. Supreme Court, the U.S. Senate either confirms or denies the nominee. The Senate Judiciary Committee gathers extensive information about the nominee, holds hearings, and eventually votes on whether to move the candidate on to a full Senate vote. The confirmation process can be quite difficult and lengthy, depending on how controversial the candidate is deemed to be by Congress, their constituents, and interested public interest groups. It only takes a majority vote for a candidate to win confirmation. However, 26

Judge Samuel A. Alito undergoes questioning by members of the Senate Judiciary Committee before his confirmation as a U.S. Supreme Court justice in 2006.

nominations by presidents have not been successful. The Senate rejected 12 appointments to the Court by formal full vote. Those 12, and the Senate's rejection vote tally, were:

John Rutledge (1795)	rejected 14-10 (for chief justice)
Alexander Wolcott (1811)	rejected 24-9
John C. Spencer (1843)	rejected 26-21
George W. Woodward (1845)	rejected 29-20
Jeremiah Black (1860)	rejected 26-25
Ebenezer R. Hoar (1870)	rejected 33-24
William B. Hornblower (1893)	rejected 30-24
Wheeler Peckham (1894)	rejected 41-32
John J. Parker (1930)	rejected 41-39
Clement F. Haynsworth (1969)	rejected 55-45
G. Harrold Carswell (1970)	rejected 51-45
Robert Bork (1986)	rejected 58-42

What justices have withdrawn their names from consideration because of senatorial opposition?

Not all U.S. Supreme Court nominees even make it to a full vote. Some of the nominees withdraw their name from consideration when it is clear that they will face significant and perhaps overwhelming senatorial opposition. The following U.S. Supreme Court nominees withdrew their names from consideration:

- Reuben H. Walworth (1844)
- Edward King (1845)
- George H. Williams (nominated in 1873, withdrawn in 1874)
- Caleb Cushing (1874)
- Justice Abe Fortas (1968 for chief justice)
- Douglas H. Ginsburg (1987)
- Harriet Miers (2005)

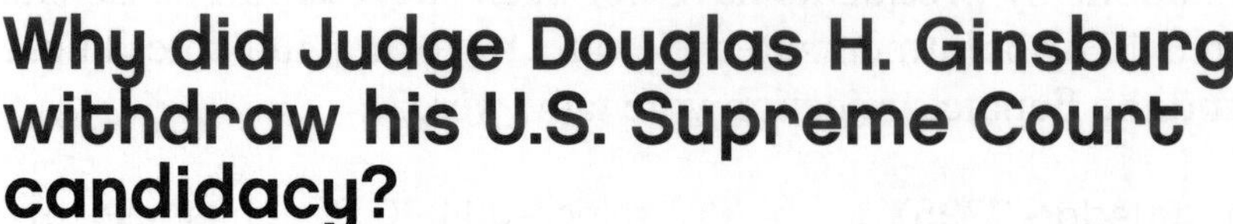

Why did Judge Douglas H. Ginsburg withdraw his U.S. Supreme Court candidacy?

Judge Douglas H. Ginsburg, who at the time was a relatively new judge on the U.S. Court of Appeals for the D.C. Circuit, withdrew his name from U.S. Supreme Court consideration when it was revealed by the media (Nina Totenberg on NPR) that Ginsburg had engaged in marijuana usage as a student and then later when he was an assistant professor of law at Harvard Law School.

Ginsburg had a stellar academic record and had worked in the Reagan administration in 1983 before being elevated to the U.S. Court of Appeals for the D.C. Circuit. However, the revelations about his personal marijuana usage, particularly as a professor, was too much at that time in the mid- to late 1980s when the Reagan administration had such a strong anti-illegal drug stance.

Ginsburg withdrew his name as mounting pressure came from both outside and inside the Reagan administration. He stated to reporters: "I have today asked President Reagan not to forward my nomination to the Supreme Court.... I was looking forward to sharing with the American people my views about justice and about the role of the courts in our society. Unfortunately, all of the attention has been focused on our personal lives, and much of that on events of many years ago. My views on the law and on what kind of Supreme Court Justice I would make have been drowned out in the clamor."

What female lawyer withdrew her nomination after significant opposition?

Harriet Miers, White House counsel to President George W. Bush, withdrew her nomination to the U.S. Supreme Court after significant opposition. Miers graduated from Southern Methodist

President George W. Bush nominates White House Counsel Harriet Miers as Supreme Court justice.

University Law School and served on law review there. She then clerked for a federal district court judge after graduation. She practiced law for decades, becoming the first female managing partner at the Dallas-based firm Locke, Liddell & Sapp.

She also was the first female president of the Dallas Bar Association and the Texas State Bar Association. Bush named her his White House counsel to succeed Alberto Gonzales, whom Bush named as his U.S. attorney general. "I've known Harriet for more than a decade," said Bush. "I know her heart. I know her character."

Many criticized Miers because she had no prior judicial experience and did not attend one of the elite law schools. Some prominent conservatives, including Robert Bork, opposed her nomination publicly. She withdrew her name from consideration after only 24 days.

In his memoir *True Faith and Allegiance*, Gonzales writes: "I failed to appreciate the difficult challenges created by the nomination of a former or current White House counsel. The U.S. Senate would want to see Harriet's internal memos, as well as sensitive documents she had reviewed.... Such a nomination sets the White House on a collision course with the Senate over access to documents the president would want to protect as privileged."

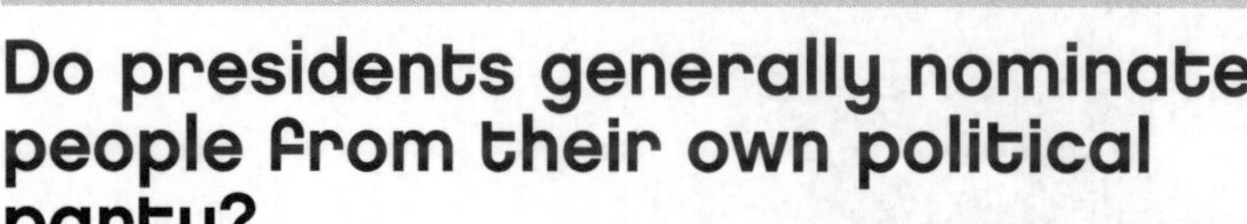

Do presidents generally nominate people from their own political party?

Yes, presidents generally nominate a person from their own political party. President Washington actually began the general process of appointing those to the Court who shared his general ideological bent. For example, President Washington was a Federalist, and he appointed fellow Federalists to the U.S. Supreme Court.

A few exceptions to this practice have occurred historically, however. For example, President John Tyler, of the Whig Party, nominated Democrat Samuel Nelson to the U.S. Supreme Court. President Franklin D. Roosevelt, a Democrat, nominated Republican Harlan Fiske Stone. President Warren Harding, a Republican, nominated Democrat Pierce Butler. President Dwight D. Eisenhower, a Republican, nominated Democrat William J. Brennan Jr.

In more modern times, it would be unthinkable for a president to nominate a person not from his or her own political party to the U.S. Supreme Court.

Who generally helps a president with selecting U.S. Supreme Court nominees?

Most presidents have delegated the selection of U.S. Supreme Court nominees to their U.S. attorney generals and other close advisors in the White House. Oftentimes, an assistant attorney general in the Office of Legal Counsel might generate a list of potential candidates. Presidents generally will have a committee who then vet these individuals and present the president with a top three. The president often will then interview those in the top three and determine whom to nominate officially.

DID YOU KNOW?

What U.S. Supreme Court justice in the 20th century did not have a law degree?

Justice Stanley Reed, who served on the Court from 1938 to 1957, did not have a law degree. He studied law at both the University of Virginia and Columbia Law School but did not graduate. He apprenticed for a lawyer in Kentucky and then was admitted to the Kentucky Bar in 1910. He began his law practice in Maysville, Kentucky, before entering politics.

However, this is a generalization. Not all presidents have operated in the same fashion when it comes to picking nominees. Some presidents have simply nominated their close friends, and other presidents have taken a very hands-on approach from the beginning.

What qualifications must a federal judge possess?

The Constitution provides no criteria or qualifications for federal judges. Technically, a person who is not a lawyer or with no legal experience could be appointed to the U.S. Supreme Court. However, Congress and the Department of Justice carefully review nominees to determine whether they have the requisite degree of professional accomplishment and experience necessary for the lofty position. Most of the judges have a record of outstanding professional achievement, key political connections, and a history of public service in some capacity. Many appellate judges have had some prior judicial experience. For example, all nine justices of the U.S. Supreme Court previously had some form of judicial experience before they served on the U.S. Supreme Court.

What is the role of the American Bar Association in the U.S. Supreme Court nomination/confirmation process?

The American Bar Association, the largest professional trade association of lawyers, has played a significant role in the nomination/confirmation process. The ABA Standing Committee on the Federal Judiciary, composed of 18 members, has conducted independent, nonpartisan, and comprehensive evaluations of the professional qualifications of nominees to the federal bench since 1953.

Until 2001, presidents generally consulted with the Standing Committee regarding proposed nominees. In March 2001, President George W. Bush took a different stance. He reasoned that "it would be particularly inappropriate ... to grant a preferential, quasi-official role to a group, such as the ABA, that takes public positions on divisive political, legal, and social issues that come before the courts." However, the Senate Judiciary Committee asked the ABA Standing Committee on the Federal Judiciary to continue reviewing those nominated for federal judgeships.

The ABA explains: "The Standing Committee does not propose, endorse or recommend nominees. Its sole function is to evaluate a nominee's integrity, professional competence and judicial temperament, and then to rate the nominee either 'Well Qualified,' 'Qualified' or 'Not Qualified.' It does not base its rating on or seek to express any view regarding a nominee's ideology or political views."

Whose confirmation process in the early part of the 20th century was especially contentious?

Justice Brandeis's confirmation was especially contentious even though everyone knew that he was eminently qualified to serve on the Court. President Woodrow Wilson nominated Justice Brandeis in January 1916, but widespread opposition to him occurred in part because he was considered to be anti-business and, sadly, because of anti-Semitism.

Many opposed Justice Brandeis because he was pro-union and fought for individuals against big business. In fact, Justice Brandeis once gave a speech in which he said that too many lawyers were working for corporations and not enough lawyers were working for the people. Sitting chief justice William Howard Taft actually wrote to President Warren G. Harding about Justice Brandeis: "Mr. Louis Brandeis is not a person to be a member of the Supreme Court."

Justice Brandeis eventually was confirmed by a vote of 47–23 and became the first Jewish justice to serve on the Court.

Does a person need prior judicial experience to serve on the U.S. Supreme Court?

No; nothing in the Constitution—or anywhere else—requires a U.S. Supreme Court justice to have had prior judicial experi-

Chief Justice Earl Warren was one of several Supreme Court Justices appointed with no prior judicial experience.

ence. In fact, Justice Frankfurter once stated: "One is entitled to say without qualification that the correlation between prior judicial experience and fitness for the Supreme Court is zero." In fact, some of the greatest justices in U.S. Supreme Court history—Chief Justice John Marshall and Chief Justice Earl Warren, to name two prime examples—had no prior judicial history before ascending to the High Court.

What judge failed to get confirmed in 1930 partly because of opposition from the NAACP?

Judge John Parker, a prominent federal appeals court judge on the U.S. Court of Appeals for the Fourth Circuit, was rejected by the U.S. Senate in 1930. The NAACP opposed Parker based on racist comments he had made 10 years earlier in a 1920 gubernatorial campaign. While running for governor of North Carolina, Parker allegedly said: "The participation of the Negro in politics is a source of evil and danger to both races and is not desired by the wise men in either race or by the Republican Party of North Carolina."

The Senate's rejection of Parker was the only time between the years 1894 and 1968 that the Senate rejected a U.S. Supreme Court nominee.

What associate justice was not confirmed to chief justice and eventually resigned from the Court altogether?

Justice Abe Fortas served as an associate justice from 1965 to 1969. President Lyndon Baines Johnson appointed him to replace Justice Arthur Goldberg, who left the Court to serve as the U.S. representative of the United Nations. President Johnson nominated him to be chief justice to replace departing chief justice Warren.

However, Justice Fortas ran into trouble during the confirmation process, as it was discovered that he had accepted $15,000 for nine lectures that he delivered at American University Washington College of Law while an associate justice. Some conservative members of Congress questioned whether it was proper for Justice Fortas to receive this money, as the money came not from the university itself but from private businesses that might have interests before the Court.

Then, another matter of controversy arose during the confirmation process. It was discovered that Justice Fortas had accepted money—a $20,000 retainer from the Wolfson Foundation—for advice. Louis Wolfson was a Wall Street financier who was a source of controversy for alleged securities law violations. Though Justice Fortas returned the money, members of Congress who opposed Justice Fortas seized upon this as evidence that Justice Fortas was unfit not only for the position of chief justice but also to sit on the Court.

Author Michael Bobelian writes in his book *Battle for the Marble Palace: Abe Fortas, Earl Warren, Lyndon Johnson, Richard Nixon and the Forging of the Modern Supreme Court*: "Fortas' nomination fundamentally altered the Court, turning the selection of justices into high-stakes contests over the future of the nation."

Under increasing congressional criticism and scrutiny, Justice Fortas resigned from the U.S. Supreme Court in 1969. However, Justice Fortas maintained that he did not do anything wrong. He wrote: "It is my opinion, however, that the public controversy relating to my association with the Foundation is likely to ... adversely affect the work and position of the Court.... In these circumstances ... it is not my duty to remain on the Court but rather to resign in the hope that this will enable the Court to proceed ... free from extraneous stress."

Historians have advanced the theory that Justice Fortas fell on his sword in part to protect his friend and mentor U.S. Supreme Court justice William O. Douglas, from being investigated about his extrajudicial activities.

What federal judges nominated by President Richard Nixon were rejected by the U.S. Senate?

President Richard Nixon's first two nominees for the U.S. Supreme Court, C. Clement Haynsworth and G. Harrold Carswell, were both rejected by the U.S. Supreme Court. Haynsworth was a judge on the U.S. Court of Appeals for the Fourth Circuit, while Carswell was a judge on the U.S. Court of Appeals for the Fifth Circuit and, before that, a federal district court judge in Florida.

The Senate rejected Haynsworth 55–45 in 1969 and Carswell 51–45 in 1970.

Why did the Senate reject Haynsworth?

Both the AFL-CIO, the influential labor union, and the NAACP opposed Haynsworth's nomination to the U.S. Supreme Court. They argued that Haynsworth made rulings that were anti-union and that supported segregation. Several Democratic senators also questioned whether Haynsworth had made rulings in cases in which he had business interests, a charge that was not proven.

Some argue that many Democrats opposed Haynsworth as payback for many of their Republican counterparts' actions against Justice Fortas. In fact, John P. Frank, in his book *Clement Haynsworth, the Senate, and the Supreme Court* (1991), wrote: "In both labor relations and civil rights, Haynsworth was no reactionary. He was not a racist, and he was not antilabor. But he did have a conservative outlook in both areas, and he had a track record of reversals which made him easy to attack."

Why did the Senate reject Carswell?

Carswell had a bad record as a segregationist. He made a series of rulings as a district court judge in civil rights cases that were reversed by the then U.S. Court of Appeals for the Fifth Cir-

DID YOU KNOW?

What U.S. Supreme Court nominee was defended by a senator as being mediocre?

Senator Roman Hruska, a Republican senator from Nebraska, famously said this of U.S. Supreme Court nominee G. Harrold Carswell, a federal judge from Florida: "Even if he is mediocre, there are a lot of mediocre judges and people and lawyers. They are entitled to a little representation, aren't they, and a little chance? We can't all have Brandeises, Cardozos and Frankfurters and stuff like that there."

The Senate rejected Carswell 45–51.

cuit. In fact, Professor William Van Alstyne of the Duke School of Law testified before the Judiciary Committee against the nomination of Carswell. This was significant, as Van Alstyne had testified earlier in support of Clement Haynsworth. Van Alstyne testified of Carswell: "There is, in candor, nothing in the quality of the nominee's work to warrant any expectation whatever that he could serve with distinction on the Supreme Court of the United States."

John P. Frank, in his book *Clement Haynsworth, the Senate, and the Supreme Court* (1991), wrote: "Carswell must be viewed historically as a bad legal joke. Like Fortas, he helped to dig his own grave with his mouth. Want of candor to a senatorial committee is rarely rewarded, and Carswell was almost disgustingly wanting in candor. But he was so demonstrably incompetent that he might well have lost no matter how much truth he told."

After the Haynsworth and Carswell rejections, what justice was unanimously confirmed by the Senate?

The U.S. Senate unanimously confirmed Justice Harry A. Blackmun by a vote of 94–0 on May 12, 1970. Justice Blackmun,

Harry Blackmun was appointed by President Nixon in 1970, serving until his retirement in 1994.

of Minnesota, had served on the U.S. Court of Appeals for the Eighth Circuit and was a close friend (at the time) of Chief Justice Warren E. Burger. In fact, the two were dubbed "the Minnesota Twins" at the time. U.S. Supreme Court scholar Henry J. Abraham writes in his book *Justices, Presidents, and Senators*: "Blackmun had served for 11 years on the federal bench. His nomination was as anticlimactic as it was noncontroversial. To the relief of the Senate he appeared to have impeccable credentials, and although he did not rank with the country's most distinguished jurists, he was quickly confirmed on May 12 by a vote of 94–0."

What other Nixon appointee to the U.S. Supreme Court faced significant opposition?

Chief Justice William H. Rehnquist, then 47 years old, faced significant opposition largely because of his conservative views. Chief Justice Rehnquist had worked for Senator Barry Goldwater in his 1964 presidential race and worked in the Office of Legal Counsel during the Nixon administration. Chief Justice Rehnquist had serious intellectual credentials, graduating first in his class from Stanford Law School and serving as a law clerk to U.S. Supreme Court justice Rob-

ert H. Jackson. The American Civil Liberties Union, for example, publicly denounced the nomination of Chief Justice Rehnquist.

Chief Justice Rehnquist also faced significant opposition when President Ronald Reagan elevated him from associate justice to chief justice in 1986. Chief Justice Rehnquist's vote was contentious because many Democratic senators believed that the chief justice was very conservative and would tilt the Court too far to the right. Chief Justice Rehnquist was the most conservative member of the Burger Court. His pattern of filing lone dissents earned him the nickname "the Lone Ranger." Much of the opposition came from allegations surfacing—or, more accurately, resurfacing—concerning Chief Justice Rehnquist's efforts in Phoenix, Arizona, in which he argued against a public accommodations law. Allegations, not proven, also came out that Chief Justice Rehnquist attempted to prevent blacks from voting in a local election. Also, concerns were raised due to a memo that Chief Justice Rehnquist authored when he was a law clerk for U.S. Supreme Court justice Robert H. Jackson in the 1952–1953 term on the *Brown v. Board of Education* school desegregation case. In the memo, Chief Justice Rehnquist wrote that the separate but equal doctrine should be upheld. During the Senate confirmation hearings, Chief Justice Rehnquist said that the memo reflected the justice's views, not his own. Many historians and legal scholars have questioned that assertion.

What famous judge did not get confirmed in 1987?

Judge Robert Bork (1927–2012), a former constitutional law professor and federal appeals court judge, did not get confirmed in 1987, as the Senate voted 58–42 against him. Many in the Senate considered Bork too conservative and too restrictive of individual rights to serve on the High Court. Senator Edward Kennedy famously impugned Bork with the following statement: "Robert Bork's America is a land in which women would be forced into back-alley abortions, blacks would sit at segregated lunch counters, rogue police could break down citizens' doors." Kennedy's comments were ex-

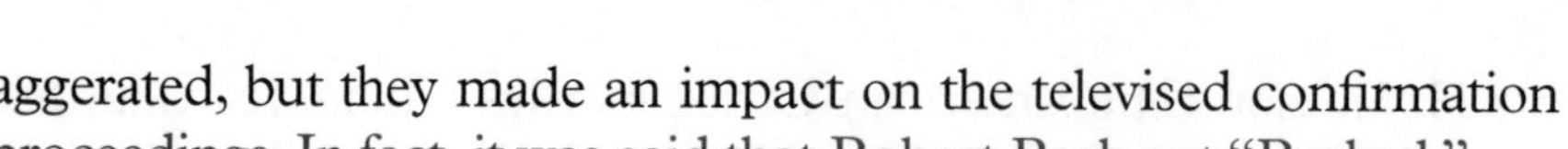

aggerated, but they made an impact on the televised confirmation proceedings. In fact, it was said that Robert Bork got "Borked."

Do the current U.S. Supreme Court justices have prior judicial experience?

Eight of the nine current U.S. Supreme Court justices have prior judicial experience. These eight are:

Name	Prior Judicial Experience
Chief Justice John G. Roberts Jr.	U.S. Court of Appeals for the D.C. Circuit
Justice Samuel A. Alito Jr.	U.S. Court of Appeals for the Third Circuit
Justice Amy Coney Barrett	U.S. Court of Appeals for the Seventh Circuit
Justice Neil M. Gorsuch	U.S. Court of Appeals for the 10th Circuit
Justice Ketanji Brown Jackson	U.S. Court of Appeals for the D.C. Circuit
Justice Brett M. Kavanaugh	U.S. Court of Appeals for the D.C. Circuit
Justice Sonia Sotomayor	U.S. District Court, Southern District of New York and U.S. Court of Appeals for the Second Circuit
Justice Clarence Thomas	U.S. Court of Appeals for the D.C. Circuit

What did U.S. senator Robert Kennedy say about Justice Thurgood Marshall in his confirmation hearings?

Senator Robert Kennedy from New York was very supportive of then Judge Marshall in his nomination to the U.S. Supreme Court.

Justice Thurgood Marshall served on the Supreme Court from his 1967 appointment by President Lyndon Johnson until his retirement in 1991.

"In nominating Judge Marshall, President Johnson has selected for our highest court a man who brings with him not only a long and distinguished career of widely varied legal experience, but also a man whose work has symbolized and spearheaded the struggle of millions of Americans for equality before the law," Kennedy said.

Kennedy spoke about how he had worked with Justice Marshall when Kennedy was U.S. attorney general. He also praised Justice Marshall for his work as solicitor general and as a judge on the U.S. Court of Appeals for the Second Circuit. He concluded: "I have known him for some period of time, and have the greatest respect for him, Mr. Chairman and members of the committee. I know what a fine judge he made, and I know what an outstanding job he did as Solicitor General of the United States. I know he is a man of integrity and a man of honesty, and a man of ability, and I recommend him to the committee."

In what context during his confirmation hearing did Justice Thurgood Marshall emphasize that the Constitution was a "living document"?

Senator Sam Ervin from North Carolina asked Justice Marshall the following question: "I wish to repeat my question: Is not

the role of the Supreme Court simply to ascertain and give effect to the intent of the Framers of the Constitution and the people who ratified the Constitution?"

Justice Marshall responded: "Yes, Senator, with the understanding that the Constitution was meant to be a living document."

What U.S. senator grilled Justice Thurgood Marshall about the history of the 13th and 14th Amendments during his confirmation hearings?

Republican Strom Thurmond of South Carolina repeatedly grilled Justice Marshall about the history of the 13th Amendment during his confirmation hearings. Among the questions that Thurmond asked Justice Marshall were the following:

- Do you know who drafted the 13th Amendment to the U.S. Constitution?
- Turning to the provision of the 13th Amendment forbidding involuntary servitude, are you familiar with any pre-1860 cases that interpreted this language?
- Under what legal theories was the constitutionality of the Civil Rights Act of 1866 supported by its proponents?
- What theories were then current in the Republican Party that gave support to the position that the Civil Rights Act of 1866 could be constitutionally passed by Congress to enforce the Privileges and Immunities Clause of Article IV, Section 2 of the original Constitution?
- What constitutional difficulties did Representative John Bingham of Ohio see, or what difficulties do you see in the congressional enforcement of the Privileges and Immunities Clause of Article IV, Section 2 through the Necessary and Proper Clause of Article I, Section 8?

DID YOU KNOW?

What was telling about Justice Thurgood Marshall's confirmation vote?

The Senate confirmed Justice Marshall by a vote of 69–11. The 11 negative votes came from conservative senators largely from the South: Robert Byrd from West Virginia, James Eastland from Mississippi, Allen J. Ellender from Louisiana, Sam Ervin from North Carolina, J. Lister Hill from Alabama, Spessard Holland from Florida, Ernest "Fritz" Hollings from South Carolina, Russell Long from Louisiana, John Sparkman from Alabama, Herman Talmadge from Georgia, and Strom Thurmond from South Carolina.

- What provisions of the Slave Codes in existence in the South before 1860 was Congress desirous of abolishing with the Civil Rights Bill of 1866?
- Why do you think the framers of the original version of the first section of the 14th Amendment added the Necessary and Proper Clause from Article I, Section 8 to the Privileges and Immunities Clause of Article IV, Section 2?
- What purpose did the framers have, in your estimation, in referring to the incident involving former representative Samuel Hoar in Charleston, South Carolina, in December 1844 as showing the need for the enactment of the original version of the 14th Amendment's first section?

Did any opposition occur to Justice Sandra Day O'Connor's nomination to the U.S. Supreme Court?

The U.S. Senate unanimously confirmed Justice O'Connor to the U.S. Supreme Court by a vote of 99–0, though initially, some opposition occurred to her nomination. Some criticized her thin record of judging. Others worried that she was either too pro-choice or too pro-life. In other words, abortion advocates on both sides of the issue expressed concern about her nomination.

What was unusual about Justice Sonia Sotomayor's confirmations to the federal bench?

Justice Sotomayor is unusual in terms of confirmations because she has been appointed to different federal judgeships by both Republican and Democratic presidents. It actually was a Republican president, President George H. W. Bush, who first appointed Justice Sotomayor to the federal bench as a federal district court judge in the Southern District of New York. While a prominent Democrat, Justice Sotomayor had the strong backing of her New York senators, including Republican senator Alphonse D'Amato, who supported her along with President Bush.

Democratic presidents elevated her both to the federal appeals court level and then to the U.S. Supreme Court. Then, in 1997, President Bill Clinton elevated her to the U.S. Court of Appeals for the Second Circuit. Finally, in 2009, Democratic president Barack Obama nominated her to the U.S. Supreme Court.

Justice Sonya Sotomayor's rise through the legal ranks was supported by both Republicans and Democrats. Nominated by President Obama, the self-described "wise Latina" was sworn in by Chief Justice Roberts on August 8, 2009.

What justice received criticism during her confirmation hearings for using the term "wise Latina" in a speech?

Some Republican senators criticized Justice Sotomayor for saying in an earlier speech that she hoped her experience as a "wise Latina" would help her in deciding cases. Several Republican senators criticized her significantly for this remark. Senator Lindsey Graham from South Carolina told her, "If I had said anything remotely like that, my career would have been over."

Justice Sotomayor got to address this when asked a friendly line of questioning from Senator Patrick Leahy.

Justice Sotomayor responded:

> Thank you for giving me an opportunity to explain my remarks. No words I have ever spoken for written have received so much attention.
>
> I gave a variant of my speech to a variety of different groups, most often to groups of women lawyers or to groups, most particularly, of young Latino lawyers and students.
>
> As my speech made clear in one of the quotes that you reference, I was trying to inspire them to believe that their life experiences would enrich the legal system, because different life experiences and backgrounds always do. I don't think that there is a quarrel with that in our society.
>
> I was also trying to inspire them to believe that they could become anything they wanted to become, just as I had. The context of the words that I spoke have created a misunderstanding, … and to give everyone assurances, I want to state up front, unequivocally and without doubt, I do not believe that any ethnic, racial or gender group has an advantage in sound judging. I do believe that every person has an equal opportunity to be a good

DID YOU KNOW?

What former justice did Justice Sotomayor say she admired as a jurist?

Justice Sotomayor specifically mentioned Justice Benjamin N. Cardozo, also of New York, as a jurist she greatly admired. Justice Sotomayor was asked which of the current justices she most identified with. She declined to answer that question but did offer Justice Cardozo as a former justice she looked up to with his approach to judging.

and wise judge regardless of their background or life experiences.

Later, when questioned by Alabama senator Jeff Sessions, Justice Sotomayor said: "I do believe that life experiences are important to the process of judging. They help you to understand and listen but that the law requires a result. And it would command you to the facts that are relevant to the disposition of the case."

Justice Sotomayor did not run away from the comment. In a meeting with Senator David Vitter from Louisiana, a perceived opponent, the following exchange took place. Vitter asked Justice Sotomayor: "I want to ask you—do you think if I was you, and I had made the wise-Latina comment that you made, that I would have deserved to be a Supreme Court Justice?"

Justice Sotomayor responded bluntly: "If you had my record, yes."

What justice's nomination was nearly derailed by charges of sexual harassment of an employee?

Justice Clarence Thomas, who has served on the U.S. Supreme Court since 1991, was barely confirmed by the U.S. Senate by a vote of 52–48. At that time, it was the closest confirmation vote of a nominee who was confirmed. Justice Thomas was a controversial nominee from the beginning, as he had strong stances against abortion. Furthermore, many Democratic senators realized that President George H. W. Bush was replacing the retiring liberal icon Justice Thurgood Marshall with a very conservative jurist in Justice Thomas.

Although somewhat controversial from the start, the controversy escalated when law professor Anita Hill, who had worked for Justice Thomas at the U.S. Department of Education and the Equal Employment Opportunity Commission (EEOC), accused Justice Thomas of sexual harassment years earlier. Hill claimed that Justice Thomas had made sexually inappropriate remarks and had asked her out on dates.

Justice Thomas vehemently denied the charges and famously referred to the proceedings as a "high-tech lynching." In one of the more memorable moments in U.S. Supreme Court confirmation history, Justice Thomas responded to Senate Judiciary Chairman Joe Biden:

> Senator, I would like to start by saying unequivocally, uncategorically, that I deny each and every single allegation against me today that suggested in any way that I had conversations of a sexual nature or about pornographic material with Anita Hill, that I ever attempted to date her, that I ever had any personal sexual interest in her, or that I in any way ever harassed her.
>
> A second, and I think more important point. I think that this today is a travesty. I think that it is disgusting. I think that this hearing should never occur in America. This is a case in which this sleaze, this dirt, was searched for by staffers of members of this committee, was then leaked to the media, and this committee and this body validated it and displayed it at prime time over our entire nation. How would any member on this committee, any person in this room, or any person in

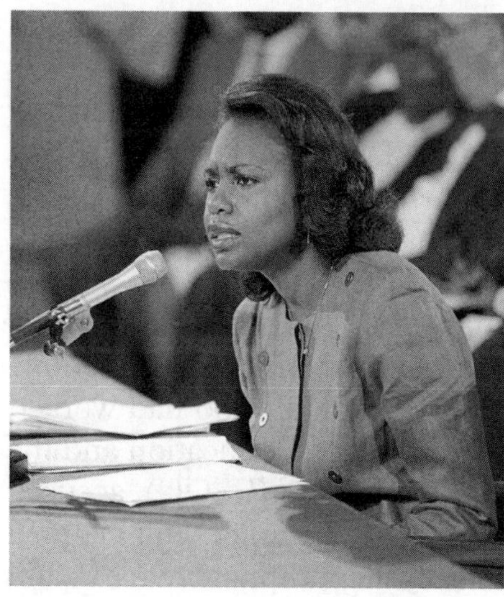

During Clarence Thomas's Supreme Court confirmation hearing, Anita Hill testified before the Senate Judiciary Committee about allegations of Thomas's misconduct.

this country, would like sleaze said about him or her in this fashion? Or this dirt dredged up and this gossip and these lies displayed in this manner? How would any person like it?

The Supreme Court is not worth it. No job is worth it. I am not here for that. I am here for my name, my family, my life, and my integrity. I think something is dreadfully wrong with this country when any person, any person in this free country would be subjected to this.

This is not a closed room. There was an FBI investigation. This is not an opportunity to talk about difficult matters privately or in a closed environment. This is a circus. It's a national disgrace.

And from my standpoint as a black American, as far as I'm concerned, it is a high-tech lynching for uppity blacks who in any way deign to think for themselves, to do for themselves, to have different ideas, and it is a message that unless you kowtow to an old order, this is what will happen to you. You will be lynched, destroyed, caricatured by a committee of the U.S.—U.S. Senate, rather than hung from a tree.

What other justice's confirmation nearly got derailed by allegations of sexual misconduct?

Justice Brett M. Kavanaugh was barely confirmed by the U.S. Senate by a 50–48 vote. Justice Kavanaugh's confirmation hearing became toxic and even salacious when it was revealed that a professor of psychology from California, Dr. Christine Blasey Ford, alleged that Justice Kavanaugh and his friend, Mark Judge, had sexually assaulted her in a bedroom at a party in high school in 1982. Dr. Ford made the allegations public in a piece published by the *Washington Post*. She later testified before the Judiciary Committee.

Justice Kavanaugh categorically denied the allegations, saying, "I did not do this back in high school or at any time." An FBI investigation did not confirm Dr. Ford's allegations. After hearing testimony from both Dr. Ford and Justice Kavanaugh, the Senate Judiciary Committee narrowly voted 11–10 to move his nomination to the full Senate. The full Senate confirmed Justice Kavanaugh by a vote of 50–48.

How did Chief Justice John G. Roberts Jr. go from being nominated as associate justice to chief justice?

When Justice Sandra Day O'Connor retired from the Court, President George W. Bush selected John G. Roberts Jr., who was then on the U.S. Court of Appeals for the D.C. Circuit, to replace Justice O'Connor. White House Counsel Alberto Gonzales recalls in his memoir *True Faith and Allegiance*: "DC Circuit judge John Roberts was young, but he was brilliant. He had been on our radar since 2003, and seemed to have a solid grasp of the Constitution combined with an impeccable, almost photographic memory of past legal cases. His relative lack of experience on the bench meant he had less of a paper trail to attack, and he had a charming, easygoing manner that masked a ferocious intellect."

Bush announced his nomination of Roberts to fill Justice O'Connor's seat as associate justice on July 19, 2005. Roberts prepared for his Senate Judiciary Committee hearing.

However, on September 3, 2005, Chief Justice Rehnquist passed away at the age of 80. President Bush now had an unexpected vacancy for chief justice. Vice President Dick Cheney, according to Gonzales, supported elevating Justice Antonin Scalia to chief justice. However, President Bush ended up nominating Roberts as chief justice.

What person was nominated to the U.S. Supreme Court but never had a hearing?

Merrick Garland was nominated to serve as an associate justice on the U.S. Supreme Court by President Barack Obama in March 2016 but went 238 days without any sort of confirmation hearing. Obama had nominated Garland after the unexpected death of Justice Scalia. However, the Republican-controlled Senate refused to take any action on his confirmation. Instead, 292 days passed until

Nominated by President Obama to fill the seat of recently deceased Associate Justice Antonin Scalia, Merrick Garland was never considered by the Republican-controlled Senate.

DID YOU KNOW?

What baseball analogy did Chief Justice John G. Roberts Jr. draw in his opening remarks at his confirmation hearing?

Chief Justice Roberts compared judges to umpires in his opening statement. He famously said:

> Judges are like umpires. Umpires don't make the rules, they apply them. The role of an umpire and a judge is critical. They make sure everybody plays by the rules, but it is a limited role. Nobody ever went to a ball game to see the umpire....
>
> I will be open to the considered views of my colleagues on the bench, and I will decide every case based on the record, according to the rule of law, without fear or favor, to the best of my ability, and I will remember that it's my job to call balls and strikes, and not to pitch or bat.

the end of the 114th Congress. A Republican president, Donald J. Trump, succeeded President Barack Obama, and he nominated Neil M. Gorsuch to the U.S. Supreme Court, who was confirmed.

What former U.S. Supreme Court justice did Justice Gorsuch identify as his life hero during his confirmation hearings?

Justice Gorsuch identified U.S. Supreme Court justice Byron White as his mentor and as "my childhood hero." He credited Justice White with making him into the lawyer and judge that he is today. Justice Gorsuch testified:

DID YOU KNOW?

What justice seemingly pointed out the inconsistency of the Establishment Clause jurisprudence during his confirmation hearings?

Justice Gorsuch spoke at his confirmation hearing about the difficulty of applying U.S. Supreme Court precedent in the Establishment Clause arena when he was a lower-court judge on the U.S. Court of Appeals for the 10th Circuit. "I can tell you as a lower court judge just trying to faithfully do what the Supreme Court wants us to do, it is a bit of a challenge in this area," Justice Gorsuch said after being asked about the state of religious expression by Senator John Corwyn. "We struggle along." He added: "The Court has struggled in Establishment Clause jurisprudence to provide a consistent, comprehensive test. I think that is a fair statement."

Justice Gorsuch identified the tension between the two religious liberty clauses of the First Amendment: The Establishment Clause and the Free Exercise Clause. He explained: "Those two commands are in tension because, to the extent we accommodate free expression, at some point the accommodation can be so great that someone is going to stand up and say you have established or you passed a law respecting an establishment of religion. It is a spectrum and it is a tension. And as in so many areas of law, judges have to mediate two competing and important values that our society holds dear."

You know, as I said, he really was my childhood hero. And to actually get picked out of the pile to spend a year with him, as Senator Mike Lee's dad did—that is something we share in common, too—was and remains the privilege of a lifetime. And it has everything to do with why I am here.

I would not have become a judge, but for watching his example. And the humility with which he approached

> the job, and I do not mean a phony humility. I mean real humility, every day. He always said two heads were better than one....
>
> And that, to me, taught me everything about what it means to be a judge and the fact that when asked his judicial philosophy in this sort of setting, he said it is to decide cases. And I know a lot of people think that is just mundane or maybe covert dishonesty in some way. It is just not true. It was the humility of the man.

Which justice was nominated by a president who specifically said he was going to place a woman of color on the bench?

President Joe Biden fulfilled his vow of nominating the first African American female to the U.S. Supreme Court when he nominated Judge Ketanji Brown Jackson to the U.S. Supreme Court. Though President Biden's specific pledge to nominate a person of a certain race and gender rankled some, Justice Ketanji Brown Jackson had impeccable credentials.

In fact, conservative former federal appeals court judge J. Michael Luttig wrote a letter of support to the Judiciary Committee that read in part:

> Judge Ketanji Brown Jackson is eminently qualified to serve on the Supreme Court of the United States. Indeed, she is as highly credentialed and experienced in the law as any nominee in history, having graduated from the Harvard Law School with honors, clerked at the Supreme Court, and served as a Federal Judge for almost a decade. Republicans and Democrats alike should give their studied advice—and then their consent—to the President's nomination. Republicans, in particular, should vote to confirm Judge Jackson.

Republicans prematurely judged President Biden's nominee when the President first announced he would nominate a black woman to the vacancy created by Justice Breyer's retirement. The President knew at the time that there were any number of highly qualified black women on the lower federal courts from among whom he could choose—including Judge Jackson—and Republicans should have known that the President would nominate one of those supremely qualified black women to succeed Justice Breyer.

Why did some Republicans attack Justice Ketanji Brown Jackson on the basis of being soft on crime?

Some Republican senators seemingly used Justice Jackson's history as a public defender against her in the hearings. For example, Senator Mitch McConnell stated: "We're in the middle of a violent crime wave, including soaring rates of homicides and carjackings. Amid all this, the soft on crime brigade is squarely in Judge Jackson's corner." Justice Jackson is the first former federal public defender to serve on the U.S. Supreme Court.

For her part, Justice Jackson stood her ground politely and responded: "As someone who has had family members on patrol and

Justice Ketanji Brown Jackson was appointed by President Biden in 2022 to replace retiring Associate Justice Stephen Breyer, who administered her Judicial Oath.

in the line of fire, I care deeply about public safety." She explained that her brother and two uncles were law-enforcement veterans.

What was Justice Ketanji Brown Jackson's comment about "staying in her lane"?

Justice Jackson testified before the Senate during her confirmation hearings that she would not go outside of her role as a judge and act as a super-legislator. She stated: "I am acutely aware that as a judge in our system, I have limited power. I am trying, in every case, to stay in my lane."

Who was the only senator to vote against confirming Justice Lewis Powell in 1971?

The U.S. Senate confirmed Justice Powell to replace Justice Hugo Black on the U.S. Supreme Court in 1971 by a vote of 89–1. The only "no" vote was cast by Senator Fred R. Harris of Oklahoma. Harris called Justice Powell "an elitist" who "has never shown any deep feelings for the little people." Harris said Justice Powell "does not have the kind of exemplary record in the fields of civil rights and civil liberties that I'd like to see in a man appointed to the Supreme Court for life."

Who were the only three "no" votes in the confirmation of Justice Ruth Bader Ginsburg?

Justice Ginsburg was confirmed by a vote of 96–3 in 1993 by the U.S. Senate. The only three "no" votes came from conservative

DID YOU KNOW?

What justice had only four "no" votes because he allegedly was a "reactionary tool of Wall Street"?

Only four Republican senators voted against Justice William O. Douglas, who was confirmed by a vote of 62–4. Those four Republican senators were Gerald P. Nye from North Dakota, Lynn J. Frazier from North Dakota, Clyde M. Reed from Kansas, and Henry Cabot Lodge Jr. from Massachusetts.

Republicans Jesse Helms from North Carolina, Don Hickles from Oklahoma, and Robert Smith from New Hampshire.

Only three senators voted against confirming Chief Justice Burger. Who were they?

The U.S. Senate confirmed then Judge Burger to the U.S. Supreme Court by a vote of 74–3. The only three "no" votes were from Senator Eugene McCarthy from Minnesota, Senator Gaylord Nelson from Wisconsin, and Senator Stephen M. Young from Ohio.

What are some suggestions for reforming the confirmation process?

The reality is that many confirmations to the U.S. Supreme Court have resulted in nominees not discussing in any depth past U.S. Supreme Court decisions and declining to answer with any specificity their views on constitutional issues. Some believe that this does not serve the process well.

For example, constitutional law expert Erwin Chemerinsky, in his book *The Case against the Supreme Court*, believes that nominees should be asked and expected to answer their opinions about challenging constitutional issues. He explains: "The confirmation process is the most important check on the unelected judiciary. Given that the nominee's views will matter significantly in how he or she decides cases, those views should be explored by the senators responsible for confirming the nominee. The Senate should insist, as a condition for confirmation, that the nominee answer detailed questions about his or her views on important constitutional questions."

Another proposal is to incorporate deadlines into the confirmation process. That would prevent something like what occurred with Merrick Garland, who is the U.S. attorney general as of this writing, though it should be acknowledged that both political parties have engaged in temporal gamesmanship at various levels of the confirmation process.

Professor Arthur S. Leonard, in a law review article, offered this proposal for improving the process: "The Judiciary Committee should resolve in the future to evaluate nominees solely upon the basis of their public record, as it reflects on their intellectual acuity, ethical probity, and political acceptability. Anything a nominee says in testimony to the Committee is by its very nature likely to be self-serving and tainted by heavy coaching from White House 'handlers.'"

Freedom of Speech

HISTORY OF FREE EXPRESSION AT THE COURT

When did the U.S. Supreme Court first start delving into the meaning of freedom of speech?

The U.S. Supreme Court first examined the First Amendment right to freedom of speech in any detail just after the time of World War I. For much of the 19th century, the U.S. Supreme Court was more focused on property rights than individual rights such as freedom of expression. Furthermore, the unique pressures generated by World War I and the perceived need to clamp down on dissenters in the United States led to the Court addressing the freedom of speech of those who disagreed with U.S. foreign policy.

Legal historian Paul Murphy explains much of this in his book *World War I and the Origins of Civil Liberties*. He writes that "[w]hat happened during World War I in the civil liberties area was a new and disturbingly different development in American history." The federal government actively began engaging in a form of social control. It was during this time period that the U.S. Congress passed the Espionage Act of 1917 and the Sedition Act of 1918. These laws criminalized the efforts of political dissenters to undermine the draft and war effort and the vociferous criticism of the government.

In hindsight, these efforts look extreme and like gross overreactions to speech, but one enduring lesson from history is that First Amendment speech rights are always fragile, particularly in times of war and other emergencies.

In what famous decision did Justice Oliver Wendell Holmes Jr. create the "clear and present danger" test?

Justice Holmes created the "clear and present danger" test in *Schenck v. United States* (1919), a case in which two members of

With World War I raging in Europe and U.S. involvement growing more likely, Congress created the Espionage Act of 1917 in response to President Woodrow Wilson's request for such legislation during his 1915 State of the Union address.

the Socialist Party—Charles Schenck and Elizabeth Baer—were convicted of violating the Espionage Act of 1917. Schenck and Baer, members of the party's executive committee, conspired to distribute 15,000 leaflets urging people to resist the draft and avoid service in World War I.

In his unanimous opinion for the Court, Justice Holmes affirmed the defendants' convictions. He asked whether the publication would create a "clear and present danger" to the U.S. war effort, the draft, and military recruiting. He noted that many things that may be said in peacetime cannot be said in times of war, concluding that the leaflets constituted a conspiracy to harm the country's war effort.

What was Justice Holmes's famous phrase from this case that involves fire in a theater?

Justice Holmes used the following analogy as an example of the idea that the First Amendment surely doesn't protect all forms of speech. He wrote: "The most stringent protection of free speech would not protect a man in falsely shouting fire in a theatre and causing a panic."

In what case were five Russians convicted of violating the Sedition Act of 1918?

The White Court ruled 7–2 in *Abrams v. United States* (1919) that several Russian immigrants could be criticized for violating the Sedition Act of 1918 for distributing pamphlets criticizing the American government and President Woodrow Wilson's decision to send troops into Russia. The anarchists distributed the two pamphlets, entitled "Revolutionists Unite for Action" and "The Hypocrisy of the United States and Her Allies," denounced the president, and urged, "Workers of the World! Awake! Rise! Put down your enemy and mine!" They were convicted and sentenced to 20 years in prison by a federal district court judge.

The Court majority, in an opinion by Justice John Hessin Clarke, affirmed the anarchists' convictions. He reasoned that "the manifest purpose" of the publications was "to create an attempt to defeat the war plans of the government of the United States." Justice Clarke wrote that "the plain purpose of their propaganda was to excite, at the supreme crisis of the war, disaffection, sedition, riots and, as they hoped, revolution."

Which two justices dissented in this sedition case?

Justice Holmes and Justice Louis Brandeis dissented in an opinion written by Justice Holmes. He wrote that "surreptitious publishing of a silly leaflet" did not create a "clear and present danger" to the American government. Instead, he found that the group of defendants "has as much right to publish [the leaflets] as the Government has to publish the Constitution of the United States now vainly invoked by them."

In his opinion, Justice Holmes made his impassioned defense of free speech as something important to the marketplace of ideas: "The best test of truth is the power of the thought to get itself accepted in the competition of the market, and that truth is the only ground upon which their wishes safely can be carried out. That is at any rate the theory of our Constitution."

Who were the five Russians convicted in the *Abrams* case, and what happened to them?

The five Russian defendants were Jacob Abrams, Hyman Lachowsky, Samuel Lipman, Jacob Schwartz, and Mollie Steimer.

Schwartz died the night before the defendants' trial, probably from beatings administered by prison guards. The other four defendants served time in federal prison until President Warren G. Harding commuted their sentences in October 1921. As part of the commutation agreement, the four defendants were shipped to Russia. Lipman, a professor in Moscow, was murdered in the Great Purges of Russian dictator Joseph Stalin in the 1930s. Lachowsky likely died in Minsk in 1941 when German leader Adolf Hitler and the Nazis conquered the city. Steimer and Abrams were exiled from Russia and eventually wound up in Mexico City. Abrams died in 1953 and Steimer in 1980.

What caused Justice Holmes to change his mind from *Schenck* to *Abrams*?

Justice Holmes received much criticism for his opinion in *Schenck* by noted experts and friends. Notably, for example, Har-

Among those criticizing Oliver Wendell Holmes's opinion in *Schenck vs. United States* was Zechariah Chafee, author of the 1919 article "Freedom of Speech in War Times."

vard law professor Zechariah Chafee, Harvard history instructor Harold Laski, and University of Chicago law professor Ernst Freund all criticized Justice Holmes's decision in *Schenck* as not protective enough of free speech. To these experts, dissent was vital to a functioning democracy. As Laski once wrote, "The price of liberty is exactly divergence of opinion on fundamental questions."

The *Schenck* opinion was decided in the spring of 1919. Justice Holmes spent much of the summer of 1919 reading about the importance of free expression. This work resulted in a fundamental change in how he approached the freedom of expression and his "clear and present danger" test. Most importantly, Justice Holmes injected the idea of imminence into the "clear and present danger" test: that the speech must lead to immediate danger or "imminent disorder" to be considered unprotected speech.

According to the Court, which presidential candidate violated the Espionage Act of 1917?

The U.S. Supreme Court—around the time it decided the *Schenck* decision—also convicted Eugene Debs, the socialist leader who ran for president of the United States multiple times, for violating the Espionage Act when he gave critical speeches of the war effort in Canton, Ohio, and St. Louis, Missouri. For example, Debs said: "We brand the declaration of war by our governments as a crime against the people of the United States and against the nations of the world. In all modern history there has been no war more unjustifiable than the war in which we are about to engage."

Writing for the Court, Justice Holmes upheld a jury instruction that told the jurors they could not find Debs guilty based on his speech "unless the words used had as their natural tendency and reasonably probable effect to obstruct the recruiting service, and unless the defendant had the specific intent to do so in his mind." This opinion conflicts with modern-day First Amendment jurisprudence, as many politicians and others condemn U.S. military action abroad in harsher language than that employed by Eugene Debs.

In what decision did the U.S. Supreme Court rule that the First Amendment Free Speech Clause be extended to the states?

The U.S. Supreme Court first ruled that the First Amendment Free Speech Clause should also limit state governments in addition to the federal government in *Gitlow v. New York* (1925). The First Amendment, by its text, only applies to limiting the federal government, as it says: "Congress shall make no law ... abridging the freedom of speech. The Founding Fathers did not extend the Bill of Rights, including the First Amendment, to limit state governments."

However, Congress later amended the Constitution by passing the 14th Amendment, in which the Due Process Clause provides that no state shall infringe on "life, liberty, or property without due process of law."

In *Gitlow*, the state of New York charged Benjamin Gitlow with violating a state criminal anarchy law that prohibited advocating the overthrow of the American government. Gitlow was a member of the left-wing section of the Socialist Party and the business manager of the party's newspaper, *The Revolutionary Age*. Gitlow believed that mass industrial revolts were necessary to overthrow the capitalistic government of the United States.

The Court affirmed Gitlow's conviction and determined that the New York anarchy law did not violate the First Amendment. The Court determined that such advocacy was not protected by the First Amendment, that the amendment "does not protect disturbances to the public peace or the attempt to subvert the government." The Court reasoned that writings such as Gitlow's *The Revolutionary Age* and "Left Wing Manifesto" are, by their very nature, a "danger to the public peace and to the security of the State." Justice Edward Terry Sanford, in his majority opinion, added: "The State cannot reasonably be required to measure the danger from every such utterance in the nice balance of a jeweler's scale. A single revolutionary spark may kindle a fire that, smoldering for a time, may burst into a sweeping and destructive conflagration."

Which two justices dissented in the *Gitlow* decision?

Justice Holmes and Justice Brandeis, sometimes called the "Fathers of the First Amendment," dissented. Justice Holmes wrote that the Court should have applied the "clear and present danger" test that he had advocated in his *Schenck v. United States* (1919) and *Abrams v. United States* (1919) opinions. Justice Holmes wrote that Gitlow's writings did not induce an immediate uprising or cause a revolution: "There was no present danger of an attempt to overthrow the government by force on the part of the admittedly small minority who shared the defendant's views."

Justice Holmes further explained: "It is said that this manifesto was more than a theory, it was an incitement. Every idea is an incitement.... The only difference between the expression of an opinion and an incitement in the narrower sense is the speaker's enthusiasm for the result. Eloquence may set fire to reason. But whatever may be thought of the redundant discourse before us, it had no chance of starting a present conflagration."

In what decision did the U.S. Supreme Court affirm a conviction under California's criminal syndicalism law?

The U.S. Supreme Court unanimously rejected a First Amendment challenge to California's criminal syndicalism law in *Whitney v. California* (1927). Criminal syndicalism laws were

passed to keep dissident political groups from disrupting industry and inciting political rebellion. The laws targeted communists, socialists, and other similar dissident groups.

Charlotte Anita Whitney was convicted of violating the law as a result of a speech she delivered in Oakland, California, on behalf of the Communist Labor Party of California, which supported the International Workers of the World. The California law prohibited people from organizing, assisting, and assembling together "to advocate, teach, aid and abet criminal syndicalism." Whitney was arrested during the height of the Red Scare when government officials were concerned about a communist uprising similar to the Bolshevik Revolution in Russia, led by Vladimir Lenin.

The Court affirmed Whitney's conviction and upheld the statute, finding that it did not violate First Amendment freedoms. Writing for the majority, Justice Sanford concluded that the law is not "an unreasonable or arbitrary exercise of the police power of the State, unwarrantably infringing any right of free speech, assembly or association, or that those persons are protected from punishment by the due-process clause who abuse such rights by joining and furthering an organization thus menacing the peace and welfare of the State."

Charlotte Anita Whitney, convicted of criminal syndicalism for delivering a speech during the Red Scare, was later pardoned by the governor of California.

DID YOU KNOW?

After the verdict, what happened to Charlotte Anita Whitney?

California governor Clement Calhoun Young pardoned Whitney, who was the niece of former U.S. Supreme Court justice Stephen Johnson Field, in June 1927. Named national party chairman of the Communist Party in 1936, she unsuccessfully ran for a U.S. Senate seat in 1950. She died in San Francisco in 1955.

However, the decision is better known for the concurring opinion of Justice Brandeis. Justice Brandeis's concurrence, which was joined by Justice Holmes, reads more like a dissent than a concurrence. Justice Brandeis's opinion became a blueprint for the justification for freedom of speech. He wrote that even advocacy of illegal conduct could not justify restricting speech unless the speech incites immediate lawless action, a test that the U.S. Supreme Court would eventually adopt in the 1969 decision *Brandenburg v. Ohio*. However, Justice Brandeis concurred with the majority because "there was other testimony which tended to establish the existence of a conspiracy, on the part of the workers of the International Workers of the World, to commit present serious crimes, and likewise to show that such a conspiracy would be furthered by the activity of the society of which Miss Whitney was a member."

Which foundational First Amendment principle did Justice Brandeis's opinion articulate?

One of the fundamental principles of First Amendment jurisprudence is that the government should respond to harmful speech by countering it with positive speech. In other words, the government should not silence negative speech but rather express a better alternative and show why the negative speech is wrong. This is called the counterspeech doctrine.

Justice Brandeis provided the justification for the counterspeech doctrine in memorable language: "If there be time to expose through discussion the falsehood and fallacies, to avert the evil by the processes of education, the remedy to be applied is more speech, not enforced silence."

In what decision did the U.S. Supreme Court invalidate the criminal conviction of an African American communist on First Amendment grounds?

The U.S. Supreme Court ruled 5–4 in *Herndon v. Lowry* (1937) that African American communist activist Angelo Herndon's conviction could not stand based on First Amendment concerns. Georgia law-enforcement officials had charged Herndon under a state law that prohibited attempting to incite an insurrection. The officials charged Herndon after learning that he had traveled from Kentucky and held three meetings in which he tried to recruit individuals to the Communist Party. The U.S. Supreme Court reversed Herndon's conviction in part due to "no evidence … by speech or written word, at meetings or elsewhere, any doctrine or action implying such forcible subversion." The Court concluded that Herndon's meetings did not fit the definition of attempting to incite an insurrection.

In his majority opinion, Justice Owen Roberts explained that Herndon's "membership in the Communist Party and his solicitation of a few members wholly fails to establish an attempt to incite others to insurrection." Justice Roberts concluded that the statute itself was too vague to withstand constitutional scrutiny, writing that it "amounts merely to a dragnet which may enmesh anyone who agitates for a change of government."

UNPROTECTED CATEGORIES OF SPEECH: FIGHTING WORDS

In what decision did the Court create the "fighting words" exception to the First Amendment?

The U.S. Supreme Court determined in *Chaplinsky v. New Hampshire* (1942) that so-called "fighting words" are not protected by the First Amendment. The case involved a former priest in Rochester, New Hampshire, named Walter Chaplinsky who denounced official religion as a "racket" and called a public marshal a "damned fascist" and a "racketeer." Chaplinsky, a Jehovah's Witness, believed that these other religions were false and was not shy about proclaiming this.

The marshal arrested Chaplinsky and charged him with violating a New Hampshire law that prohibited calling people annoying or offensive or derisive names in public. The Court rejected Chaplinsky's First Amendment defense, reasoning that its protections did not apply to "fighting words."

Justice Frank Murphy explained:

> There are certain well-defined and narrowly limited classes of speech, the prevention of which has never been thought to raise any Constitutional problem. These include the lewd and obscene, the profane, the libelous, and the insulting or fighting words—those which by their very utterance inflict injury or tend to incite an immediate breach of the peace. It has been well observed that such utterances are no essential part of any exposition of ideas, and are of such slight social value as a step to truth that any benefit that may be derived from them is clearly outweighed by the social interest in order and morality.

The U.S. Supreme Court in later years limited—but never overruled—the *Chaplinsky* decision. The "fighting words" doctrine remains a part of First Amendment jurisprudence.

In what decision did the Court limit *Chaplinsky* and the "fighting words" doctrine?

Nearly three decades later, the U.S. Supreme Court limited the "fighting words" doctrine in *Cohen v. California* (1971). The case involved a man named Paul Robert Cohen who wore a jacket bearing the words "Fuck the Draft" on the back. Cohen wore the jacket into a Los Angeles courthouse.

A police officer charged Cohen with violating a state breach of the peace law. The state justified the law in part on the "fighting words" doctrine, reasoning that Cohen's jacket was as much of an offensive insult as Chaplinsky's comments to the marshal. But the U.S. Supreme Court reversed its opinion, finding that Mr. Cohen did not target a specific recipient when he wore the jacket. He simply wore it and expressed the message. Justice John Marshall Harlan II famously wrote in his majority opinion that "one man's vulgarity is another's lyric."

The *Cohen* decision thus limited *Chaplinsky* to direct, face-to-face personal insults.

What U.S. Supreme Court decision said that the government must be careful in targeting only certain types of fighting words?

The U.S. Supreme Court ruled in *R.A.V. v. City of St. Paul* (1992) that a St. Paul, Minnesota, ordinance was unconstitutional because it targeted only a certain type of fighting words: displays that aroused anger or resentment on the basis of race, color, creed, or gender. The ordinance targeted a type of hate speech. The city charged and convicted juvenile Robert Alan Viktoria (R.A.V.) because he burned a cross in the yard of an African American neighbor.

Justice Antonin Scalia wrote the majority opinion in *R.A.V. v. City of Saint Paul* on the basis that the city's Bias-Motivated Crime Ordinance violated the First Amendment.

The Court reversed the conviction because it found that the ordinance in question was discriminating on the basis of viewpoint. In other words, it targeted, for example, forms of racist hate speech but not hate speech based on political affiliation, sexual orientation, or other categories. "St. Paul has no such authority to license one side of a debate to fight freestyle, while requiring the other to follow Marquis of Queensbury Rules," Justice Antonin Scalia wrote.

INCITEMENT TO IMMINENT LAWLESS ACTION

What is incitement to imminent lawless action?

The Court explained this First Amendment exception in *Brandenburg v. Ohio* (1969), a case involving a Ku Klux Klan leader named Clarence Brandenburg who spoke at a Klan rally in front of about a dozen other Klan members and a television crew in Hamilton County, Ohio.

Brandenburg stated, "We're not a revengent [*sic*] organization, but if our President, our Congress, our Supreme Court, continues to suppress the white Caucasian race, it's possible that there might have to be some revengence." Officials charged Brandenburg with violating an Ohio state criminal syndicalism law. The U.S. Supreme Court reversed Brandenburg's conviction, finding that the Ohio law violated the First Amendment. The Court reasoned that "the constitutional guarantees of free speech and free press do not permit a State to forbid or proscribe advocacy of the use of force or of law violation except where such advocacy is directed to inciting or producing imminent lawless action and is likely to incite or produce such action."

Why is timing so important in incitement cases?

Timing is important because incitement to imminent lawless action requires that the resulting unlawful action take place immediately after the inciting expression. The Court applied this principle in *Hess v. Indiana* (1973). Antiwar demonstrator Gregory Hess was protesting with many others on the campus of Indiana University. A police officer told Hess to move off the street onto the sidewalk. Hess responded: "We'll take the fucking street later."

Hess was charged with disorderly conduct. However, the U.S. Supreme Court reversed his conviction because the Court reasoned that his statement about taking the street later at most amounted to advocacy of illegal conduct at some indefinite point of time in the future. In other words, imminence was not sufficient to support his conviction.

TRUE THREATS

When did the Court create an exception for true threats?

The U.S. Supreme Court ruled in *Watts v. United States* (1969) that true threats are not protected by the First Amendment.

However, the Court reversed the conviction of Robert Watts because it found that his statements were more rhetorical hyperbole than unprotected, true threats. Watts was charged under a federal law prohibiting threats against the president after he stated at an antiwar rally in Washington, D.C., in conversation with people nearby: "I am not going. If they ever make me carry a rifle the first man I want to get in my sights is L. B. J. They are not going to make me kill my black brothers." An undercover federal agent heard the comments, leading to the charges against Watts. The Court agreed with Watts that his statement was a "kind of very crude offensive method of stating political opposition to the President." The Court also said that what was a true threat needed to be distinguished from protected speech.

How did the Court address true threats in a cross-burning case out of Virginia?

The U.S. Supreme Court ruled in *Virginia v. Black* (2003) that true threats could come in the form of burning a cross if the intent of the person doing the burning was to intimidate others. The Court addressed a Virginia law that provided: "It shall be unlawful for any person or persons, with the intent of intimidating any person or group of persons, to burn, or cause to be burned, a cross on the property of another, a highway or other public place."

The case involved two separate prosecutions that were consolidated or combined. The first involved a Ku Klux Klan leader named Barry Elton Black who burned a cross in a field with the permission of the property owner. The other case involved two individuals, Richard Elliott and Jonathan O'Mara, who burned a cross outside the home of James Jubilee, the lone African American person in the neighborhood.

The Court ended up reversing Barry Elton Black's conviction but affirming the convictions of Elliott and O'Mara. The difference was that Black burned the cross in a field with the permission of

the property owner, while Elliott and O'Mara were targeting and terrorizing an African American neighbor and his family.

Writing for the majority, Justice Sandra Day O'Connor opined:

> "True threats" encompass those statements where the speaker means to communicate a serious expression of an intent to commit an act of unlawful violence to a particular individual or group of individuals. The speaker need not actually intend to carry out the threat. Rather, a prohibition on true threats protect[s] individuals from the fear of violence and "from the disruption that fear engenders," in addition to protecting people "from the possibility that the threatened violence will occur." Intimidation in the constitutionally proscribable sense of the word is a type of true threat, where a speaker directs a threat to a person or group of persons with the intent of placing the victim in fear of bodily harm or death.

The Court did invalidate a part of the Virginia law that said that cross burning is prima facie evidence of the intent to intimidate. In other words, the law had a presumption that all cross

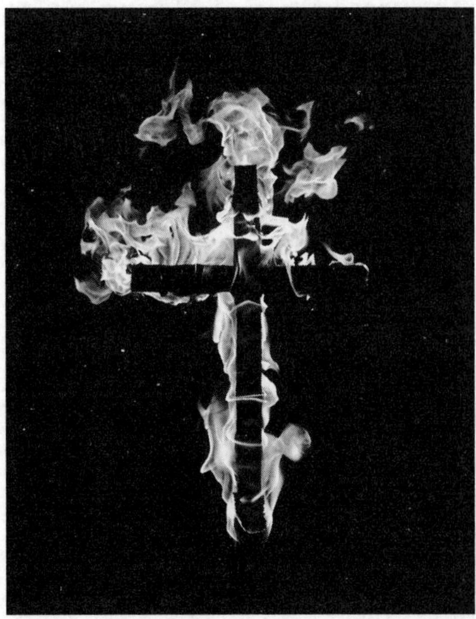

In *Virginia v. Black* the Court considered two convictions for cross burning, distinguishing between the constitutionality of the prosecutions based on the where and why of each instance.

burners had this nefarious intent to intimidate others and commit a true threat. Justice O'Connor disagreed, reasoning that all cross burnings are not the same.

OBSCENITY CASES

What case established the test still used in obscenity cases today?

The U.S. Supreme Court established the leading standard for obscenity cases in its *Miller v. California* (1973) decision. Chief Justice Warren E. Burger's majority opinion established a three-prong test to guide jurors in obscenity cases. The test provides this: "(a) the average person, applying contemporary community standards, would find that the work, taken as a whole, appeals to the prurient interest; (b) whether the work depicts or describes, in a patently offensive way, sexual conduct specifically defined by the applicable state law; and (c) whether the work, taken as a whole, lacks serious literary, artistic, political, or scientific value."

The case applied the test to the prosecution of Marvin Miller, the owner of a mail-order business in California, that trafficked in pornography. Miller mailed catalogs that advertised several adult-oriented books, including *Intercourse*, *Man–Woman*, *Sex Orgies Illustrated*, and *An Illustrated History of Pornography*. He also advertised a film entitled *Marital Intercourse.* He mailed the brochures to families in Newport Beach, California, who did not request them. This led to his prosecution.

The Court narrowly affirmed his conviction by a 5–4 vote. The Court rejected Miller's argument that a national standard for obscenity needed to be established. Chief Justice Burger responded to that argument, writing: "It is neither realistic nor constitutionally sound to read the First Amendment as requiring that the people of Maine or Mississippi accept public depiction of conduct found tolerable in Las Vegas, or New York City."

DID YOU KNOW?

What U.S. Supreme Court justice famously changed his mind on the obscenity question?

Justice William J. Brennan Jr. changed his mind regarding obscenity in *Miller v. California* and its companion case, *Paris Adult Theatre I v. Slaton* (1973). Justice Brennan had authored the Court's majority or main opinion in several obscenity cases, including *Roth v. United States* (1957). However, in *Slaton,* Justice Brennan changed course, writing: "I am convinced that the approach initiated 16 years ago in *Roth v. United States* (1957) and culminating in the Court's decision today, cannot bring stability to this area of the law without jeopardizing fundamental First Amendment values, and I have concluded that the time has come to make a significant departure from that approach."

What movie starring Jack Nicholson became the subject of an obscenity prosecution?

The U.S. Supreme Court determined in *Jenkins v. Georgia* (1974) that the film *Carnal Knowledge* was not obscene. The film starred not only Jack Nicholson but also such mainstream movie stars as Art Garfunkel, Ann-Margaret, Rita Moreno, and Carol Kane. It was considered a top 10 movie of the year and even received an Oscar nomination. However, the film contained scenes of nudity, and, thus, movie theater manager Billy Jenkins was prosecuted in Albany, Georgia, for obscenity for showing the film in Georgia.

Justice William H. Rehnquist wrote the Court's main opinion, finding that the film was not obscene: "We hold that the film could not, as a matter of constitutional law, be found to depict sexual conduct in a patently offensive way, and that it is therefore not outside the protection of the First and Fourteenth Amendments."

He added that "nudity alone is not enough to make material legally obscene under the Miller standards."

What famous comedian's case formed the basis for an important U.S. Supreme Court case on indecency?

George Carlin's "Filthy Words" monologue, in which he elaborates on the seven dirty words that are not to be said on television, led to the important U.S. Supreme Court decision on indecency, *F.C.C. v. Pacifica Foundation* (1978). Indecency is a much lesser category of sexual expression than obscenity. Obscenity is unprotected expression, while indecency can sometimes be limited for children but often cannot be banned for adults.

The case involved a New York–based radio station playing Carlin's "Filthy Words" monologue during daytime hours. A father heard the afternoon broadcast with his young son in their car. The father filed a complaint with the Federal Communications Com-

The daytime broadcast of George Carlin's "Filthy Words" monologue prompted the Supreme Court to affirm the right of the FCC to regulate indecent content on the airwaves.

mission (FCC), and the FCC ultimately fined Pacifica Foundation, saying that the company had violated FCC standards against the broadcast of indecent communications. The Court ruled 5–4 that in order to protect children, the FCC can prohibit indecent material in the broadcast medium.

How has the Roberts Court resisted the creation of new unprotected categories of speech?

In recent years, the U.S. Supreme Court, under Chief Justice John G. Roberts Jr., has rejected the creation of new unprotected categories of speech. Specifically, the Court ruled that violent video games were not, per se, unprotected in *Entertainment Merchants Association v. Brown* (2011); that images of animal cruelty were not, per se, unprotected in *United States v. Stevens* (2010); that false speech was not, per se, unprotected in *United States v. Alvarez* (2012); and that protests at military funerals were not, per se, unprotected in *Snyder v. Phelps* (2011).

In each of these four cases, the government argued that violent video games, images of animal cruelty, false speech, and protests at military funerals lacked social value and caused harm. But Chief Justice Roberts explained in the *Stevens* case that the Court lacks "freewheeling authority" to create new unprotected categories of speech that are not rooted in history or tradition.

What was *Snyder v. Phelps* about?

The case of *Snyder v. Phelps* involved the father of a slain marine, Albert Snyder, suing the Westboro Baptist Church and its founder, Fred Phelps, for causing him emotional distress for protesting at his son's funeral. The Westboro Baptist Church made it a habit of traveling all over the country and protesting at military funerals. The Church believed that God was punishing the United

States of America by killing its soldiers because the United States was tolerating and promoting homosexuality. Members of the Church, largely Phelps's family, would peacefully protest near funerals and hold up awful signs with hateful messages like "God Hates Fags."

Snyder sued the defendants in federal court and prevailed with a more than $10 million jury verdict. However, the Fourth Circuit reversed its decision and, on further appeal, so did the U.S. Supreme Court. In his majority opinion, Chief Justice John G. Roberts Jr. wrote in majestic language: "Speech is powerful. It can stir people to action, move them to tears of both joy and sorrow, and—as it did here—inflict great pain. On the facts before us, we cannot react to that pain by punishing the speaker. As a Nation we have chosen a different course—to protect even hurtful speech on public issues to ensure that we do not stifle public debate. That choice requires that we shield Westboro from tort liability for its picketing in this case."

STUDENT EXPRESSION

What did the U.S. Supreme Court hold with regard to forced flag salutes for kids in public schools?

The Court initially upheld, by an 8–1 vote, a Pennsylvania law that required public school students to stand, salute the flag, and recite the Pledge of Allegiance in *Minersville School District v. Gobitis* (1940). The Court reasoned that the flag salute was a constitutional patriotic exercise rather than an unconstitutional infringement on the freedom of religion rights of the Jehovah's Witnesses students who had challenged the law. Justice Felix Frankfurter wrote the Court's majority opinion, reasoning that "national unity is the basis of national security" and that "the ultimate foundation of a free society is the binding tie of cohesive sentiment."

However, the Court reversed its decision only three years later in *West Virginia Board of Education v. Barnette* (1943). This time, the Court ruled 6–3 that a West Virginia school's forced flag-salute law for schoolkids was unconstitutional. The Court agreed with the Jehovah's Witnesses, reasoning that the state could not coerce patriotism. In his majority opinion, Justice Robert H. Jackson wrote: "If there is any fixed star in our constitutional constellation, it is that no official, high or petty, can prescribe what shall be orthodox in politics, nationalism, religion, or other matters of opinion or force citizens to confess by word or act their faith therein."

Why did the Court overrule itself so soon, only three years later?

The *Gobitis* decision upholding the Pennsylvania law unfortunately caused a wave of violence against Jehovah's Witnesses in various parts of the country. In his book *To the Flag: The History of the Pledge of Allegiance*, author Richard J. Ellis writes: "The persistent patter of expulsions, arbitrary arrests, and violent intimidation led to a rethinking among the Supreme Court justices of the wisdom of the *Gobitis* decision." Ellis also relates that thousands of Jehovah's Witnesses had been expelled from school.

What was ironic about the date of the Court's decision in the *Barnette* case?

The U.S. Supreme Court issued its decision in *Barnette* on June 14, 1943. June 14 is Flag Day.

In what decision did the Court rule that students don't lose their rights at the schoolhouse gate?

The U.S. Supreme Court ruled in *Tinker v. Des Moines Independent Community School District* (1969) that students do possess

First Amendment rights at public school. The *Barnette* flag-salute decision had established that students had some level of First Amendment protection, but the Court did not provide any type of real test.

But in *Tinker*, the Court explained that public school officials cannot censor student expression unless they can reasonably forecast that the student expression will cause a substantial disruption or material interference with school activities. The case involves several students in Des Moines, Iowa, who wore black peace armbands to their respective schools to protest U.S. involvement in Vietnam, to support Robert Kennedy's Christmas truce, and to mourn those who had perished in the conflict.

However, school officials learned of the impending protest and passed a district-wide rule that barred the wearing of armbands. School officials selectively targeted a particular symbol associated with a particular viewpoint, as they allowed students to wear other forms of symbolic speech such as political campaign buttons or Iron Crosses. Mary Beth Tinker wore the armband to her middle school, while John Tinker (Mary Beth's brother) and Christopher Eckhardt wore the armbands to their high schools. All three were suspended by school officials.

Des Moines's Theodore Roosevelt Senior High School suspended student Christopher Eckhardt for wearing an armband in a protest. *Tinker v. Des Moines Independent Community School District* (1969) established that students do possess First Amendment rights at public schools.

With help from the American Civil Liberties Union, they sued in federal court, contending that their First Amendment free-speech rights were violated. However, a federal district judge and a federal appeals court ruled against them (though the federal appeals court was split 4–4).

But the U.S. Supreme Court reversed its decision by a 7–2 vote. Writing for the majority, Justice Abe Fortas reasoned that public schools are not "enclaves of totalitarianism" and that public school officials should not punish speech simply because they do not like it or wish students to hold another point of view.

How did the U.S. Supreme Court create exceptions to student expression and *Tinker* in later rulings?

The U.S. Supreme Court created exceptions or carve-outs to the *Tinker* ruling in three subsequent decisions: *Bethel School District v. Fraser* (1986), *Hazelwood School District v. Kuhlmeier* (1988), and *Morse v. Frederick* (2007). The Court ruled in *Fraser* that public school officials can prohibit student speech that is vulgar and lewd. The student in question, Matthew Fraser, had delivered a speech before a 600-member school assembly nominating a fellow student for vice president. Fraser used sexual innuendo in his speech that caused laughter but no real disruption. The lower courts, applying *Tinker*, found that Fraser's speech was protected because no proof existed that it caused a substantial disruption of school activities. But the U.S. Supreme Court—in Chief Justice Burger's last opinion on the bench—created a new rule saying that public school officials can prohibit such vulgar and lewd speech because they have the ability to "teach students the boundaries of socially appropriate behavior."

Then, two years later in *Hazelwood School District v. Kuhlmeier* (1988), the Court created a new rule for so-called school-sponsored student speech, or student speech that observers would think the school is promoting or endorsing. The case involved two articles in the school newspaper that the school principal ordered to be excised or removed. The articles addressed the sensitive topics of teen pregnancy and the impact of divorce upon teens. The principal reasoned that the pregnant students at school might be further ostracized and that the article on teen pregnancy included comments on some parents who allegedly were not given a chance to respond. The Eighth Circuit below had ruled that these articles were not disruptive under *Tinker* and should be protected. However, the U.S. Supreme Court ruled 5–3 that the principal had legitimate educational reasons to order the articles to be removed and that the principal did not need to show a reasonable forecast of a substantial disruption when it came to such school-sponsored student speech, like the student newspaper at issue in *Hazelwood*.

Finally, the Court ruled in *Morse v. Frederick* (2007) that public schools could discipline students for student speech that they reasonably regarded as advocating the illegal use of drugs. The student in question, Joseph Frederick, had displayed a banner right near the school on a public street with the message "Bong Hits 4 Jesus!" The principal believed that such a message was inappropriate and suspended him. The Court sanctioned the principal's action under its new rationale.

How did the U.S. Supreme Court rule with regard to a public school student's profane rant on Snapchat off campus?

The U.S. Supreme Court ruled in *Mahanoy School District v. B.L.* (2021) that public school officials exceeded their constitutional authority when they disciplined a public school student for a profane Snapchat post that she made off the school campus near a convenience store on the weekend. Brandi Levy, the student, was upset that she did not make the school's varsity cheerleading squad and was also upset that she did not get her preferred position on a softball team not affiliated with her school. She posted a series of F-bombs, venting her frustration.

Mahanoy School District v. B.L. (2021) extended the free speech protection for students, ruling that schools cannot regulate off-campus student speech.

The school learned of the profane Snapchat post and suspended Levy from the cheerleading squad for a year. She and her parents sued, believing that the school district had violated her First Amendment free-speech rights and that any discipline should have come from the parents, not school officials.

The Court ruled that Levy's off-campus rant was more a matter of parental than school discipline and that school officials failed to show how such an off-campus rant reasonably could have led to any substantial disruption at school.

PUBLIC EMPLOYEES

When did the Court first explicitly rule that public employees retain First Amendment rights?

The U.S. Supreme Court formally explained in *Pickering v. Board of Education* (1968) that public employees do not lose all of their First Amendment free-speech rights when they accept public employment. For much of the 20th century and before, the basic

rule was that a public employee willingly relinquished their free-speech rights when they accepted public employment. In fact, the Court relied on reasoning supplied by Justice Holmes when he was a justice on the Supreme Judicial Court of Massachusetts. Justice Holmes famously wrote in a Massachusetts case, *McAuliffe v. City of New Bedford* (1892): "Petitioner may have a constitutional right to talk politics but he does not have a constitutional right to be a police officer."

However, the Court changed course in the case of Marvin Pickering, a high school teacher from Illinois who believed that his school board was spending too much money on athletics instead of academics, so Pickering wrote a highly critical letter to the editor of his local newspaper. In response, school officials fired him. Pickering took his case all the way to the U.S. Supreme Court, and the Court ruled in his favor 8–1.

Writing for the majority, Justice Thurgood Marshall reasoned that public employees are often in the best position to inform the public about important issues. He said that in these cases, the courts must balance the public employee's right to free speech on matters of public concern (or importance) against the employer's efficiency interests in a disruptive-free workplace. Justice Marshall emphasized that Pickering did not speak negatively about people he worked with on a day-to-day basis such as his principal or fellow teachers.

How did the U.S. Supreme Court in the Roberts era change the Pickering test?

The Court created a new categorical rule for public employee First Amendment cases in *Garcetti v. Ceballos* (2006). The Court ruled that when public employees make statements related to their official job duties, they have no First Amendment protection. The case involved a deputy district attorney in Los Angeles named Richard Ceballos who wrote a memorandum to his superiors say-

DID YOU KNOW?

What is the Pickering balancing test?

The Pickering balancing test was the dominant test that the U.S. Supreme Court used in public employee free-speech cases for years. It involved an initial question of whether a public employee spoke on a matter of public concern or a private grievance. If the employee's speech was only a private grievance, then no First Amendment claim could be made. However, if the public employee spoke on a matter of public concern, then one must balance the employee's right to speak out on important issues versus the employer's interests in maintaining an efficient, disruptive-free workplace.

For example, the U.S. Supreme Court applied this test in the case of *Connick v. Myers* (1983), a case involving a New Orleans assistant district attorney named Sheila Myers who was upset that she got transferred to a different division. In response, she circulated a questionnaire to fellow employees at work that asked various questions, including one about whether employees in the district attorney's office felt compelled to support candidates supported by District Attorney Harry Connick Sr. (the father of the legendary jazz musician). Connick fired Myers for circulating the questionnaire, and Myers then sued.

The U.S. Supreme Court ruled that most of Myers's questionnaire involved private matters, and thus, no First Amendment claim could be made. However, the Court found that one question about whether employees felt pressured to support a particular political candidate did touch on a matter of public importance. Thus, the Court had to balance Myers's right to speak out versus Connick's interest in maintaining an efficient workplace. The Court reasoned that Myers's questionnaire was too disruptive and ruled in favor of Connick.

ing that a criminal case should be dismissed because of perjured law-enforcement testimony on an affidavit. His superiors, including Gil Garcetti, apparently did not appreciate the memo and demoted Ceballos.

Ceballos alleged First Amendment retaliation, and the Ninth Circuit agreed with him, applying the Pickering balancing test. However, the U.S. Supreme Court reversed its decision by a narrow 5–4 ruling, finding that it was Ceballos's job to write the memo, and no First Amendment cause of action could ensue from such a form of government employee work.

The case has been widely criticized by First Amendment scholars and plaintiffs' attorneys, who refer to the phenomena of public employees as being "Garcettized."

FREEDOM OF THE PRESS

In what decision did the Court create a very high standard to sue newspapers who write about public officials for defamation?

The Court created a high standard of defamation in *New York Times Co. v. Sullivan* (1964), one of the most important First Amendment decisions in history. The Court's decision gave the press breathing room to make mistakes when reporting about important issues and public officials. The case involved a March 1960 editorial advertisement published in the *New York Times* called "Heed Their Rising Voices." The ad referred to violations of civil rights in the South. However, the ad contained several errors. For example, the ad said that police in Montgomery, Alabama, had padlocked a dining hall at Alabama State College. The ad also said that Dr. Martin Luther King Jr., the prominent civil rights leader, had been arrested seven times (he had been arrested only four times). Montgomery police commissioner L. B. Sullivan

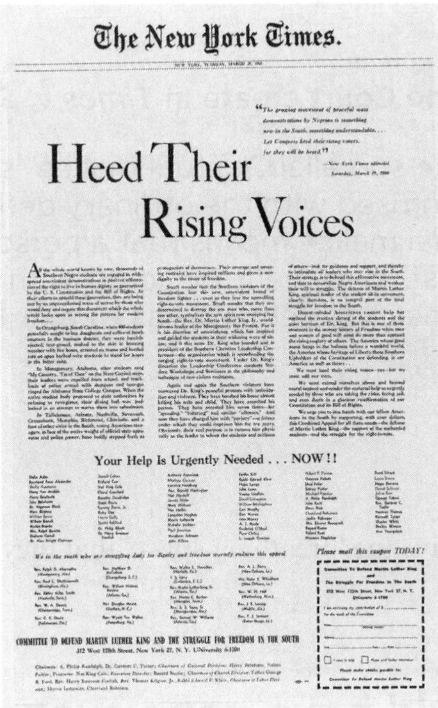

The New York Times.

"The growing movement of peaceful mass demonstrations by Negroes is something new in the South, something understandable. . . . Let Congress heed their rising voices, for they will be heard."

—New York Times editorial

Heed Their Rising Voices

Your Help Is Urgently Needed . . . NOW!!

Please mail this coupon TODAY!

COMMITTEE TO DEFEND MARTIN LUTHER KING AND THE STRUGGLE FOR FREEDOM IN THE SOUTH

312 West 125th Street, New York 27, N. Y. UNiversity 6-1700

After a full-page newspaper ad spurred a successful defamation case by a police commissioner, the Supreme Court unanimously overturned the decision in *New York Times Co. v. Sullivan* (1964), helping protect the freedom of the press.

sued for libel in Alabama state court, and an all-white jury awarded him $500,000 in damages.

Why did the Court reverse the state court libel judgment?

The Court recognized that the central purpose of the First Amendment was to ensure the ability of citizens to criticize the government and government officials. The Court considered the case "against the background of a profound national commitment to the principle that debate on public issues should be uninhibited, robust, and wide-open, and that it may well include vehement, caustic, and sometimes unpleasantly sharp attacks on government and public officials." The Court also reasoned that sometimes, the press would veer away from reporting on important matters if it could be punished for every mistake—"[t]hat erroneous statement is inevitable in free debate, and that it must be protected if the

DID YOU KNOW?

What standard did the Court create in *Times v. Sullivan?*

The Court created the so-called "actual malice" standard, which is not to be confused with the ordinary definition of malice or ill will. Actual malice means that a person knowingly published a false statement or acted with reckless disregard as to whether a statement was true or false.

freedoms of expression are to have the 'breathing space' that they 'need ... to survive.'"

Which justices would have gone even further than the majority in protecting the press in *Times v. Sullivan*?

Justice Hugo Black, Justice William O. Douglas, and Justice Arthur Goldberg would have given the press even more freedom under the First Amendment than the majority gave in Justice Brennan's decision. Justice Black wrote a concurring opinion that was joined by Justice Douglas. Justice Black expressed the view that the newspaper had "an absolute, unconditional right to publish in the *Times* advertisement their criticisms of the Montgomery agencies and officials." Justice Black explained that the First Amendment flatly prohibited such libel suits. Justice Goldberg also wrote a concurring opinion (which Justice Douglas also joined) that expressed a similar view. He explained: "In my view, the First and Fourteenth Amendments to the Constitution afford to the citizen and to the press an absolute, unconditional privilege to criticize official conduct despite the harm which may flow from excesses and abuses."

Why was the case so important to the civil rights movement?

The case was important to the civil rights movement because it allowed the press to continue to report on civil rights abuses without fear of crushing libel lawsuits for every error. Justice Black explained that at the time of the decision, 11 suits existed against the *New York Times* and five libel suits against CBS for reporting on similar civil rights abuses. Justice Black explained: "Moreover, this technique for harassing and punishing a free press—now that it has been shown to be possible—is by no means limited to cases with racial overtones; it can be used in other fields where public feelings may make local as well as out-of-state newspapers easy prey for libel verdict seekers."

In what decision did the U.S. Supreme Court first declare that prior restraint of a newspaper is forbidden under the First Amendment?

The Court first ruled that prior restraint of a news publication was an impermissible form of a prior restraint in *Near v. Minnesota* (1931). The case involved the application of a Minnesota law that allowed government officials to declare a newspaper a public nuisance for publishing scandalous material. The Court ruled that such a scheme was "the essence of censorship."

The case involved the *Saturday Press*, a publication owned by Jay Near. The paper published several articles alleging that city officials turned a blind eye to crimes committed by Jewish gangsters. Much of the material in the article was anti-Semitic, including the following statement: "There have been too many men in this city and especially those in official life, who HAVE been taking orders and suggestions from JEW GANGSTERS, therefore we HAVE Jew Gangsters, practically running Minneapolis."

Hennepin County, Minnesota, officials objected to the articles and sought to close down the newspaper pursuant to the law that allowed newspapers to be declared public nuisances if they were "malicious, scandalous and defamatory." Near contended that the statute violated his First Amendment free-press rights. The state courts disagreed, but he appealed all the way to the U.S. Supreme Court.

Chief Justice Charles Evans Hughes, writing for the majority, explained that the First Amendment severely limited the ability of government officials to limit the publication of newspapers. The proper remedy, if any, was for government officials to sue the publisher for libel; it was not to silence the publication and prevent it from being published at all. Chief Justice Hughes noted that any charge of official corruption creates a scandal and would allow the closing of many publications. "The fact that the liberty of the press may be abused by miscreant purveyors of scandal does not make any less necessary the immunity of the press from previous restraint in dealing with official misconduct," Chief Justice Hughes

Chief Justice Charles Evans Hughes wrote the majority opinion for *Near v. Minnesota* (1931), protecting newspaper publishers from being shuttered by politicians.

wrote for the 5–4 majority. "Subsequent punishment for such abuses as may exist is the appropriate remedy, consistent with conditional privilege."

Did the U.S. Supreme Court say that all prior restraints on publications were unconstitutional?

No, the Court said that the government "might prevent actual obstruction to the recruiting service or the publication of the sailing dates of transports or the number and location of troops." In other words, instances could occur where national security would allow the government to prevent the publication of military secrets.

What famous decision involving the publication of a secret Vietnam study by two major newspapers led to a test case on the national security exception to the prior restraint doctrine?

The U.S. Supreme Court tested the national security exception to the prior restraint doctrine in the famous "Pentagon Papers" case, styled *New York Times Co. v. United States* (1971). The High Court examined whether the federal government could prohibit the *New York Times* and the *Washington Post* from publishing a classified study of U.S. involvement in the Vietnam War.

The newspapers contended that allowing the government to halt the publication on matters of urgent public interest would constitute an invalid prior restraint on free expression. The government contended that further publication of the study would compromise U.S. intelligence and possibly endanger U.S. troops.

The Court ruled 6–3 for the newspapers. The majority reasoned that prior restraints are presumptively invalid and that the government failed to carry its burden that such a prior restraint was justified in this case. Three justices dissented, emphasizing that more time was needed to carefully evaluate the thousands of pages in the Pentagon Papers to determine whether the government's national security interests were compelling.

What exactly were the Pentagon Papers?

The Pentagon Papers referred to a 7,000-page study commissioned by Secretary of Defense Robert S. McNamara. He ordered a study that traced the history of U.S. involvement in the Vietnam conflict. Only 15 copies of this classified study existed.

How did the newspapers acquire a copy of the Pentagon Papers?

Daniel Ellsberg, one of the authors of the study, made a copy of the study for Neil Sheehan, a reporter with the *New York Times*. Ellsberg, a former Marine and consultant to the Department of Defense and the State Department, believed that the study needed to be released in order to expose government dishonesty. Ellsberg had access to the study because he worked at the Rand Corporation, a research institution specializing in national security issues that worked with the federal government. He also gave copies of parts of the story to other newspapers, including the *Washington Post*.

What happened to Daniel Ellsberg?

Ellsberg was first indicted on theft of government property charges on June 29, 1971 (the day before the U.S. Supreme Court

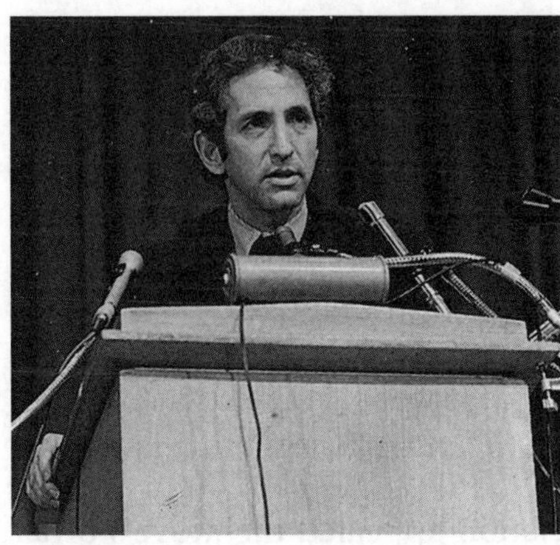

Daniel Ellsberg, the whistle-blower responsible for leaking the Pentagon Papers to the press, was prosecuted under the Espionage Act. The case was dismissed due to the government's illegal surveillance campaign against Ellsberg.

decision in the *New York Times Co. v. United States* decision). He faced a second indictment in Los Angeles in December 1971 for 13 counts, ranging from conspiracy to espionage to theft of government property. Ellsberg and codefendant Anthony Russo faced a trial beginning in January 1973. The trial lasted 89 days. U.S. district court judge William Matthew Byrne Jr. dismissed the charges after a series of disclosures, including the revelation that White House operatives had engineered a burglary of Ellsberg's psychiatrist in order to obtain his file. The FBI had intercepted Ellsberg's phone conversations, and, apparently, President Richard Nixon spoke to Judge Byrne about him becoming the new FBI director. The judge determined that "the bizarre events have incurably infected the prosecution of this case … the only remedy available that would assure due process and a fair administration of justice is that this trial be terminated and the defendants' motion for dismissal be granted and the jury discharged." In 2002, Ellsberg published a book about the Pentagon Papers entitled *Secrets: A Memoir of Vietnam and the Pentagon Papers.*

How did the U.S. Supreme Court rule with respect to gag orders on the press?

The U.S. Supreme Court ruled in *Nebraska Press Association v. Stuart* (1976) that gag orders on the press represented prior restraints on expression that should be tolerated only under extremely limited circumstances. The case began in a small Nebraska town when Edwin Charles Simants murdered six members of the Henry Kellie family in Sutherland, Nebraska. The attorneys in the case (both the prosecution and the defense) asked the judge to limit the pretrial publicity. Both a county and a district judge limited pretrial publicity in the case. The district judge, Hugh Stuart, wrote that "because of the nature of the crimes charged in the complaint that there is a clear and present danger that pre-trial publicity could impinge upon the defendant's right to a fair trial."

The Nebraska Press Association appealed the judge's order limiting pretrial publicity to the U.S. Supreme Court. The Court determined that the trial judge's order violated the press's First Amendment rights. Chief Justice Burger wrote that "prior restraints on speech and publication are the most serious and the least tolerable infringement on First Amendment rights."

In order for a trial judge to issue a prior restraint, the U.S. Supreme Court said that a trial judge must make three determinations: (1) the nature and extent of pretrial news coverage; (2) whether other measures (change of venue, jury sequestration) would lessen the effects of pretrial publicity; and (3) how effective the prior restraint would be to prevent the threatened danger.

What alternatives did the Court say that trial judges must consider before issuing a gag order on the press?

Chief Justice Burger said that trial judges should consider the following alternatives: a change of trial venue (location of the trial), postponement of the trial, intensive questioning of prospective jurors, clear and emphatic jury instructions, and sequestration (separation and isolation) of the jurors. Chief Justice Burger also wrote that "trial courts in appropriate cases may limit what the contending lawyers, the police and witnesses may say to anyone."

What did the U.S. Supreme Court rule with respect to reporters' privilege to withhold confidential sources?

The U.S. Supreme Court ruled 5–4 in *Branzburg v. Hayes* (1972) that reporters do not have a First Amendment right to avoid testifying before a grand jury pursuant to a subpoena issued in good faith. The reporters involved in the cases contended that forcing reporters to testify and reveal their confidential sources would burden the reporters' news-gathering efforts. The result, according to the press, would be that sources would be less willing to talk to reporters and the public would receive less information about important events. The government officials countered that the public's compelling interest in combatting crime outweighed any speculative harm on the reporters' news-gathering process.

Justice Byron White reasoned that "we see no reason to hold that these reporters, any more than other citizens, should be excused from furnishing information that may help the grand jury in arriving at its initial determination." The majority concluded that reporters were not entitled to special constitutionally based privilege in order to avoid their civic duty to testify to grand juries any more than other citizens.

Four justices dissented, with Justice Potter Stewart, Justice Douglas, and Justice Brennan each writing separate dissents. Justice Stewart's opinion became the most influential. He said that before a reporter could be forced to testify before the grand jury regarding his or her confidential sources, the government must "(1) show that there is probable cause to believe that the newsman has information that is clearly relevant to a specific probable violation of the law; (2) demonstrate that the information sought cannot be obtained by alternative means less destructive of First Amendment rights; and (3) demonstrate a compelling and overriding interest in the information." Justice Stewart's opinion became the blueprint for states passing so-called reporter shield laws, providing a degree of protection to reporters.

Who were the actual reporters in the *Branzburg* case?

The reporters in the consolidated cases were Paul Branzburg of the *Louisville Courier-Journal*; Paul Pappas, a television reporter from New Bedford, Massachusetts; and Nat Caldwell of the *New York Times*. Branzburg wrote stories, such as "The Hash They Make Isn't to Eat," about two young people from Kentucky growing and selling hash. Pappas filed a report about a Black Panthers headquarters in a boarded-up store. Caldwell wrote a series of articles about the Black Panthers and other black militant groups.

What decision involving a pornographer extended the protections for freedom of the press?

The U.S. Supreme Court's celebrated decision in 1988 extended protection to pornographer Larry Flynt and other publishers. The case *Hustler Magazine Co. v. Falwell* involved a battle

After prominent televangelist Jerry Falwell was targeted in a lurid *Hustler* magazine parody, Falwell successfully sued the magazine and its publisher for libel. The Supreme Court later reversed the decision.

between Flynt, the pornographer, and Jerry Falwell, the prominent televangelist and preacher. Flynt had lampooned Falwell in his *Hustler* magazine through a parody of the Campari Liquor ads where celebrities talked about their "first times," with a double entendre referring to the first time they tasted the liquor but playing on their first sexual experience. Flynt wrote that Jerry Falwell's "first time" was an incestuous rendezvous with Falwell's mother in an outhouse.

Though obviously not factual, the ad incensed Falwell, who sued Flynt for libel, invasion of privacy, and intentional infliction of emotional distress. A jury awarded Falwell damages on the intentional infliction of emotional distress claim. The U.S. Supreme Court reversed its decision and ruled in favor of Flynt, reasoning that his parody, though offensive, was a form of protected speech and even a "distant cousin" to political cartoons of the past.

Writing for the Court, Chief Justice Rehnquist reasoned that because the parody could not be interpreted as conveying actual facts about Falwell, it was protected. Chief Justice Rehnquist also reasoned that outrage was far too subjective of a standard to protect freedom of expression.

FREEDOM OF ASSEMBLY

In what decision did the U.S. Supreme Court protect the free-assembly rights of a communist?

The U.S. Supreme Court unanimously ruled 8–0 in *De Jonge v. Oregon* (1937) that "peaceable assembly for lawful discussion cannot be made a crime." The case involved Oregon-based communist Dirk De Jonge, who was sentenced to seven years for participating in a Communist Party meeting. No evidence existed of any violence or rebellion at the meeting, only lawful political discussions. The Court concluded that the "holding of meetings for peaceable political action cannot be subscribed." The case is also important because for the first time, the Court clarified that the First Amendment freedom of assembly is extended to the states via the 14th Amendment's Due Process Clause.

What U.S. Supreme Court decision laid the foundation for the public forum doctrine?

The Court's decision in *Hague v. Committee for Industrial Organization* (1939) laid the foundation for the public forum doctrine: the idea that First Amendment rights often depend upon place and are increased if the expression takes place on a traditional public forum.

The Court invalidated a Jersey City, New Jersey, ordinance that allowed the director of public safety to deny permits for the use of city halls for public meetings. Jersey City officials also prohibited labor organizations from distributing printed material on the public street while allowing other groups to distribute printed material without interference. The Court majority determined that this violated the labor group's constitutional rights.

In his plurality opinion, Justice Owen Roberts wrote that public streets and parks were places that by tradition should be open to the public to exercise their constitutional rights to assembly, petition, and speech. This statement formed the historical basis for the public forum doctrine, which gives increased First Amendment protection in certain public places.

In what decisions did the U.S. Supreme Court rule that a First Amendment right to burn an American flag exists?

In two decisions, *Texas v. Johnson* (1989) and *U.S. v. Eichman* (1990), the U.S. Supreme Court ruled 5–4 that individuals have

"Radical lawyer" William Kunstler, shown with *Texas v. Johnson* defendant Gregory Johnson, also represented the defendants in *United States v. Eichman.*

a First Amendment right to burn the American flag as a form of political dissent. In *Texas v. Johnson*, the Court struck down a Texas flag-desecration law prohibiting such treatment of the flag. In *Eichman*, the Court invalidated the federal law, the Flag Protection Act of 1990, which the U.S. Congress passed in response to the Court's decision in *Texas v. Johnson*.

Justice Brennan wrote the majority opinion in both cases. He stated in oft-quoted language in *Texas v. Johnson*: "If there is a bedrock principle underlying the First Amendment, it is that the government may not prohibit the expression of an idea simply because it finds it offensive or disagreeable."

In response to these decisions, Congress introduced several amendments to the Constitution prohibiting the burning of the American flag. Several times, these amendments passed the House of Representatives, but they failed to garner the necessary two-thirds majority in the Senate. In June 2006, a flag protection amendment passed the House but failed in the Senate by a single vote. The amendment needed 67 votes in the Senate (the necessary number for two-thirds) but received 66.

Freedom of Religion

THE FREE EXERCISE CLAUSE

In what decision did the Court initially address the meaning of the Free Exercise Clause?

The U.S. Supreme Court addressed the meaning of the Free Exercise Clause in *Reynolds v. United States* (1878), a case involving a Mormon from Utah named George Reynolds who faced prosecution for polygamy. Reynolds argued that it violated his religious liberty rights because a central tenet of his religion was to have multiple wives.

By practicing polygamy, Reynolds, a member of the Church of Jesus Christ of Latter-day Saints (also known as the Mormon Church), was following what was then one of the central tenets of his religion. Appealing his case to the U.S. Supreme Court, Reynolds argued that the antibigamy law violated his free-exercise rights.

However, the U.S. Supreme Court was not convinced. It reasoned that the state had an interest in regulating morality and punishing conduct, even religiously inspired conduct that violated those state interests.

"To permit this would be to make the professed doctrines of religious belief superior to the law of the land, and, in effect, to permit every citizen to become a law unto himself," wrote Chief Justice Morrison Waite for the Court. "Government could exist only in name under such circumstances."

What decision reversed the conviction of a phonograph playing Jehovah's Witnesses propaganda?

The Hughes Court unanimously (9–0) ruled in *Cantwell v. Connecticut* (1940) that Jesse Cantwell did not commit breach of the peace when he walked door to door in a Catholic neighborhood soliciting for Jehovah's Witnesses. Jesse Cantwell, his brother Russell, and his father Newton walked down Cassius Street in a Catholic neighborhood and asked the residents if they would listen to one of their records. These records attacked official religions, including Catholicism. City officials cited the three men for failing to obtain a permit to solicit door to door and for breach of the peace.

The Court unanimously ruled that the city law requiring solicitors to obtain a permit violated the First Amendment. The Court focused on the fact that the secretary of the welfare council would determine the merits of the solicitation and religious causes before making the permit decision. To the Court, this was unacceptable: "But to condition the solicitation of aid for the perpetuation of religious views or systems upon a license, the grant of which rests in the exercise of a determination by state authority as to what is a religious cause, is to lay a forbidden burden upon the exercise of liberty protected by the Constitution." The Court then addressed Jesse Cantwell's conviction for breach of the peace, finding that his conduct did not merit official sanction.

DID YOU KNOW?

In what decision did the Court protect the religious liberty rights of a Seventh-day Adventist female worker?

In *Sherbert v. Verner* (1963), the Warren Court ruled 7–2 in favor of Seventh-day Adventist Adele Sherbert, who was denied unemployment compensation by South Carolina officials for refusing to work on her Sabbath day of Saturday. The state courts rejected Sherbert's free-exercise claims, finding that she could still practice her religious faith. The U.S. Supreme Court reversed its opinion, writing that the state rulings infringed her religious liberty rights and that the state could not justify such an infringement by a compelling state interest. "Significantly, South Carolina expressly saves the Sunday worshipper from having to make the kind of choice which we here hold infringes the Sabbatarian's religious liberty," Justice William J. Brennan Jr. wrote for the Court.

The state had argued that the denial of benefits was justified because the state had a compelling interest in preventing fraudulent claims. The U.S. Supreme Court ruled that the state had failed to carry its burden of showing a danger of such claims.

In famous language, the Court wrote:

In the realm of religious faith, and in that of political belief, sharp differences arise. In both fields the tenets of one man may seem the rankest error to his neighbor. To persuade others to his point of view, the pleader, as we know, at times, resorts to exaggeration, to vilification of men who have been, or are, prominent in church or state, and even to false statement. But the people of this nation have ordained in the light of history, that, in spite of the probability of excesses and abuses, these liberties are, in the long view, essential to enlightened opinion and right conduct on the part of the citizens of a democracy.

What did the U.S. Supreme Court say about Sunday closing laws?

The Warren Court upheld the constitutionality of Sunday closing laws, or Sunday blue laws, in a pair of 1961 decisions: *McGowan v. Maryland* and *Braunfeld v. Brown.* In *McGowan*, the Court determined that such a law did not violate the Establishment Clause of the First Amendment by preferring the Christian Sabbath day of Sunday. Instead, the Court reasoned that the closing laws had a valid, secular purpose: to provide a day of rest for everyone in the community. In *Braunfeld*, the Court ruled that a closing law did not violate the free-exercise rights of Orthodox Jews who shut their businesses down on their Sabbath day of Saturday and then were forced to shut down on Sundays as well. Chief Justice Earl Warren wrote that the closing law "does not make unlawful any religious practices" and "simply regulates a secular activity."

In what ruling did the U.S. Supreme Court protect the Amish from a compulsory education law?

The U.S. Supreme Court ruled in *Wisconsin v. Yoder* (1972) that application of a compulsory education law against members of the Old Amish Order, including Jonas Yoder, violated their religious liberty rights under the Free Exercise Clause.

Wisconsin's compulsory education law required parents to send their children to school until the age of 16. However, some of the Amish—including the Yoder family—declined to send their children to school after they completed the eighth grade. Instead, the children would help their families by working on farms.

On the basis of the First Amendment's Free Exercise Clause, the Supreme Court ruled in favor of Amish families who refused to send their children to public school after eighth grade. Besides the benefit of another hand on the family farm, many Amish believe higher education endangers their faith and lifestyle.

In Green County, Wisconsin, authorities charged Yoder and Wallace Miller of the Amish religion and Adin Yutzy of the Old Mennonite Order of violating the law. They were all convicted and fined. However, the Wisconsin Supreme Court ruled that this violated their religious liberty rights.

On appeal, the U.S. Supreme Court agreed in an opinion written by Chief Justice Warren E. Burger. "Amish objection to formal education beyond the eighth grade is firmly grounded in these central religious concepts," he wrote. "They object to the high school, and higher education generally, because the values they teach are in marked variance with Amish values and the Amish way of life; they view secondary school education as an impermissible exposure of their children to a 'worldly' influence in conflict with their beliefs."

Chief Justice Burger elaborated:

> Formal high school education beyond the eighth grade is contrary to Amish beliefs, not only because it places Amish children in an environment hostile to Amish beliefs with increasing emphasis on competition in class work and sports and with pressure to conform to the styles, manners, and ways of the peer group, but also be-

> cause it takes them away from their community, physically and emotionally, during the crucial and formative adolescent period of life. During this period, the children must acquire Amish attitudes favoring manual work and self-reliance and the specific skills needed to perform the adult role of an Amish farmer or housewife. They must learn to enjoy physical labor. Once a child has learned basic reading, writing, and elementary mathematics, these traits, skills, and attitudes admittedly fall within the category of those best learned through example and "doing" rather than in a classroom. And, at this time in life, the Amish child must also grow in his faith and his relationship to the Amish community if he is to be prepared to accept the heavy obligations imposed by adult baptism. In short, high school attendance with teachers who are not of the Amish faith—and may even be hostile to it—interposes a serious barrier to the integration of the Amish child into the Amish religious community.

Chief Justice Burger acknowledged that the state had a strong interest in the education of children but said that this must be balanced against the fundamental right to free exercise of religion. He added: "In sum, the unchallenged testimony of acknowledged experts in education and religious history, almost 300 years of consistent practice, and strong evidence of a sustained faith pervading and regulating respondents' entire mode of life support the claim that enforcement of the State's requirement of compulsory formal education after the eighth grade would gravely endanger if not destroy the free exercise of respondents' religious beliefs."

Who wrote a dissenting opinion in the case?

Justice William O. Douglas wrote an opinion dissenting in part. He agreed that the Amish had a fundamental right under the free exercise of religion. However, he emphasized that the rights of the Amish children—not just the parents—should be taken into account.

"On this important and vital matter of education, I think the children should be entitled to be heard," Justice Douglas wrote. "While the parents, absent dissent, normally speak for the entire family, the education of the child is a matter on which the child will often have decided views. He may want to be a pianist or an astronaut or an oceanographer. To do so he will have to break from the Amish tradition."

Did the Rehnquist Court change Free Exercise Clause jurisprudence?

Yes, the Rehnquist Court changed Free Exercise Clause jurisprudence with its controversial 1990 decision *Employment Division v. Smith.* The Free Exercise Clause is the clause designed to ensure that people have the right to practice their religious faith free from governmental interference. Traditionally, the U.S. Supreme Court, since the time of the Warren Court, had held that the government could not infringe upon a person's free-exercise rights unless the government met strict scrutiny showing that their regulation was advancing a compelling governmental interest in the least restrictive way possible. In the 1963 decision *Sherbert v. Verner*, the Court ruled that the state of South Carolina violated the free-exercise rights of Seventh-day Adventist Adele Sherbert by denying her unemployment compensation when she was terminated for refusing to work on Saturday, her Sabbath day. *Sherbert v. Verner* stated the law of the land in the free-exercise area until *Employment Division v. Smith.*

In *Smith*, two Native American drug counselors, Alfred Smith and Galen Black, were terminated from their jobs in Oregon and denied unemployment compensation for using a hallucinogenic drug (peyote) for religious reasons. The state asserted that it had a clear interest in preventing illegal drug use. Smith and Black argued that the denial of unemployment benefits infringed on their free-exercise rights to use peyote for religious reasons. Justice Antonin Scalia wrote that "[w]e have never held that an individual's religious beliefs [494 U.S. 879] excuse him from compliance with an otherwise valid law prohibiting conduct that the State is free to regulate."

Justice Scalia ruled that the government does not violate the Free Exercise Clause when it acts pursuant to a generally applicable law that does not target religion but merely has an incidental effect. The decision lowered the standard of review in many Free Exercise Clause cases. In her opinion, Justice Sandra Day O'Connor opined that Justice Scalia's opinion is "incompatible with our Nation's fundamental commitment to individual religious liberty."

In what decision did the Court rule that a Florida city intentionally targeted unpopular religious beliefs?

The U.S. Supreme Court ruled in *Church of the Lukumi Babalu v. Hialeah* (1993) that the city of Hialeah, Florida, intentionally passed an animal cruelty law to target the Santeria religion, which believed that animal sacrifices are "directly commanded by the gods."

When a new Santeria church was planned in Hialeah, city leaders passed an ordinance that prohibited sacrificing animals "in a public or private ritual or ceremony not for the primary purpose of food consumption." Licensed establishments could, however, slaughter animals that were "specifically raised for food purposes."

The city of Hialeah, Florida, passed an animal cruelty law specifically targeting Santeria's animal sacrifices such as this chicken sacrifice at a 2017 ceremony in Havana, Cuba.

The Santeria Church contended that the law was targeted against it specifically. The city argued that under *Employment Division v. Smith* (1990), the city's law was a neutral and generally applicable law against animal sacrifices. The Court ruled unanimously, in an opinion by Justice Anthony Kennedy, that the law was not natural and generally applicable and instead directly targeted the Santeria religion.

The Court thus applied strict scrutiny instead of the rational basis–type standard outlined in *Smith*. The Court reasoned that "the legitimate governmental interests in protecting the public health and preventing cruelty to animals could be addressed by restrictions stopping far short of a flat prohibition of all Santeria sacrificial practice."

Justice Kennedy concluded: "Legislators may not devise mechanisms, overt or disguised, designed to persecute or oppress a religion or its practices. The laws here in question were enacted contrary to these constitutional principles, and they are void."

How did Congress and the Court disagree over the Free Exercise Clause?

The *Smith* decision caused great uproar in the religious liberty community, who felt that the decision would have a dramatic negative impact on free-exercise protections in the country. This led to Congress passing a 1993 law called the Religious Freedom Restoration Act (RFRA), which restored the compelling-interest test articulated in the *Sherbert* decision. Under RFRA, the government cannot substantially burden free exercise of religion rights unless the government advances a compelling governmental interest in the least restrictive means. Congress passed RFRA in direct response to the *Smith* decision. In a sense, RFRA represented a congressional overturning of the Court's decision. This led to another U.S. Supreme Court decision in *City of Boerne v. Flores* (1997), which dealt with a land zoning dispute involving a church that wanted to ex-

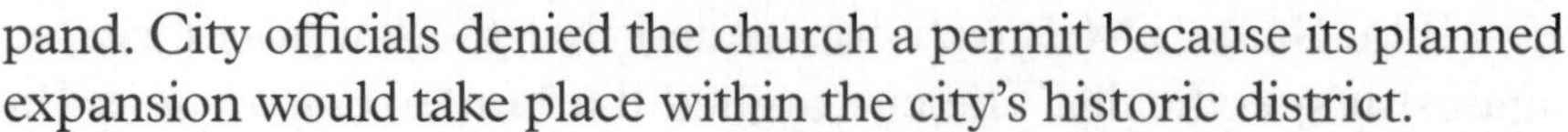

pand. City officials denied the church a permit because its planned expansion would take place within the city's historic district.

The city contended that Congress exceeded its constitutional power under Section 5 of the 14th Amendment in passing RFRA and applying it to the states. The Court majority determined that RFRA swept too broadly, particularly because Congress did not have sufficient evidence of discrimination against religious freedoms in the states. In his concurring opinion, Justice John Paul Stevens added that RFRA violated the Establishment Clause by creating a governmental preference for religion. The Court's opinion also reaffirmed the fundamental principle articulated in *Marbury v. Madison* that the U.S. Supreme Court has the ultimate power to determine the meaning of the Constitution:

> Our national experience teaches that the Constitution is preserved best when each part of the Government respects both the Constitution and the proper actions and determinations of the other branches. When the Court has interpreted the Constitution, it has acted within the province of the Judicial Branch, which embraces the duty to say what the law is. When the political branches of the Government act against the background of a judicial interpretation of the Constitution already issued, it must be understood that in later cases and controversies the Court will treat its precedents with the respect due them under settled principles, including stare decisis, and contrary expectations must be disappointed. RFRA was designed to control cases and controversies, such as the one before us; but as the provisions of the federal statute here invoked are beyond congressional authority, it is this Court's precedent, not RFRA, which must control.

In response to this decision, Congress passed a second law called the Religious Land Use and Institutionalized Persons Act (RLUIPA), which was similar to RFRA but not quite as broad. It applied in land use and prisoner cases but was grounded on Congress's Commerce Clause and Spending Clause powers rather than just Congress's powers under Section 5 of the 14th Amendment. In 2005, the U.S. Supreme Court ruled in *Cutter v. Wilkinson* that RLUIPA did not violate the Establishment Clause but represented a permissible accommodation of prisoners' religious liberty rights. However, other constitutional questions remain as to whether RLUIPA is constitutional. The U.S. Supreme Court likely will have to address this controversy in later cases.

In what decision did the U.S. Supreme Court rule that closely held corporations had rights under RFRA?

The U.S. Supreme Court ruled 5–4 in *Burwell v. Hobby Lobby Stores* (2014) that closely held for-profit corporations, in this case Hobby Lobby, had a right under RFRA to refuse to comply with a mandate under the Affordable Care Act (often called "Obamacare") to provide contraceptive services to its employees.

David Barbara Green, who founded Hobby Lobby, provided an insurance policy that covered most forms of birth control. However, Hobby Lobby decided not to provide certain forms of birth control, such as those they deemed to be abortion-inducing drugs, or abortifacients.

Hobby Lobby challenged the contraceptive mandate in federal court, arguing that it violated its sincerely held religious beliefs under RFRA. The Court ruled 5–4 in favor of Hobby Lobby. The Court ruled that complying with the contraceptive mandate imposed a substantial burden on Hobby Lobby's religious liberty rights.

In *Burwell v. Hobby Lobby*, the closely held corporation asserted its right to not cover specific types of birth control through its employees' health insurance plan under the First Amendment's free exercise of religion clause.

DID YOU KNOW?

Who wrote the Court's primary dissenting opinion in the *Hobby Lobby* case?

Justice Ruth Bader Ginsburg wrote the Court's primary dissenting opinion. She reasoned that RFRA should not protect a for-profit corporation and that the law's protections should extend only to nonprofits that are primarily religious in nature. She also questioned whether female employees should be treated differently when they work for a corporation like Hobby Lobby or the "shop next door."

The Court ultimately sided with Hobby Lobby because it felt that the contraceptive mandate could have been applied in a less restrictive way, similar to how the mandate applied to nonprofit corporations like the Little Sisters of the Poor. Under the ACA, the government, not the nonprofit, paid for the contraceptive coverage that violated the religious tenets of the nonprofit.

Writing for the majority, Justice Samuel A. Alito Jr. reasoned that "this system constitutes an alternative that achieves all of the Government's aims while provided greater respect for religious liberty."

THE ESTABLISHMENT CLAUSE

In what decision did the U.S. Supreme Court define the meaning of the Establishment Clause?

The U.S. Supreme Court addressed the meaning of the Establishment Clause—"Congress shall make no law respecting an Establishment of Religion"—in *Everson v. Board of Education* (1947). The case concerned a New Jersey law that allowed school

Justice Hugo Black wrote the majority decision in *Everson v. Board of Education,* which helped shape the application of the First Amendment's Establishment Clause.

districts to reimburse parents for the costs of bus transportation to and from schools. The town of Ewing applied this law to allow reimbursements for all parents, including those whose children attended private religious schools. Arch Everson sued, contending that the practice of paying monies to parents whose children attended private religious schools violated the Establishment Clause.

The Court determined that the Establishment Clause meant to ensure that a "wall of separation" existed between church and state. However, a narrow majority of the Court determined that the wall did not prevent the town from paying the bus transportation costs of all of its students from both public and private schools. Justice Hugo Black, writing for the majority, explained: "We must be careful, in protecting the citizens of New Jersey against state-established churches, to be sure that we do not inadvertently prohibit New Jersey from extending its general State law benefits to all its citizens without regard to their religious beliefs." He concluded: "The First Amendment has erected a wall between church and state. That wall must be kept high and impregnable. We could not approve the slightest breach. New Jersey has not breached it here."

In what passage in *Everson* did Justice Black most directly address the meaning of the Establishment Clause?

Justice Black addressed the meaning of the Establishment Clause in the following passage:

> The "establishment of religion" clause of the First Amendment means at least this: neither a state nor the Federal Government can set up a church. Neither can pass laws which aid one religion, aid all religions, or prefer one religion over another. Neither can force nor influence a person to go to or to remain away from church against his will or force him to profess a belief or disbelief in any religion. No person can be punished for entertaining or professing religious beliefs or disbeliefs, for church attendance or non-attendance. No tax in any amount, large or small, can be levied to support any religious activities or institutions, whatever they may be called, or whatever form they may adopt to teach or practice religion. Neither a state nor the Federal Government can, openly or secretly, participate in the affairs of any religious organizations or groups, and vice versa. In the words of Jefferson, the clause against establishment of religion by law was intended to erect "a wall of separation between church and State."

Who wrote the Court's dissenting opinions in *Everson v. Board of Education*?

Justice Robert H. Jackson and Justice Wiley Blount Rutledge both wrote dissenting opinions. Justice Jackson emphasized that the government was paying for bus transportation to largely Catholic schools. "I should be surprised if any Catholic would deny that the parochial school is a vital, if not the most vital, part of the

Roman Catholic Church," he wrote. "Catholic education is the rock on which the whole structure rests, and to render tax aid to its Church school is indistinguishable to me from rendering the same aid to the Church itself."

Justice Rutledge also wrote a dissenting opinion. "Not simply an established church, but any law respecting an establishment of religion, is forbidden," he wrote. "The Amendment's purpose was not to strike merely at the official establishment of a single sect, creed or religion, outlawing only a formal relation such as had prevailed in England and some of the colonies. Necessarily, it was to uproot all such relationships. But the object was broader than separating church and state in this narrow sense. It was to create a complete and permanent separation of the spheres of religious activity and civil authority by comprehensively forbidding every form of public aid or support for religion."

What did the Warren Court say about government-sponsored prayer in public schools?

The Warren Court ruled that teacher-led prayer in public schools violated the Establishment Clause of the First Amendment, which is designed to ensure a degree of separation between church and state. The Court first reached this conclusion in its 1962 decision *Engel v. Vitale*. The Court dealt with a New York Board of Regents prayer that read: "Almighty God, we acknowledge our dependence upon Thee, and we beg Thy blessings upon us, our parents, our teachers, and our Country."

"The New York laws officially prescribing the Regents' prayer are inconsistent both with the purposes of the Establishment Clause and with the Establishment Clause itself," Justice Black wrote for the Court majority. "It is neither sacrilegious nor antireligious to say that each separate government in this country should stay out of the business of writing or sanctioning official prayers and leave that purely religious function to the people themselves and to those the people choose to look to for religious guidance."

The Court reached a similar ruling in the companion cases *School District of Abington Township v. Schempp* and *Murray v. Curlett* (1963). These cases came from the states of Pennsylvania and Maryland, respectively. The Pennsylvania law required the reading of 10 Bible verses a day. The Maryland law required a reading of a chapter of the Holy Bible and the reading of the Lord's Prayer. The school district defendants argued that the prayer exercises advanced the secular purposes of promoting morality, contradicting a "materialistic trend" in society and teaching literature. The Court invalidated both state laws, describing them as "religious exercises … in violation of the command of the First Amendment that the Government maintain strict neutrality, neither aiding nor opposing religion."

Who was the only justice on the Warren Court to dissent in the school prayer decisions?

Justice Potter Stewart was the lone dissenter in both *Engel v. Vitale* and *Abington School District v. Schempp*. He explained his

School District of Abington Township v. Schempp helped firm up the hazy line between acceptable study of religious materials in school versus state establishment of religion.

Did the U.S. Supreme Court say that the Bible could not be discussed in public schools?

No, the Court did not rule that the Bible was banned from public schools. Popular opposition to the U.S. Supreme Court grew after the school prayer decisions, as some alleged that the Court had "kicked God out of the public schools." However, a close reading of the Court's decision in *Abington Township* reveals the opposite. Justice Tom C. Clark explained: "In addition, it might well be said that one's education is not complete without a study of comparative religion or the history of religion and its relationship to the advancement of civilization. It certainly may be said that the Bible is worthy of study for its literary and historic qualities. Nothing we have said here indicates that such study of the Bible or of religion, when presented objectively as part of a secular program of education, may not be effected consistently with the First Amendment."

DID YOU KNOW?

view in *Engel*: "With all respect, I think the Court has misapplied a great constitutional principle. I cannot see how an 'official religion' is established by letting those who want to say a prayer say it. On the contrary, I think that to deny the wish of these school children to join in reciting this prayer is to deny them the opportunity of sharing in the spiritual heritage of our Nation."

What famous, or infamous, test did the U.S. Supreme Court use beginning in the 1970s to evaluate Establishment Clause cases?

The U.S. Supreme Court used the so-called Lemon Test, a test developed by the Court in *Lemon v. Kurtzman* (1971). The

case involved challenges to state laws in Pennsylvania and Rhode Island that permitted tax-funded reimbursement to church-affiliated schools, covering expenses such as teacher salaries and the costs of textbooks and other instructional materials. Because educational costs were rapidly increasing, subjecting parochial schools to increasing budget constraints, the states offered financial-assistance programs in an effort to secure the quality of education at church-affiliated schools.

The Court established a three-part test to determine whether a government action violates the Establishment Clause. The test requires that (1) the action have a secular purpose; (2) its primary effect neither advance nor inhibit religion; and (3) no excessive government entanglement be present.

Chief Justice Burger, who wrote the Court's opinion in *Lemon*, did not create the test out of whole cloth. Instead, he borrowed tests from several different previous decisions. Though oft-criticized, the Lemon Test remained the dominant Establishment Clause test for decades.

In what decision did the Court first not use the Lemon Test and instead rely on history and tradition?

The Supreme declined to use the Lemon Test in *Marsh v. Chambers* (1983), instead upholding the Nebraska Legislature's long-standing practice of opening legislative sessions with a chaplain-led prayer.

"The opening of sessions of legislative and other deliberative public bodies with prayer is deeply embedded in the history and tradition of this country," wrote Chief Justice Burger for the majority. "From colonial times through the founding of the Republic and ever since, the practice of legislative prayer has coexisted with the principles of disestablishment and religious freedom."

Chief Justice Burger noted that the Continental Congress opened sessions with prayer, as did the U.S. Congress since its ini-

tial opening in 1789. He concluded: "This unique history leads us to accept the interpretation of the First Amendment draftsmen who saw no real threat to the Establishment Clause arising from a practice of prayer similar to that now challenged."

Justice Brennan authored a dissenting opinion. "I now believe that the practice of official invocational prayer, as it exists in Nebraska and most other state legislatures, is unconstitutional," he wrote. "It is contrary to the doctrine as well the underlying purposes of the Establishment Clause, and it is not saved either by its history or by any of the other considerations suggested in the Court's opinion."

Justice Stevens wrote a separate dissenting opinion. "Prayers may be said by a Catholic priest in the Massachusetts Legislature and by a Presbyterian minister in the Nebraska Legislature, but I would not expect to find a Jehovah's Witness or a disciple of Mary Baker Eddy or the Reverend Moon serving as the official chaplain in any state legislature," he pointed out. "Regardless of the motivation of the majority that exercises the power to appoint the chaplain, it seems plain to me that the designation of a member of one religious faith to serve as the sole official chaplain of a state legislature for a period of 16 years constitutes the preference of one faith over another in violation of the Establishment Clause of the First Amendment."

What did Justice Scalia famously write in criticism of the Lemon Test years later?

In the 1993 decision *Lamb's Chapel v. Center Moriches* (1993), Justice Scalia famously wrote of the Lemon Test: "As to the Court's invocation of the Lemon Test: like some ghoul in a late-night horror movie that repeatedly sits up in its grave and shuffles abroad after being repeatedly killed and buried, *Lemon* stalks our Establishment Clause jurisprudence once again, frightening the little children and school attorneys of Center Moriches Union Free School District."

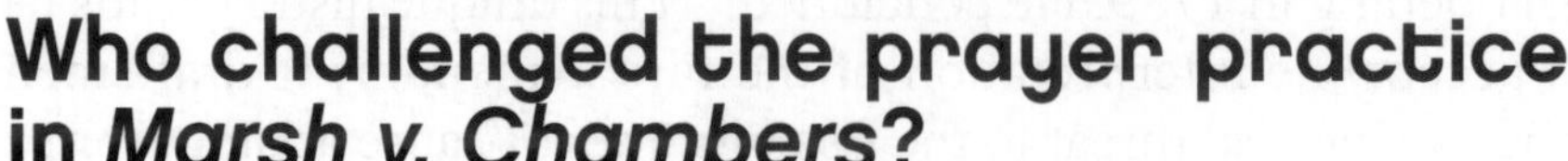

Who challenged the prayer practice in *Marsh v. Chambers*?

Nebraska legislator Ernest Chambers, known as "the Maverick of Omaha," filed the lawsuit challenging the practice of prayer in the legislature. Chambers, an atheist, was for many years the only African American member of the Nebraska House, and he also is the longest-serving member in history, having served for more than 45 years. Chambers actually filed a federal lawsuit against God, contending that God had caused countless acts of destruction in the world. A judge dismissed the lawsuit, finding that God had no known address.

In what decision did the U.S. Supreme Court invalidate a law requiring the Ten Commandments in every classroom?

The U.S. Supreme Court ruled 5–4 in *Stone v. Graham* (1980) that a Kentucky law requiring the posting of the Ten Commandments in every elementary- and secondary-school classroom violated the Establishment Clause of the First Amendment. The state of Kentucky argued that the law had a secular purpose, emphasizing that the following notation was added to all the Ten Commandment postings: "The secular application of the Ten Commandments is clearly seen in its adoption as the fundamental legal code of Western Civilization and the Common Law of the United States."

However, the five-member majority, in a per curiam (for the Court) opinion, ruled that the Kentucky law violated the purpose prong of the Lemon Test because the law had a plainly religious purpose. "The pre-eminent purpose for posting the Ten Commandments on schoolroom walls is plainly religious in nature," the Court wrote. "The Ten Commandments are undeniably a sacred text in the Jewish and Christian faiths, and no legislative recitation of a supposed secular purpose can blind us to that fact."

In 1980 the Court found that the state of Kentucky could no longer require classrooms to display the Ten Commandments in schoolrooms as had previously been the state law.

What was unusual about the Court's decision?

The Court reversed the Kentucky court's opinion without hearing the oral argument or requiring briefs on the merits. In other words, the Court summarily reversed the lower-court decision. Furthermore, the Court majority wrote its opinion *per curiam*, which means "for the Court." In other words, no single justice was noted as the author of the Court's opinion. Instead, it was ostensibly a collective decision.

Which justice wrote a dissenting opinion questioning the majority's interpretation of the Establishment Clause?

Chief Justice William H. Rehnquist wrote a dissenting opinion. "The Establishment Clause does not require that the public sector be insulated from all things which may have a religious significance or origin," he wrote.

In what decision did the Court uphold the display of a crèche as part of a larger Christmas display?

The U.S. Supreme Court ruled in *Lynch v. Donnelly* (1984) that the display of a crèche in Pawtucket, Rhode Island, in the context of a larger secular celebration of Christmas did not violate the Establishment Clause.

"The narrow question is whether there is a secular purpose for Pawtucket's display of the crèche," wrote Chief Justice Burger. "The display is sponsored by the City to celebrate the Holiday and to depict the origins of that Holiday. These are legitimate secular purposes. The District Court's inference, drawn from the religious nature of the crèche, that the City has no secular purpose was, on this record, clearly erroneous."

Crucial to the Court's decision was that the clearly religious symbol of the crèche was surrounded by secular Christmas symbols, like reindeer, Santa Claus, and candy canes. To the majority, these additional symbols showed that the display was not religious.

"We are satisfied that the City has a secular purpose for including the crèche, that the City has not impermissibly advanced religion, and that including the crèche does not create excessive entanglement between religion and government," he wrote. "We hold that, notwithstanding the religious significance of the crèche, the City of Pawtucket has not violated the Establishment Clause of the First Amendment."

What justice wrote a concurring opinion in the case and created a new test?

In a concurring opinion, Justice O'Connor offered what she termed a "clarification" of the Lemon Test, what became known as the Endorsement Test. Justice O'Connor explained: "Endorsement

sends a message to nonadherents that they are outsiders, not full members of the political community, and an accompanying message that they are insiders, favored members of the political community. Disapproval sends the opposite message.... Focusing on institutional entanglement and on endorsement or disapproval of religion clarifies the Lemon test as an analytical device.... The purpose prong of the Lemon test asks whether government's actual purpose is to endorse or disapprove of religion. The effect prong asks whether, irrespective of government's actual purpose, the practice under review in fact conveys a message of endorsement or disapproval."

The Endorsement Test remains a staple of modern Establishment Clause jurisprudence, particularly in religious display cases.

In what case did the Court uphold one display and strike down another?

The U.S. Supreme Court ruled in *Allegheny County v. ACLU* (1989) that a crèche placed on the Grand Staircase of the Allegheny County Courthouse in Pittsburgh violated the Establish-

In *Allegheny County v. ACLU* the Supreme Court issued a very nuanced double opinion about what type of religious displays may appear on public property and in what context.

DID YOU KNOW?

How did the U.S. Supreme Court rule on a Moment of Silence Law in public schools?

The Burger Court ruled 6–3 in *Wallace v. Jaffree* (1985) that Alabama's Moment of Silence Law violated the Establishment Clause of the First Amendment, which is designed to ensure separation between church and state. The Alabama legislature had a law that provided students in Alabama with a one-minute period of silence "meditation." A few years later, the legislature amended the statute to provide the one-minute period for "meditation or voluntary prayer." The sponsor of the new legislation said that the purpose of the law was "an effort to return voluntary prayer" to public schools. The majority of the U.S. Supreme Court determined that the law violated the Establishment Clause because the clear purpose of the law was religious rather than secular. The law represented an endorsement of religion that was "not consistent with the established principle that the government must pursue a course of complete neutrality toward religion."

ment Clause, but that a Chanukah menorah placed just outside the City–County Building, next to a Christmas tree and a sign saluting liberty, was permissible.

The Court reasoned that the crèche display in the courthouse, though adorned with flowers, was religious in nature and sent a clear message of governmental advancement of religion. On the other hand, the menorah was surrounded by numerous secular symbols. "Furthermore, the crèche sits on the Grand Staircase, the 'main' and 'most beautiful part' of the building that is the seat of county government," the Court wrote. "No viewer could reasonably think that it occupies this location without the support and approval of the government. Thus, by permitting the display of the crèche in this particular physical setting, the county sends an unmistakable message that it supports and promotes the Christian praise to God that is the crèche's religious message."

The other menorah display was secondary to a large, 45-foot Christmas tree, which was the dominant symbol in the overall context. "Given this configuration, it is much more sensible to interpret the meaning of the menorah in light of the tree, rather than vice versa," the Court explained. "In the shadow of the tree, the menorah is readily understood as simply a recognition that Christmas is not the only traditional way of observing the winter-holiday season. In these circumstances, then, the combination of the tree and the menorah communicates, not a simultaneous endorsement of both the Christian and Jewish faiths, but instead, a secular celebration of Christmas coupled with an acknowledgment of Chanukah as a contemporaneous alternative tradition."

Which of the three dissenters criticized the Court's entire Establishment Clause jurisprudence since 1947?

Chief Justice Rehnquist noted that the U.S. Supreme Court in 1947 had quoted former president Thomas Jefferson's phrase "wall of separation between church and state" to describe the meaning of the Establishment Clause. Chief Justice Rehnquist said that "the Establishment Clause has been expressly freighted with Jefferson's misleading metaphor for nearly 40 years." Chief Justice Rehnquist cited many examples of religious influences in public life and said that "no historical foundation" existed for the Court's interpretation of the Establishment Clause.

How did the Rehnquist Court deal with the issue of school prayer?

The Court addressed the issue of school prayer in two decisions. In both decisions, the Court struck the policies down as violations of the Establishment Clause. In the first decision, *Lee v. Weisman* (1992), the Court struck down 5–4 a middle school grad-

The Supreme Court Justices who decided *Wallace v. Jaffee* (1985) pose with President Reagan in 1981. Left to right: Blackmun, Marshall, Brennan, Chief Justice Burger, President Reagan, O'Connor, White, Powell, Rehnquist, and Stevens.

uation prayer in Rhode Island. Even though the prayer was nonsectarian, the Court reasoned that it amounted to psychological coercion on the students attending the ceremony, who were a captive audience. "The undeniable fact is that the school district's supervision and control of a high school graduation ceremony places public pressure, as well as peer pressure, on attending students to stand as a group or, at least, maintain respectful silence during the invocation and benediction," Justice Kennedy wrote in his majority opinion. "This pressure, though subtle and indirect, can be as real as any overt compulsion."

Then, in *Santa Fe Independent School District v. Doe* (2000), the U.S. Supreme Court invalidated, by a 6–3 vote, a Texas high school's practice of student-sponsored prayers being announced over the loudspeakers at high school football games. "In this context the members of the listening audience must perceive the pregame message as a public expression of the views of the majority of the student body delivered with the approval of the school administration," Justice Stevens wrote in his majority opinion.

Can the Ten Commandments be posted on government property?

A sharp dispute remains over this matter even after two U.S. Supreme Court decisions on this subject in 2005. The Burger

DID YOU KNOW?

Quotable: The Justices in *Wallace v. Jaffree* (1985)

Justice John Paul Stevens (majority): "The legislative intent to return prayer to the public school is, of course, quite different from merely protecting every student's right to engage in voluntary prayer during an appropriate moment of silence during the schoolday."

Justice Sandra Day O'Connor (concurring): "A state-sponsored moment of silence in the public schools is different from state-sponsored vocal prayer or Bible reading. First, a moment of silence is not inherently religious. Silence, unlike prayer or Bible reading, need not be associated with a religious exercise. Second, a pupil who participates in a moment of silence need not compromise his or her beliefs.... It is difficult to discern a serious threat to religious liberty from a room of silent, thoughtful schoolchildren."

Chief Justice Warren E. Burger (dissenting): "Some who trouble to read the opinions in these cases will find it ironic—perhaps even bizarre—that on the very day we heard arguments in the cases, the Court's session opened with an invocation for Divine protection."

Chief Justice William H. Rehnquist (dissenting): "It is impossible to build sound constitutional doctrine upon a mistaken understanding of constitutional history, but unfortunately the Establishment Clause has been expressly freighted with Jefferson's misleading metaphor for nearly 40 years."

Court had ruled 5–4 in *Stone v. Graham* that a Kentucky law requiring the posting of the Ten Commandments in public school classrooms violated the Establishment Clause. The ruling focused on the special environment of the school and the impressionable young ages of the viewers (the students). Lower courts continued to divide over the constitutionality of the posting of the Ten Commandments on other government property. On June 27, 2005, the Court issued decisions in *Van Orden v. Perry* (docket no. 03-1500) and *McCreary County v. ACLU of Kentucky* (docket no. 03-1693).

The Court issued two 5–4 decisions, one upholding a Ten Commandments monument on government property in *Van Orden* and the other striking down such a monument in a Kentucky courthouse in *McCreary*. In his plurality opinion, Chief Justice Rehnquist noted that 21 historical markers and 17 monuments surrounded the Texas state capital, that the monument was placed there in 1961, and that even the challenger had walked by the monument for many years before filing a lawsuit. Chief Justice Rehnquist also noted the large number of government buildings in Washington, D.C., that contained religious displays or monuments. "We need only look within our own Courtroom," the chief justice wrote. "Since 1935, Moses has stood, holding two tablets that reveal portions of the Ten Commandments written in Hebrew, among other lawgivers in the south frieze."

In *McCreary*, Justice David Souter wrote the Court's plurality opinion, finding that the display in the courthouse violated the Establishment Clause. He noted that initially, the Ten Commandments plaque was placed by itself in the courthouse: "When the government initiates an effort to place this statement alone in public view, a religious object is unmistakable." The decisions seem to indicate that context, history, and the purpose behind the placing of the Ten Commandments are key factors. A look at the Court's decisions shows that eight justices ruled the same way in each case, with Justice Stephen Breyer providing the key fifth vote in both cases. It may well take more litigation to clarify the constitutionality of such displays.

What has the Rehnquist Court ruled on the issue of teaching evolution in public schools?

The Rehnquist Court has issued only one opinion on the divisive issue of the evolution–creationism debate. In *Edwards v. Aguil-*

lard (1987), the Court struck down a Louisiana law that required public school teachers to give "balanced time" to the teaching of evolution and creationism. Under Louisiana's Balanced Treatment for Creation-Science and Evolution-Science in Public School Instruction Act, if a science teacher taught about evolution, she would have to also give nearly equal time to discussing the creationism theory. A teacher could not teach just evolution. The state argued that the purpose of the law was to enhance academic freedom. The U.S. Supreme Court disagreed 7–2, writing that the "preeminent purpose of the Louisiana Legislature was clearly to advance the religious viewpoint that a supernatural being created humankind." The latest dispute in the evolution–creationism debate is the teaching of intelligent design: the theory that life's origins point to a designer or creator. Intelligent design is a more modern-day version of creationism. The teaching of intelligent design has led to a lawsuit in federal court in Pennsylvania. The U.S. Supreme Court has not had the opportunity to weigh in on the issue of intelligent design.

Did the U.S. Supreme Court strike down the Pledge of Allegiance in public schools?

No; the U.S. Supreme Court did not rule that the inclusion of the words "under God" amounted to a church–state violation. The Court did decide *Elk Grove Unified School District v. Newdow* (2004), which dealt with a claim by Dr. Michael Newdow that the Pledge of Allegiance was unconstitutional. A divided three-judge panel of the U.S. Court of Appeals for the Ninth Circuit had ruled that the Pledge was unconstitutional. The U.S. Supreme Court reversed its opinion, though it did not reach the underlying First Amendment issue. Instead, the Court decided that Michael Newdow did not have standing to file the lawsuit because he was not the primary custodial parent of his daughter. Though the Court did not reach the Establishment Clause issue, Justice Stevens's majority opinion seemed to cast doubt on Newdow's argument. For example, Justice Stevens referred to the Pledge as a "patriotic exercise designed to foster national unity" as opposed to a religious

After the Ninth Circuit found that mandatory participation in classroom Pledge of Allegiance recitation was unconstitutional, the Supreme Court weakly reversed the ruling on a point of procedure.

ceremony. It also seemed ironic to at least some Court observers that the Court issued the *Newdow* decision on June 14th: Flag Day.

What did the U.S. Supreme Court say with respect to Bible clubs in public schools?

The Court ruled in *Westside Community Board of Education v. Mergens* (1990) that an Omaha, Nebraska, public school district violated the Equal Access Act when it prohibited high school student Bridgette Mergens from forming a student Bible club. The school allowed other student clubs, such as a scuba diving club and a chess club, to meet at school during noninstructional time. The Court determined that under the 1984 federal Equal Access Act, schools cannot discriminate against student clubs based on their religious or philosophical viewpoints. The school board had argued that it prohibited giving official recognition to the student Bible club because it did not want to violate the Establishment Clause. The U.S. Supreme Court determined that the Equal Access Act did not violate the Establishment Clause. "We think that secondary school students are mature enough and are likely to understand that a school does not endorse or support student speech that it merely permits on a nondiscriminatory basis," the Court wrote.

Did the Rehnquist Court rule on the constitutionality of a school voucher program?

Yes; a narrow majority of the U.S. Supreme Court upheld a school voucher program in Cleveland, Ohio, in *Zelman v. Simmons-Harris* (2002). The case involved a program that provided tuition assistance to low-income parents. The vast majority of the participating schools in the program were private religious schools. In fact, a majority of the students in the program attended Catholic schools. A constitutional challenge was filed, contending that the state of Ohio violated the Establishment Clause by funding a program that gave substantial benefits to private religious schools. A federal district judge and a federal appeals court ruled that the voucher program violated the Establishment Clause, reasoning that the primary effect of the program was to benefit religion. However, the U.S. Supreme Court reversed its opinion, focusing on private choice and neutrality. Chief Justice Rehnquist wrote that the program was one of "true private choice." He added: "Program benefits are available to participating families on neutral terms, with no reference to religion. The only preference stated anywhere in the program is a preference for low-income families, who receive greater assistance and are given priority for admission at participating schools."

In what more recent decision did the U.S. Supreme Court uphold the display of a large Latin cross?

The U.S. Supreme Court upheld the display of a large Latin cross—a preeminent symbol of Christianity—in *American Legion*

The large cross marking the World War I memorial in Bladensburg, Maryland, was the focus of *American Legion v. American Humanist Association,* in which the Court decided 7-2 to let the monument stand due to its historical status.

v. American Humanist Association (2019). The display was erected in 1925 to honor the World War I veterans from Prince George's County, Maryland, who lost their lives in the conflict. The cross sat on a pedestal with the following message: "Dedicated to the heroes of Prince George's County, Maryland who lost their lives in the Great War for the liberty of the world."

The American Humanist Association filed suit in federal court, contending that the public display of the huge Latin cross—the preeminent symbol of Christianity—represented a stark violation of the Establishment Clause.

However, the U.S. Supreme Court ruled 7–2 that the cross did not violate the Establishment Clause. "Although the cross has long been a preeminent Christian symbol, its use in the Bladensburg memorial has a special significance," Justice Samuel A. Alito Jr. wrote for the majority. "After the First World War, the picture of row after row of plain white crosses marking the overseas graves of soldiers who had lost their lives in that horrible conflict was emblazoned on the minds of Americans at home, and the adoption of the cross as the Bladensburg memorial must be viewed in that historical context."

Justice Alito concluded:

> The cross is undoubtedly a Christian symbol, but that fact should not blind us to everything else that the Bladensburg Cross has come to represent. For some, that monument is a symbolic resting place for ancestors who never returned home. For others, it is a place for the community to gather and honor all veterans and their sacrifices for our Nation. For others still, it is a historical landmark. For many of these people, destroying or defacing the Cross that has stood undisturbed for nearly a century would not be neutral and would not further the ideals of respect and tolerance embodied in the First Amendment. For all these reasons, the Cross does not offend the Constitution.

What became of the Lemon Test?

It remains to be seen whether the Lemon Test will survive. In the *American Legion* case, several justices attacked it. In this decision, the U.S. Supreme Court criticized the Lemon Test significantly. In his majority opinion, Justice Alito explained why the test has little significance or use in religious display cases. He also noted that numerous justices and scholars have criticized the test. Justice Brett M. Kavanaugh, in his concurring opinion, said that the Lemon Test was no longer good for the law, writing: "And the court's decisions over the span of several decades demonstrate that the Lemon test is not good law and does not apply to Establishment Clause cases in any of the five categories."

Justice Neil M. Gorsuch also criticized the Lemon Test, calling it a "misadventure." Justice Gorsuch added that "[t]oday not a single member of the court even tries to defend Lemon against these criticisms—and they don't because they can't."

In *Kennedy v. Bremerton School District* (2022), the Court appeared to formally overrule Lemon. Justice Gorsuch, in his majority opinion, wrote that "this Court long ago abandoned Lemon and its endorsement test offshoot."

Criminal Justice

FOURTH AMENDMENT SEARCH AND SEIZURE LAW

When did the Court create the automobile exception to the Fourth Amendment?

The U.S. Supreme Court created the automobile exception in *Carroll v. United States* (1925). One of the key exceptions concerns automobiles. In fact, it is called the automobile exception. The idea behind the automobile exception is that due to the inherent mobility of automobiles, law-enforcement officials do not have sufficient time to obtain a warrant to search the contents of an automobile. The Court examined whether the police could stop a vehicle on the highway that officers reasonably believed was carrying illegal liquor. The Court upheld the warrantless stop and search of the vehicle because of what it identified as a "necessary difference" between searching "a store, dwelling house or other structure" and searching "a ship, motor boat, wagon or automobile." The difference, according to the Court, was that a "vehicle can be quickly moved out of the locality or jurisdiction in which the warrant must be sought."

When did the Court rule that the exclusionary rule applied to the states?

The Warren Court ruled in *Mapp v. Ohio* (1961) that the Fourth Amendment–based exclusionary rule—which holds that evidence illegally seized by law-enforcement officials must be excluded from trials—applies to the states through the 14th Amendment Due Process Clause. In 1949, the Court had ruled in *Wolf v. Colorado* that "in a prosecution in a State court for a State crime the Fourteenth Amendment does not forbid the admission of evidence obtained by an unreasonable search and seizure." The Court overruled that aspect of its *Wolf* decision 12 years later in *Mapp*.

Justice Tom C. Clark, a former prosecutor, wrote: "We hold that all evidence obtained by searches and seizures in violation of the Constitution is, by that same authority, inadmissible in a state court."

Who was the defendant in *Mapp v. Ohio*, and what other events brought her into the public eye?

The case of *Mapp v. Ohio* began when at least seven Cleveland police officers searched the home of Dollree Mapp looking for gambling paraphernalia. Instead, the officers found pornographic books, which they labeled obscene. Mapp was found not guilty of gambling charges but was convicted on the obscenity charges. The case eventually reached the U.S. Supreme Court, which reversed her conviction because the police officers failed to produce a search warrant before rummaging through Mapp's home.

Mapp was known in boxing circles. She used to be married to former top-ranked light-heavyweight and heavyweight boxer Jimmy Bivins. Then, in 1956, Mapp filed a $750,000 lawsuit against world light-heavyweight champion Archie Moore. She claimed that Moore broke a promise to marry her and physically assaulted her. Mapp then moved to Queens, New York. In 1970, police officers seized $250,000 in drugs and stolen property. Mapp was convicted and sentenced to a prison term of 20 years to life. Mapp claimed that the charges were stemming from a vendetta made against her after her famous case. In 1981, Governor Hugh Carey commuted Mapp's sentence. She had served more than nine years in a women's prison in New Bedford, New York.

When did the U.S. Supreme Court create the good-faith exception to the exclusionary rule?

The U.S. Supreme Court limited the exclusionary rule in its 1984 decision *U.S. v. Leon* by holding that the rule would not apply when a police officer acted in reasonably good faith on the validity of a search warrant. The good-faith exception provides that "evidence need not be suppressed when police obtain the evidence through objective good faith reliance on a facially valid warrant that later is found to lack probable cause." The Court did not eviscerate the exclusionary rule. *Leon* applied to search warrants, but not to all search warrants that were found to be lacking in probable cause. The Court noted several exceptions to the good-faith exception, including (1) where the magistrate issued the warrant based on a deliberately or recklessly false affidavit; (2) where the issuing magistrate failed to act in a neutral and detached manner; (3) where a warrant was based on an affidavit so lacking in indicia of probable cause as to render official belief in its existence entirely unreasonable; and (4) where a warrant was so facially deficient that the executing officers could not reasonably presume it to be valid.

What Warren Court decision became the leading search and seizure precedent dealing with privacy rights?

The U.S. Supreme Court established in *Katz v. United States* (1967) that the Fourth Amendment privacy protections applied to "people, not places." The case involved the wiretapping of a public phone booth to record the gambling phone calls of defendant Charles Katz. The Federal Bureau of Investigation (FBI) wiretapped the phone without obtaining a warrant. Katz contended that he had a right to privacy in his telephone calls. He alleged that government officials violated the Fourth Amendment because they did not seek a warrant backed by probable cause and had illegally wiretapped the phone. The government argued to the Court that Katz had no Fourth Amendment rights in the phone calls because he made such calls from a public phone. The Court agreed with Katz, finding that the government should have obtained a warrant based on probable cause from a magistrate before eavesdropping on the phone calls.

In Justice John Marshall Harlan II's concurring opinion in *Katz,* the most important question was whether a person had a "reasonable expectation of privacy," which became known as the *Katz* test.

What Fourth Amendment standard emerged from the Court's *Katz* decision?

The prevailing standard that still dominates the U.S. Supreme Court's current Fourth Amendment jurisprudence came from Justice John Marshall Harlan II's concurring opinion in *Katz*. Justice Harlan wrote that the important question was whether a person had a "reasonable expectation of privacy." He explained that this was a two-part test: first, that a person exhibited an actual (subjective) expectation of privacy, and second, that the expectation be one that society is prepared to recognize as reasonable.

DID YOU KNOW?

Justice Potter Stewart, in his majority opinion, explained: "For the Fourth Amendment protects people, not places. What a person knowingly exposes to the public, even in his own home or office, is not a subject of Fourth Amendment protection. But what he seeks to preserve as private, even in an area accessible to the public, may be constitutionally protected." Justice Stewart continued: "No less than an individual in a business office, in a friend's apartment, or in a taxicab, a person in a telephone booth may rely upon the protection of the Fourth Amendment. One who occupies it, shuts the door behind him, and pays the toll that permits him to place a call is surely entitled to assume that the words he utters into the mouthpiece will not be broadcast to the world."

How did the Warren Court increase the power of the police in street-level encounters?

The Warren Court strengthened the authority of the police by upholding the practice of "stop and frisk" in its 1968 deci-

sion *Terry v. Ohio*. The Court noted that the Fourth Amendment does not prohibit all searches and seizures but only "unreasonable searches and seizures." The Court reasoned that if a police officer reasonably believes that individuals pose a safety risk to the officer or to the general public, the officer may "conduct a carefully limited search of the outer clothing of such persons in an attempt to discover weapons which might be used to assault him."

What happened in this case?

In *Terry v. Ohio* (1968), Martin McFadden, a more than 30-year veteran of the Cleveland police department, observed two men repeatedly walking back and forth past a jewelry store and peering through the store's window. The two men then met a third man and conversed with him on the street. McFadden approached the men, including defendant John Terry, frisked them, and found a weapon. Terry argued that the officer lacked any individualized suspicion to pat him down. The U.S. Supreme Court disagreed, reasoning that if a police officer reasonably believes that individuals pose a safety risk to the officer or to the general public, the officer may "conduct a carefully limited search of the outer clothing of such persons in an attempt to discover weapons which might be used to assault him."

In applying this standard, the Court reasoned that Officer McFadden did not violate John Terry's Fourth Amendment rights.

"The scope of the search in this case presents no serious problem in light of these standards. Officer McFadden patted down the outer clothing of petitioner and his two companions," the Court wrote. "He did not place his hands in their pockets or under the outer surface of their garments until he had felt weapons, and then he merely reached for and removed the guns.... Officer McFadden confined his search strictly to what was minimally necessary to learn whether the men were armed and to disarm them once he discovered the weapons."

What single justice objected to the Court's decision in *Terry v. Ohio*?

Justice William O. Douglas filed the lone dissent in *Terry v. Ohio*. Justice Douglas believed that police should not be able to search and seize a person unless they had probable cause. He explained:

> To give the police greater power than a magistrate is to take a long step down the totalitarian path. Perhaps such a step is desirable to cope with modern forms of lawlessness. But if it is taken, it should be the deliberate choice of the people through a constitutional amendment. Until the Fourth Amendment, which is closely allied with the Fifth, is rewritten, the person and the effects of the individual are beyond the reach of all government agencies until there are reasonable grounds to believe (probable cause) that a criminal venture has been launched or about to be launched.

How did the Court protect Fourth Amendment interests in the context of the warrantless use of GPS technology?

The U.S. Supreme Court ruled in *United States v. Jones* (2012) that the use of enhanced technology could threaten privacy rights under the Fourth Amendment. Police had engaged in warrantless surveillance of an individual through the use of a Global Positioning System (GPS) tracking device that law-enforcement officials placed on the vehicle of Antoine Jones, a Washington, D.C., nightclub owner that they suspected of running a cocaine distribution ring. The government placed the device on Jones's car and monitored his movements for 28 days.

The U.S. Supreme Court unanimously ruled that this warrantless action violated the Fourth Amendment. Once again, Jus-

The Court's decision in *Riley v. California*, prompted by the warrantless search of a motorist's cell phone, strengthened the individual's right to privacy.

tice Antonin Scalia was at the forefront of protecting Fourth Amendment freedoms. "It is important to be clear about what occurred in this case," Justice Scalia wrote. "The government physically occupied private property for the purpose of obtaining information. We have no doubt that such a physical intrusion would have been considered a 'search' within the meaning of the Fourth Amendment when it was adopted."

How did the U.S. Supreme Court emphasize privacy protection for cell phone searches?

The U.S. Supreme Court protected digital privacy in the context of cell phones when it ruled in *Riley v. California* (2014) that generally, the police need a warrant before they can search through a person's cell phone. San Diego police had stopped a vehicle driven by Leon Riley and then later searched his cell phone without a warrant, trying to find information to connect him to a gang shooting. At that time, lower courts were divided on whether police needed a search warrant to search the cell phone of someone who was arrested. The theory used by law-enforcement officials was that a search incident leading to a lawful arrest applied to cell phones. Other lower courts held that the police needed a warrant in order to search cell phones.

In his majority opinion, Chief Justice John G. Roberts Jr. ruled that generally, police need a warrant. The Court emphasized the ubiquity of cell phones in modern life, writing that they are "such a pervasive and insistent part of daily life that the proverbial visitor from Mars might conclude they were an important feature of human anatomy." Chief Justice Roberts also emphasized how much private information people carry on their cell phones and noted that the term "cell phone" may be a misnomer; they "could just as easily be called cameras, video players, rolodexes, calendars, tape recorders, libraries, diaries, albums, televisions, maps, or newspapers."

The government argued that the search of the cell phone was justified under a concept known as search incident to a lawful arrest. Chief Justice Roberts disagreed with this argument, noting: "Digital data stored on a cell phone cannot itself be used as a weapon to harm an arresting officer or to effectuate the arrestee's escape. Law-enforcement officers remain free to examine the physical aspects of a phone to ensure that it will not be used as a weapon—say, to determine whether there is a razor blade hidden between the phone and its case. Once an officer has secured a phone and eliminated any potential physical threats, however, data on the phone can endanger no one."

FIFTH AMENDMENT PRIVILEGE AGAINST SELF-INCRIMINATION LAW

When did the U.S. Supreme Court establish so-called Miranda rights?

The U.S. Supreme Court ruled in four 1966 consolidated cases—*Miranda v. Arizona*, *Vignera v. New York*, *Westover v. United States*, and *California v. Stewart*—that law-enforcement officials could not use statements that were obtained from a police interrogation "unless it demonstrates the use of procedural safeguards effective to secure the privilege against self-incrimination." The Court held that police violate the Fifth Amendment if they do not inform a suspect prior to questioning that he or she (1) has a right to remain silent; (2) that any statement he or she makes can be used against them in a court of law; (3) that he or she has the right to have an attorney present during questioning; and (4) that if he or she cannot afford an attorney, one will be provided to them. If law-enforcement officials fail to provide these procedural safeguards, the Court can say that evidence obtained during such interrogations cannot be used against the suspect.

Who was Miranda?

Ernesto A. Miranda was a criminal defendant convicted of rape who challenged his conviction in a U.S. Supreme Court case that bears his name. Miranda was arrested on suspicion of robbery. During a two-hour interrogation at a Phoenix police station, Miranda not only confessed to the robbery but also to sexually assaulting and raping a woman 11 days earlier. The police officers never informed Miranda that he had a right to have a lawyer present during questioning. A jury convicted Miranda of kidnapping and rape and sentenced him to 20–30 years for each offense. Miranda's lawyers argued that their client's Fifth Amendment right against self-incrimination was violated by the coercive interrogation. In *Miranda v. Arizona* (1966), the U.S. Supreme Court agreed.

Law enforcement officials must inform suspects of their Fifth Amendment rights, as outlined in the Supreme Court's ruling in *Miranda v. Arizona*.

What happened to Miranda after the U.S. Supreme Court decision?

Prosecutors retried Miranda without the evidence obtained from his confession. The prosecution presented the testimony of Miranda's common-law wife, who testified that during a prison visit, Miranda confessed to her that he had raped the victim. A jury convicted him again on charges of kidnapping and rape in 1966. Miranda was paroled in 1972. However, in 1976, Miranda was stabbed to death in a bar fight.

How did the U.S. Supreme Court limit the Warren Court's *Miranda* decision?

The U.S. Supreme Court, in the Burger Court era, never overruled *Miranda*, but it created exceptions to it in several decisions. In *Harris v. New York* (1971), the Court ruled that prosecutors can impeach defendants at trial with statements they previously made without receiving their Miranda warnings. The Court ruled that *Miranda* should not be read as sanctioning perjury. In *Quarles v. New York* (1984), the Court created a public-safety exception to *Miranda* in cases when police officers do not have time to deliver Miranda warnings. Then, in *Oregon v. Elstad* (1985), the Court ruled that an initial failure to deliver Miranda warnings does not prevent the use of confessions and admissions made after Miranda warnings have been given.

Why was *Miranda* considered so controversial at the time?

Miranda was considered controversial by many who felt that the Court was legislating from the bench. In other words, they argued that the Court should not be dictating what statements the police should make to suspects and that such policy should be determined by the legislative branch of government.

However, others defended the ruling, including U.S. attorney general Ramsey Clark in his book *Crime in America: Observations on Its Nature, Causes, Prevention and Control.* Clark wrote: "All Miranda means is that we must not take advantage of the poor, the ignorant and the distracted—that government will be fair and has self-confidence. Are the rights of the poor and uneducated so unimportant that they are not to be accorded what others cannot be denied?"

Similarly, attorney Al Knight, in his book *The Life of the Law*, explains the importance of the Fifth Amendment. He writes that "[d]espite the scorn that has been heaped upon it, the privilege against self-incrimination seems neither irrational nor silly when viewed objectively. Its essence is a citizen, arms folded, confronting the state and saying, 'Prove it.'"

Can a criminal defendant or former criminal defendant sue for a Miranda violation?

No, the U.S. Supreme Court ruled in *Vega v. Tekoh* (2022) that a person may not sue a police officer for the improper admission of an "un-Mirandized" statement in a criminal prosecution. The case involved the interrogation of Terence Tekoh by Los Angeles County Sheriff's deputy Carlos Vega.

In March 2014, Tekoh was working as a certified nursing assistant at a Los Angeles medical center. A female patient accused Tekoh of sexually assaulting her. Vega questioned Tekoh in the hospital. Vega did not read Tekoh his Miranda warnings. At some point during the questioning, Tekoh provided a written statement apologizing for inappropriately touching a patient's genitals.

Tekoh was arrested and charged with unlawful sexual penetration. His case proceeded to trial, and his first trial resulted in a mistrial. Prosecutors re-tried Tekoh. During the trial, Tekoh's attorneys sought to exclude the statement in which he allegedly confessed. The judge denied that request. However, a jury found Tekoh not guilty.

DID YOU KNOW?

How did Chief Justice William H. Rehnquist end up supporting *Miranda*?

In the landmark *Miranda v. Arizona* (1966) decision, the Warren Court ruled inadmissible a confession by a suspect because he had not been given warnings about his constitutional rights despite being under arrest. These came to be known as Miranda rights. Chief Justice Rehnquist had criticized the *Miranda* decision while being a member of the Burger Court. For this reason, many assumed that when Rehnquist announced that he had written the decision in *Dickerson v. U.S.* for the Court in 2000, the Court would overrule *Miranda*. To the surprise of many, he refused to overrule *Miranda*, writing that "*Miranda* has become embedded in routine police practice to the point where the warnings have become part of our national culture."

Tekoh then sued Vega and other government officials for alleged violations of his constitutional rights, including his right to be free from self-incrimination. Tekoh alleged that the Miranda violation committed by Vega was a cognizable claim under 42 U.S.C. Section 1983, the federal law that serves as the vehicle for the assertion of constitutional claims.

Tekoh argued that a violation of Miranda constitutes a violation of the Fifth Amendment right against compelled self-incrimination. The U.S. Supreme Court disagreed by a vote of 6–3. In his majority opinion, Justice Samuel Alito reasoned that "Miranda did not hold that a violation of the rules it established necessarily constitutes a Fifth Amendment violation."

Alito continued: "Allowing the victim of a Miranda violation to sue a police officer for damages under Section 1983 would have little additional deterrent value and permitting such claims would cause many problems."

Justice Elena Kagan—joined by Justices Stephen Breyer and Sonia Sotomayor—dissented. She explained that Miranda is a constitutional rule that gives suspects like Terence Tekoh rights. These rights include the right to sue for a constitutional violation under Section 1983. She wrote: "Today, the Court strips individuals of the ability to seek a remedy for violations of the right recognized in Miranda."

SIXTH AMENDMENT RIGHT TO A SPEEDY TRIAL LAW

How did the U.S. Supreme Court determine whether a defendant's Sixth Amendment right to a speedy trial was violated?

The Court addressed the speedy-trial right at length in a case involving the delayed murder prosecution of Kentucky inmate Willie Barker in the case *Barker v. Wingo* (1972). The Court identified several factors that were important to determining whether a violation of the right to a speedy trial occurred. These factors were (1) length of the delay; (2) reason for the delay; (3) whether the defendant asserted his or her speedy-trial rights; and (4) prejudice to the defendant.

The Court explained that the length of the delay was "the triggering mechanism" in that if a significant delay does not occur, then it is unnecessary to address the other factors. If a significant delay occurs, then a reviewing court has to balance the other factors. The next factor is the government's reason for the delay. In other words, did a legitimate reason for the delay exist, or was the prosecution playing games or engaging in some improper motive in delaying the matter? The third factor also is important: whether the defendant asserted his or her speedy-trial rights. The Court noted that "failure to assert the right will make it difficult for a defendant to prove that he was denied a

Justice Lewis Franklin Powell Jr. wrote the majority opinion in *Barker v. Wingo* that helped define a defendant's right to a speedy trial.

speedy trial." Finally, the fourth factor, prejudice, is perhaps the most important factor. The Court identified three concerns regarding a long delay: (1) to prevent oppressive pretrial incarceration; (2) to minimize the anxiety and concern of the accused; and (3) to limit the possibility that the defense will be impaired. The last concern is the most significant, as a defendant could be prejudiced by a long delay: his witnesses may have been lost, have died, or have lost recall of significant events. In other words, a long delay could impair a defendant's right to an effective defense.

SIXTH AMENDMENT RIGHT TO COUNSEL LAW

How did the Warren Court expand the right to counsel in criminal cases?

The Warren Court expanded the right to counsel by ruling that criminal defendants charged with felonies in state courts do

have a fundamental right to an attorney even if they cannot afford one. The Sixth Amendment provides that "in all criminal prosecutions, the accused shall enjoy the right ... to have the Assistance of Counsel for his defence." In *Johnson v. Zerbst* (1938), the U.S. Supreme Court ruled that indigent criminal defendants charged with crimes in federal court have the right to counsel. However, the Sixth Amendment applied only to the federal government, meaning that only those charged with federal crimes were entitled to legal representation. The legal question was whether the Sixth Amendment right to counsel should be extended to the states through the 14th Amendment's Due Process Clause, which provides that states shall not deprive individuals of "life, liberty or property without due process of law." In 1942, the U.S. Supreme Court answered "no" in *Betts v. Brady*, writing that the "appointment of counsel is not a fundamental right, essential to a fair trial." This meant that criminal defendants who were not charged with capital (death penalty) crimes did not have a constitutional right to the appointment of counsel. The Warren Court changed all of this in its 1963 decision *Gideon v. Wainwright*.

What did the Court rule in *Gideon v. Wainwright*?

The story of *Gideon v. Wainwright* began when prosecutors in Florida charged Clarence Earl Gideon with breaking into the Bay Harbor Poolroom in Panama City, Florida. Gideon was not a man who was likely to change the legal system. He had spent time in prison for four different felonies. Gideon asked the state court judge to appoint him counsel, saying: "The United States Supreme Court says I am entitled to be represented by Counsel." The trial judge denied his request. Gideon appealed all the way to the U.S. Supreme Court. The U.S. Supreme Court accepted his case and appointed Washington, D.C., attorney Abe Fortas to argue the case for Gideon before the High Court. (Fortas later became a justice on the U.S. Supreme Court.) The U.S. Supreme Court overruled *Betts v. Brady* and determined that state criminal

Quotable: Justice Hugo Black in *Gideon v. Wainwright* (1963)

"That government hires lawyers to prosecute and defendants who have the money hire lawyers to defend are the strongest indications of the widespread belief that lawyers in criminal cases are necessities, not luxuries. The right of one charged with crime to counsel may not be deemed fundamental and essential to fair trials in some countries, but it is in ours. From the very beginning, our state and national constitutions and laws have laid great emphasis on procedural and substantive safeguards designed to assure fair trials before impartial tribunals in which every defendant stands equal before the law. This noble idea cannot be realized if the poor man charged with crime has to face his accusers without a lawyer to assist him."

defendants who were charged with felonies have a constitutional right to the assistance of counsel.

Writing for the Court, Justice Hugo Black wrote that "in our adversary system of criminal justice, any person hauled into court, who is too poor to hire a lawyer, cannot be assured a fair trial unless counsel is provided to him." The Court reversed Gideon's conviction. This meant that the state would have to appoint Gideon counsel if it sought to prosecute him again.

Author Anthony Lewis, in his book *Gideon's Trumpet*, famously wrote of the Court's decision: "The case of *Gideon v. Wainwright* is in part a testament to a single human being. Against all the odds of inertia and ignorance and fear of state power, Clarence Earl Gideon insisted that he had a right to a lawyer and kept on insisting all the way to the Supreme Court of the United States. His triumph there shows that the poorest and least powerful of men—a convict with not even a friend to visit him in prison—can take his cause to the highest court in the land and bring about a fundamental change in the law."

What happened to Clarence Earl Gideon after the U.S. Supreme Court's decision?

The U.S. Supreme Court's decision meant that Gideon would be retried again, this time with the benefit of counsel. Lawyer Abe Fortas told Gideon that he would be better off with local (Florida) counsel. He recommended that Gideon write to the ACLU of Florida, asking for the assistance of counsel. The ACLU sent two lawyers to meet with Gideon. However, much to their (and the Court's) surprise, Gideon did not want to be represented by these lawyers. Local Panama City attorney Fred Turner was appointed to represent Gideon. Turner effectively cross-examined one of the state's chief witnesses during the second trial. The jury voted "not guilty," and Gideon was freed after serving two years in prison. He died in 1972.

What were the ironies in the *Gideon v. Wainwright* case?

Several ironies in the *Gideon v. Wainwright* case occurred. One dealt with Justice Black. In 1942, Justice Black had dissented

Abe Fortas, the lawyer who represented Gideon before the U.S. Supreme Court in 1963, was appointed an Associate Justice of the Supreme Court in 1965 by President Lyndon Johnson.

in *Betts v. Brady* when the Court had ruled that the Constitution did not afford state criminal defendants the benefit of counsel in noncapital cases. The irony was that Justice Black wrote the Court's decision in *Gideon v. Wainwright*, overruling the *Betts* decision. Anthony Lewis writes in his book *Gideon's Trumpet* that Justice Black told a friend after the ruling: "When *Betts v. Brady* was decided, I never thought I'd live to see it overruled." Another irony was that the lawyer who represented Gideon before the U.S. Supreme Court was none other than Abe Fortas. Fortas became a U.S. Supreme Court justice in 1965. Still another irony related to Gideon's attorney in his second trial, Fred Turner. During that trial, Turner effectively cross-examined the state's witness, Henry Cook. Turner performed well during his examination, probably in part because he twice previously had represented Cook in a divorce and in beating a man out of $1.98 at none other than the Bay Harbor Poolroom.

What did the U.S. Supreme Court say about ineffective assistance of counsel?

The U.S. Supreme Court explained that an individual has a Sixth Amendment right to counsel; this means that the person should receive the reasonably effective assistance of counsel. Many times, inmates argue in what are called state post-conviction proceedings, or federal habeas corpus actions, that they should be entitled to a new trial because their attorney failed to provide the effective assistance of counsel. In essence, the defendant is arguing that they received the ineffective assistance of counsel.

The U.S. Supreme Court's leading standard in ineffective assistance of counsel claims comes from the Court's decision in *Strickland v. Washington* (1984). Under this standard, an inmate must show two things: (1) that his attorney's performance was deficient and (2) that the attorney's deficient performance rises to the level of prejudice. These are known as the deficiency and prejudice prongs.

In what decision did the Court find ineffective assistance of counsel for failing to inform a defendant about immigration-related consequences of pleading guilty?

The U.S. Supreme Court ruled in *Padilla v. Kentucky* (2010) that criminal defense attorneys can commit ineffective assistance of counsel by failing to advise noncitizen clients of deportation risks. Professor Juliet Stumpt coined the phrase "crimimigration" to discuss the melding or intersection between criminal and immigration law.

Padilla v. Kentucky involved the case of Jose Padilla, a native of Honduras who was a lawful permanent resident—but not a citizen—of the United States. Though he lived in the United States for decades and even served in Vietnam, he faced deportation after pleading guilty to drug charges. He pled guilty because his attorney told him that he would not face deportation if he pled guilty. Unfortunately, his attorney gave him bad legal advice, and deportation was automatic for such drug offenses.

Padilla filed a claim for ineffective assistance of counsel. Lower courts rejected Padilla's claim, but the U.S. Supreme Court reversed their decision. The Court reasoned that criminal defense attorneys must inform their noncitizen clients about deportation risks associated with a conviction or guilty plea.

Padilla eventually became a U.S. citizen in March 2019.

How does the Court determine whether a double-jeopardy violation has occurred?

The Court created a test to determine whether a double-jeopardy problem has occurred in *Blockburger v. United States* (1932).

Under the Blockburger test, the first question is whether the different charges arise out of the same act or transaction. If so, then the next question is whether each law has a distinct element that is not found in the other law. If the charges arise out of the same act and a distinct element in one law is not found in the other, then a double-jeopardy problem has occurred.

For example, the Court found a double-jeopardy problem in *Brown v. Ohio* (1977). The case involved a defendant who had stolen a car in East Cleveland, Ohio; nine days later, he was caught in Wickliffe, Ohio. He pled guilty to joyriding in Wickliffe, but then, later prosecutors charged him with both auto theft and joyriding in East Cleveland. The Court found that joyriding was a lesser included offense of auto theft under Ohio law, and thus, prosecutors could not charge him again with either joyriding or auto theft because the defendant already had pled guilty to joyriding in another Ohio county.

To the Court, joyriding and auto theft were "the same statutory offense," and thus, prosecutors could not add on successive and cumulative punishments for conduct to which the defendant already had pled guilty. Thus, a double-jeopardy problem had occurred.

What did the Court decide with respect to the criminal three-strikes law?

The U.S. Supreme Court upheld California's Career Criminal Punishment Act (also known as the "three-strikes law") sentencing law in *Ewing v. California* (2003) and *Lockyer v. Andrade* (2003). Under the California law, if a criminal defendant is convicted of at least three felonies, he is subject to the three-strikes law, which carries a penalty of 25 years to life.

The cases involved Gary Ewing, who stole three golf clubs, and Leandro Andrade, who stole $150 worth of videotapes. However, both defendants had multiple criminal convictions in their past, including burglaries, that made them eligible as recidivist of-

When Gary Ewing stole three golf clubs from a pro shop in Southern California, the state examined his criminal career and locked him up for life under the three-strikes law. The Supreme Court upheld the sentence in *Ewing v. California.*

fenders under the state law. They challenged their sentences and the three-strikes law as a violation of the Eighth Amendment's cruel and unusual punishment clause.

The Court rejected the argument that the defendants' sentences violated the Eighth Amendment's prohibition against cruel and unusual punishment. "The gross disproportionality principle reserves a constitutional violation for only the extraordinary case," Justice Sandra Day O'Connor wrote for the Court in *Andrade*. In her *Ewing* opinion, Justice O'Connor explained that states have the right to pass laws protecting the public from career criminals: "When the California Legislature enacted the three strikes law, it made a judgment that protecting the public safety requires incapacitating criminals who have already been convicted of at least one serious or violent crime. Nothing in the Eighth Amendment prohibits California from making that choice." She also cited statistics showing that a disturbing number of inmates committed repeat offenses upon release from incarceration.

Has the U.S. Supreme Court addressed constitutional issues related to sexual predators?

Yes; the Court has addressed many legal issues related to sexual predators. In its 1994 decision *Kansas v. Hendricks*, the Court

upheld the constitutionality of Kansas's Sexually Violent Predator Act. This law allowed the state to initiate civil commitment proceedings for sexual predators who suffer from a mental abnormality or personality disorder that makes them likely to commit other acts of sexual violence. The state sought to commit offender Leroy Hendricks, a career child abuser who admitted that he couldn't control his urges, under this law. Hendricks, who had nearly completed a long sentence for sexually offending two youths, contended that the law violated his due-process rights and amounted to double jeopardy by punishing him for the same act twice. The Court rejected those constitutional challenges. It reasoned that the civil commitment proceedings didn't violate double jeopardy because the statute was a civil law, not a criminal one, with the primary goal of punishment. "If detention for the purpose of protecting the community from harm necessarily constituted punishment, then all involuntary civil commitments would have to be considered punishment," the Court wrote. "But we have never so held." The Court also noted that Hendricks was placed under the supervision of the state department of health and social and rehabilitative services, which was segregated from the general prison population and not manned by employees of the department of correction.

Eight years later, the U.S. Supreme Court addressed the very same Kansas law in *Crane v. Kansas* (2002). This case required the Court to address whether a sexual predator could be civilly confined under the state sexual predator law if the state did not prove that the sexual offender had some difficulty in controlling his behavior. The Court ruled that the Constitution required the state of Kansas to prove that the sexual offender has "serious difficulty" controlling his behavior before seeking civil commitment proceedings under the sexual predator law. Otherwise, according to the Court, the civil law could be used as "a mechanism for retribution or general deterrence." In another case—*Seling v. Young* (2001)—the U.S. Supreme Court upheld Washington's Community Protection Act of 1990, another law that provided for the civil confinement of certain sexual predators.

The Court also addressed another type of law—called Megan's Law—that informs the public about the location of sex offenders living in the community. The Court upheld Alaska's Sex

Offender Registration Act in its 2003 decision *Smith v. Doe*. The Alaska law requires former sex offenders to register with the state. The law provides notification to the community about these sex offenders through a publicly accessible database on the internet. Two former sex offenders, who already served their prison terms before the law was passed, challenged the law on ex post facto and due-process grounds.

These former offenders argued that the law violates the Ex Post Facto Clause because it imposes additional punishment on them for conduct that occurred before the passage of the law. The state countered that the law does not violate the clause because it is not intended to punish offenders but to protect and inform the public. The Court sided with the state, finding that fundamentally, the law was civil rather than criminal.

The Court refused to rule otherwise even though the offenders' information was disseminated on the internet. "It must be acknowledged that notice of a criminal conviction subjects the offender to public shame, the humiliation increasing in proportion to the extent of the publicity," the Court wrote. "And the geographic reach of the Internet is greater than anything which could have been designed in colonial times. These facts do not render Internet notification punitive. The purpose and the principal effect of notification are to inform the public for its own safety, not to humiliate the offender."

Megan's Law provides for the collection of data on the location of sex offenders and makes it available to the public through a database on the internet.

The Court also upheld Connecticut's Megan's Law from constitutional attack in its 2003 decision *Connecticut Department of Public Safety v. Doe*, reasoning that Connecticut had the right to disseminate information on all sex offenders to the public, even particular sex offenders who posed no threat to the community.

THE DEATH PENALTY

When did the U.S. Supreme Court invalidate the death penalty?

The U.S. Supreme Court ruled 5–4 in *Furman v. Georgia* (1972) that capital punishment was unconstitutional. The five justices in the majority joined in a one-paragraph, per curiam opinion and then each wrote separately. In fact, all nine justices wrote separately, making the decision one of the longest in U.S. Supreme Court history. The *Furman* decision effectively ended capital punishment in America for more than four years.

The opinion stated: "The Court holds that the imposition and carrying out of the death penalty in these cases constitute cruel and unusual punishment in violation of the Eighth and Fourteenth Amendments." Justice Douglas, Justice William J. Brennan Jr., and Justice Thurgood Marshall broadly attacked the death penalty. Justice Douglas wrote that the states' death penalty laws were "pregnant with discrimination." Justice Brennan and Justice Marshall reasoned that capital punishment inherently constituted cruel and unusual punishment. Justice Brennan wrote that the death penalty was "condemned as fatally offensive to human dignity," while Justice Marshall said it was "morally unacceptable."

Justice Stewart and Justice Byron White wrote narrower opinions, focusing on the fact that the state laws in question did not provide sufficient guidance to jurors in capital sentencing in order to determine who should live and who should die. Justice Stewart captured this sentiment in oft-quoted language: "These death sentences are cruel and unusual in the same way that being struck by lighting is cruel and unusual."

Among the majority-opinion justices were these quotes:

Justice William O. Douglas: "Thus, these discretionary statutes are unconstitutional in their operation. They are pregnant with discrimination and discrimination is an ingredient not compatible with the idea of equal protection of the laws that is implicit in the ban on 'cruel and unusual' punishments."

Justice William J. Brennan Jr.: "Death is truly an awesome punishment. The calculated killing of a human being by the State involves, by its very nature, a denial of the executed person's humanity."

Justice Potter Stewart: "These death sentences are cruel and unusual in the same way that being struck by lightning is cruel and unusual."

Justice Byron White: "That conclusion, as I have said, is that the death penalty is exacted with great infrequency even for the most atrocious crimes and that there is no meaningful basis for distinguishing the few cases in which it is imposed from the many cases in which it is not."

Justice Thurgood Marshall: "There is but one conclusion that can be drawn from all of this—i.e., the death penalty is an excessive and unnecessary punishment that violates the Eighth Amendment. The statistical evidence is not convincing beyond all doubt, but it is persuasive.... In addition, even if capital punishment is not excessive, it nonetheless violates the Eighth Amendment because it is morally unacceptable to the people of the United States at this time in their history."

Dissenters made these remarks:

Chief Justice Warren E. Burger: "In the 181 years since the enactment of the Eighth Amendment, not a single decision of this Court has cast the slightest shadow of a doubt on the constitutionality of capital punishment. In rejecting Eighth Amendment attacks on particular modes of execution, the Court has more than once implicitly denied that capital punishment is impermissibly 'cruel' in the constitutional sense."

Justice Harry Blackmun: "Athough personally I may rejoice at the Court's result, I find it difficult to accept or to justify as a matter of history, of law, or of constitutional pronouncement. I fear the Court has overstepped. It has sought and has achieved an end."

Justice Lewis F. Powell Jr.: "In terms of the constitutional role of this Court, the impact of the majority's ruling is all the greater because the decision encroaches upon an area squarely within the historic prerogative of the legislative branch—both state and federal—to protect the citizenry through the designation of penalties for prohibitable conduct. It is the very sort of judgment that the legislative branch is competent to make and for which the judiciary is ill-equipped."

Justice William H. Rehnquist: "The task of judging constitutional cases imposed by Art. III cannot for this reason be avoided, but it must surely be approached with the deepest humility and genuine deference to legislative judgment. Today's decision to invalidate capital punishment is, I respectfully submit, significantly lacking in those attributes."

How did the Court change their opinion on the death penalty four years after *Furman v. Georgia*?

In *Gregg v. Georgia* (1976), the Burger Court changed course by upholding 7–2 Georgia's new capital punishment statute. Georgia's new law, according to the Court, focused the jury's attention on the "particularized nature of the crime" and the "particularized characteristics of the individual defendant." Since

DID YOU KNOW?

When did the U.S. Supreme Court rule the death penalty as constitutional again?

The *Furman* decision caused many states to pass new death penalty statutes that would provide more guidance to jurors on whether a defendant should be sentenced to death. Georgia's new statute required jurors to focus on aggravating and mitigating factors that were associated with the capital crime. In 1976, the U.S. Supreme Court ruled 7–2 that this Georgia law was constitutional in *Gregg v. Georgia*. Because it focused on these aggravating and mitigating factors, Justice Stewart wrote: "No longer can a jury wantonly and freakishly impose the death sentence; it is always circumscribed by the legislative guidelines." Justice Stewart wrote that the new statute focused the jury on "the particularized nature of the crime and the particularized characteristics of the individual defendant." Since *Gregg*, the U.S. Supreme Court has never ruled that the death penalty is, per se, unconstitutional. Only Justice Brennan and Justice Thurgood Marshall dissented.

Gregg, the majority of states have implemented the death penalty, and a majority of U.S. Supreme Court justices have ruled that the death penalty, per se, is constitutional.

In what decision did the U.S. Supreme Court rule that death by electrocution was not cruel and unusual punishment?

The Court ruled unanimously in *In Re Kemmler* (1890) that the state of New York could execute convicted murderer William Kemmler by a relatively new method of execution called electrocution. "Electrocution" comes from the combination of the two words "execution" and "electricity." Attorneys for Kemmler argued that the punishment violated the Eighth Amendment because this punishment certainly was unusual. However, the Court noted that while the punishment could be classified as unusual because it was so new, it was not cruel.

The Court explained that the New York legislature had the authority to pass a law authorizing this new form of execution, writing: "The enactment of this statute was, in itself, within the legitimate sphere of the legislative power of the state, and in the observance of those general rules prescribed by our systems of jurisprudence; and the legislature of the state of New York determined that it did not inflict cruel and unusual punishment."

In what decision did the U.S. Supreme Court invalidate the death sentence in the 1920s because of a moblike atmosphere during the trial?

The U.S. Supreme Court ruled 7–2 in *Moore v. Dempsey* (1923) that five African American men had the right to a new hear-

The Supreme Court ruled in William Kemmler's case that death by the then-new electric chair would not be "cruel and unusual punishment." Witness accounts of Kemmler's clumsy and gruesome execution would suggest otherwise.

ing in federal court regarding whether their constitutional rights were violated as a result of a sham trial in Arkansas state court. The underlying incident arose in 1919 in Philips County, Arkansas, after a white sheriff's deputy fired upon a group of black cotton farmers who were meeting to discuss ways to organize and better their shabby economic position. After the white sheriff's deputy was killed, an outraged white community formed a mob and killed more than 200 blacks. Law-enforcement officials also arrested 12 black men, including Frank Moore, and charged them with murder.

In the proceeding, the men were tried without the benefit of adequate counsel in 45 minutes. Their lawyer did not call any witnesses on their behalf, and an all-white jury convicted them after only five minutes of deliberation. After losing in state court and the lower federal courts, the defendants—with backing from the National Association for the Advancement of Colored People (NAACP)—appealed to the U.S. Supreme Court. The High Court sent the case back to the federal district court with instructions to allow the men to present their constitutional claims. Justice Oliver Wendell Holmes Jr. wrote: "But if the case is that the whole proceeding is a mask—that counsel, jury, and judge were swept to the fatal end by an irresistible wave of public passion, and that the State Courts failed to correct the wrong, neither perfection in the machinery for correction nor the possibly that the trial court and counsel saw no other way can prevent this Court from securing to the petitioners their constitutional rights."

Justice James Clark McReynolds and Justice George Sutherland dissented, finding that the U.S. Supreme Court should not overrule the judgment of state courts: "The delays incident to enforcement of our criminal laws have become a national scandal and give serious alarm to those who observe."

What death penalty defendants were the Scottsboro Boys?

The Scottsboro Boys were a group of nine African American youths who were wrongfully charged and later convicted of raping

two white women in 1931 on a train traveling from Tennessee to Alabama. The youths were immediately arraigned and tried without adequate legal counsel after only six days. The defendants were not provided with an attorney until the morning of the trial. Nearly all of the defendants were convicted immediately, and another had a hung jury after most of the jurors held out for the death penalty when the prosecution had only sought a term of life imprisonment.

The U.S. Supreme Court ruled in *Powell v. Alabama* (1932) that the conviction of several of the Scottsboro Boys, including Ozzie Powell, was invalid because they had been deprived of due process. The Court ruled 7–2 that the defendants' due-process rights were invalidated because the Court failed to provide them with the meaningful assistance of counsel in their own defense. Defendants facing capital crimes have a constitutional right to an attorney, the majority wrote.

After the convictions were invalidated, the state filed rape charges against most of the defendants again. Clarence Norris, another of the Scottsboro Boys, challenged his second conviction on appeal because the state failed to allow blacks to serve on juries. The evidence established that in Jackson County, Alabama, no

The nine defendants of the Scottsboro Boys case—shown here with Juanita Jackson Mitchell (the first African American woman to practice law in Maryland) and another woman—would appeal their convictions all the way to the Supreme Court. Along the way, their cases highlighted glaring failures of the justice system, and most avoided prison terms.

black had ever served on any grand or petit (trial) jury. "That testimony in itself made out a prima facie case of the denial of the equal protection which the Constitution guarantees," Chief Justice Charles Evans Hughes wrote for the Court in *Norris v. Alabama* (1937). The Court ruled 8–0 in favor of Norris.

Who were the nine Scottsboro Boys?

The nine Scottsboro Boys were Olen Montgomery, Clarence Norris, Haywood Patterson, Ozzie Powell, Willie Roberson, Charley Weems, Eugene Williams, Andy Wright, and Roy Wright.

What happened to the Scottsboro Boys after these ordeals?

The Scottsboro Boys went to prison, though they were all eventually released. Andy Wright stayed in prison the longest, until 1950. Roy Wright, the youngest of the nine, shot his wife and then killed himself in 1959. But the other defendants managed to overcome their hardships and unfairness to lead productive lives. Clarence Norris, who later coauthored a book titled *The Last of the Scottsboro Boys*, lived until the age of 76. He received a pardon from Alabama governor George Wallace in 1976.

In what decision did the Court reverse the death penalty convictions of African American men in Florida because of illegally forced confessions?

The U.S. Supreme Court unanimously reversed the death penalty convictions of several African American men in Broward County, Florida, in *Chambers v. Florida* (1940). Law-enforcement officials, upset over the robbery and murder of an elderly white man, began a pattern of rounding up and questioning the African American men in the county over a period of several hours. Four men, after a week of repeatedly denying the crime, finally confessed after hours and hours of all-night interrogation.

Writing for the Court, Justice Black explained: "To permit human lives to be forfeited upon confessions thus obtained would make of the constitutional requirement of due process of law a meaningless symbol."

When did the U.S. Supreme Court rule that it was unconstitutional to execute the criminally insane?

The Court first determined that it would be a violation of the Eighth Amendment and the concept of the "evolving standards of decency" to execute an inmate who truly was insane in *Ford v. Wainwright* (1986). The case involved a defendant named Alvin Bernard Ford who, when he was convicted of murder in 1984, did not exhibit signs of insanity. However, in later years on death row, Mr. Ford's mental condition deteriorated significantly. He referred to himself as the Pope, began speaking in code, and became obsessed with a delusion that the Klan and numerous guards were conspiring against him.

His attorneys had Ford evaluated by a psychiatrist who determined that Ford suffered from paranoid schizophrenia and delusional thinking. Florida law at the time required the Florida governor to appoint three psychological experts to evaluate the inmate in order to determine the sanity of the inmate.

The three state experts all evaluated Ford and deemed him competent. However, their examinations were relatively cursory. Ford's attorneys managed to obtain an evidentiary hearing in order to determine Ford's sanity. A federal district court ruled against Ford, but a federal appeals court reversed the decision.

On further appeal, the U.S. Supreme Court unanimously ruled that the state of Florida could not execute Ford because it violated the Eighth Amendment to execute the insane. Writing for the Court, Justice Thurgood Marshall noted that a long-standing history in English common law existed against executing the insane.

Justice Marshall also noted that the Florida law in this case that provided for the appointment of three medical experts was problematic. First, the law did not allow any cross-examination of the three experts. Even worse, the Florida statute allowed the state governor to appoint his own experts instead of individuals who might be more naturally impartial. In sum, the Florida law did not provide enough safeguards to ensure that the evaluation of the inmate would be an accurate fact-finding mission.

Instead, the Court reasoned that the statute was deficient, writing: "Rather, consistent with the heightened concern for fairness and accuracy that has characterized our review of the process requisite to the taking of a human life, we believe that any procedure that precludes the prisoner or his counsel from presenting material relevant to his sanity or bars consideration of that material by the factfinder is necessarily inadequate."

Justice Marshall also emphasized that it offended humanity to execute an inmate who was insane. "Similarly, the natural abhorrence civilized societies feel at killing one who has no capacity to come to grips with his own conscience or deity is still vivid today," he wrote. "And the intuition that such an execution simply offends humanity is evidently shared across this Nation. Faced with such widespread evidence of a restriction upon sovereign power, this Court is compelled to conclude that the Eighth Amendment prohibits a State from carrying out a sentence of death upon a prisoner who is insane."

How has the U.S. Supreme Court dealt with intellectually disabled death penalty defendants?

In 1989, the Court ruled in *Penry v. Lynaugh* (1989) that it did not violate the Eighth Amendment to execute an inmate who was

Associate Justice John Paul Stevens, who authored the majority opinion in *Atkins v. Virginia,* was appointed by President Gerald Ford in 1975 and served until his retirement in 2010.

mentally retarded. This decision paved the way for the state of Texas to execute Johnny Paul Penry even though he had a very low IQ. Fortunately for Penry, a further appeal led to another decision by the Court, *Penry v. Johnson* (2001), which held that the trial court's instructions on mitigating evidence was inadequate. Later, in 2008, Penry agreed to a plea bargain that gave him three life sentences without parole.

But the Court's earlier decision still allowed for the execution of inmates who were intellectually disabled. That all changed in the case of Virginia inmate Daryl Renard Atkins, who had a tested IQ of only 59, well below the line for intellectual disability. His lawyers did not argue that his low level of intellectual functioning justified his criminal actions. Rather, they argued that his low IQ should prohibit the state of Virginia from executing him.

The U.S. Supreme Court ruled 6–3 in *Atkins v. Virginia* (2002) that it violates the Eighth Amendment to execute those who truly are intellectually disabled. In his majority opinion, Justice John Paul Stevens reasoned that an emerging legislative trend in the states prohibited the execution of those who are intellectually disabled. Since the Court's decision in *Penry* in 1989, at least 16 different states had amended their death penalty laws to prohibit such executions.

Justice Stevens explained that those who are intellectually disabled are less able to appreciate the gravity of harm their criminal actions cause. He also explained that intellectually disabled defendants are less able to assist their attorneys, express remorse for their actions, or understand the Court proceedings and are more likely to be subject to wrongful executions.

The Court's decision ultimately led to Daryl Atkins's death sentence being commuted to a life sentence. The Court's decision also spawned a new array of litigation over whether inmates truly are intellectually disabled. Obviously, after the Court's decision in *Atkins*, a host of other inmates filed petitions, arguing that they also should be removed from death row because they are intellectually disabled.

How has the U.S. Supreme Court dealt with the death penalty for juveniles?

While juveniles were not executed with nearly the same level of frequency as adult criminal defendants, the U.S. Supreme Court did not erect a per se bar against doing so until 2005. In fact, in the 1989 decision *Stanford v. Kentucky*, the Court ruled that no Eighth Amendment violation existed for the state of Kentucky to impose a death sentence. Defendant Kevin Stanford was convicted of murdering a 20-year-old female when he was 17 years old in Jefferson County, Kentucky. The crime was brutal, and the jury imposed a sentence of death.

The case was consolidated in *State v. Wilkins* (1987), a case out of Missouri involving defendant Heath Wilkins, who murdered a 26-year-old female store clerk when he was 16 years old.

In both cases, the lawyers for the men who committed murder when they were 17 and 16 years old argued to the U.S. Supreme Court that the Eighth Amendment's prohibition against cruel and unusual punishment should bar the execution of those who committed their crimes under the age of 18. However, the U.S. Supreme Court disagreed, and Justice Scalia wrote the plurality opinion.

Justice Scalia explained that the common law in the history of the United States did not include executing juveniles. In fact, he cited a legal historian for the proposition that 281 juveniles had been executed in the United States.

"We discern neither a historical nor a modern societal consensus forbidding the imposition of capital punishment on any person who murders at 16 or 17 years of age," Justice Scalia wrote. "Accordingly, we conclude that such punishment does not offend the Eighth Amendment's prohibition against cruel and unusual punishment."

However, the U.S. Supreme Court overruled its *Stanford* decision in *Roper v. Simmons* (2005). The case involved a brutal murder committed by 17-year-old Christopher Simmons in Missouri. He kidnapped a woman, tied her up, and then took her to a bridge and dumped her into the water on September 9, 1993. The crime undoubtedly was horrific, and prosecutors sought the death penalty.

Associate Justice Anthony Kennedy, who penned the majority opinion in *Roper v. Simmons,* was appointed to the Supreme Court by President Reagan, serving from 1988 until his retirement in 2018.

The U.S. Supreme Court agreed with this position in its decision in *Roper v. Simmons*. Writing for the majority, Justice Anthony Kennedy noted that juveniles were different from adults in three significant ways: (1) juveniles are less mature than adults; (2) juveniles are more susceptible to peer pressure than adults; and (3) the character of juveniles is not as well developed as adults.

Justice Kennedy explained:

> The differences between juvenile and adult offenders are too marked and well understood to risk allowing a youthful person to receive the death penalty despite insufficient culpability. An unacceptable likelihood exists that the brutality or cold-blooded nature of any particular crime would overpower mitigating arguments based on youth as a matter of course, even where the juvenile offender's objective immaturity, vulnerability, and lack of true depravity should require a sentence less severe than death.…
>
> Our determination that the death penalty is disproportionate punishment for offenders under 18 finds confirmation in the stark reality that the United States is the only country in the world that continues to give official sanction to the juvenile death penalty.

What international aspect of the decision in *Roper v. Simmons* inspired significant criticism from Justice Scalia?

The part of Justice Kennedy's opinion that outraged Justice Scalia was the reliance on international sources of law and what other countries did. Justice Kennedy emphasized that the United States was about the only country in the world that regularly executed those who committed murder as juveniles. Justice Kennedy wrote that since 1990, only seven other countries—Iran, Pakistan, Saudi Arabia, Yemen, Nigeria, the Democratic Republic of Congo, and China—have executed defendants who were juveniles at the time of their crime.

Justice Scalia was outraged at this, writing: "More fundamentally, however, the basic premise of the Court's argument—that American law should conform to the laws of the rest of the world—ought to be rejected out of hand. In fact, the Court itself does not believe it. In many significant respects the laws of most other countries differ from our law—including not only such explicit provisions of our Constitution as the right to jury trial and grand jury indictment, but even many interpretations of the Constitution prescribed by this Court itself."

Race Issues

What infamous subject led to the U.S. Supreme Court's first decisions on race?

The subject of slavery led to the Court's initial decisions that discuss or relate to the subject of race. The U.S. Constitution did not mention the word slavery, but several provisions related to slavery and sanctioned its practice. For example, the Constitution contained the Fugitive Slave Clause, which read: "No person held to service or labour in one state, under the laws thereof, escaping into another, shall, in consequence of any law or regulation therein, be discharged from such service or labor, but shall be delivered up on claim of the party to whom such service or labour may be due." This provision meant that if a slave escaped from a slave state and went to free territory, the person was still not free.

In several early decisions in the 19th century, the U.S. Supreme Court addressed the status of individuals as either slaves or free people. Sadly, the Court's earlier decisions viewed slaves more as property than as people. Today, these decisions are viewed as blots on the Court's history.

In what decision did the Court affirm the release of Africans enslaved by Spaniards?

In *United States v. Schooner Amistad* (1841), the U.S. Supreme Court affirmed a lower-court judgment that 43 enslaved Africans who washed ashore in Connecticut on the Spanish ship *La Amistad* should be returned to their native land free from the shackles of slavery by their Spanish captors.

The controversy arose when the Spanish ship sailed from Havana, Cuba, to Porte Principe, another town in Cuba. The Africans revolted and killed the ship's captain, Ramon Ferrer, along with a few other members of the crew. Two crewmembers, Jose Ruiz and Pedro Montes, momentarily escaped but were captured. The Africans did not kill Ruiz and Montes. Apparently, the two Spaniards promised to sail the ship back to Africa but instead headed for America. The ship was discovered by Lieutenant Thomas Gedney of the U.S. Coast Guard and by sea captains Henry Green and Peletiah Fordham.

Ruiz and Montes told authorities of the African mutiny, which led to the imprisonment of the Africans. The Spanish men, Gedney, Green, and Fordham all filed claims for either all or parts of the ship and its cargo's value. Meanwhile, President Martin Van

Death of Capt. Ferrer, the Captain of the Amistad, July, 1839.
Don Jose Ruiz and Don Pedro Montez, of the Island of Cuba, having purchased fifty-three slaves at Havana, recently imported from Africa, put them on board the Amistad, Capt. Ferrer, in order to transport them to Principe, another port on the Island of Cuba. After being out from Havana about four days, the African captives on board, in order to obtain their freedom, and return to Africa, armed themselves with cane knives, and rose upon the

In a contemporaneous illustration, enslaved Africans are depicted mutinying against their Spanish captors aboard the vessel *La Amistad*. The Supreme Court would rule in favor of the rights of the Africans.

Buren pressured the U.S. attorney in Connecticut to file a claim on behalf of the Spanish government. The Africans—the so-called "Amistads"—were placed on trial for murder.

The civil claims proceeded first, as the courts had to figure out whether the Africans were property or free men. A federal trial court judge determined that the Amistads were free men who were unlawfully transported by the Spanish and should be returned to their native land. The United States appealed the decision to circuit judge Smith Thompson, who affirmed. Then, the United States appealed to the U.S. Supreme Court.

The U.S. Supreme Court ruled that the Amistads "never were the lawful slaves of Ruiz or Montes, or of any other Spanish subjects." The government attorney argued that the Amistads should still be returned to Spain pursuant to the obligations of a treaty between the two nations. Writing for the Court, Justice Joseph Story rejected that argument, noting that the Africans were aboard the ship on a fraud that was in violation of even Spanish law. He added that Africans have just as many rights as Spanish subjects.

What two attorneys argued on behalf of the Amistads before the U.S. Supreme Court?

Roger Baldwin and John Quincy Adams argued on behalf of the Amistads. Baldwin was the future governor of Connecticut and U.S. senator. Meanwhile, the venerable Adams was the former president of the United States, who later served nearly 30 years in the U.S. House of Representatives after leaving the Oval Office.

In what decision did the U.S. Supreme Court uphold the Fugitive Slave Act of 1793?

The Court upheld the Fugitive Slave Act of 1793 in *Prigg v. Pennsylvania* (1842), ruling that the federal law was justified under the Fugitive Slave Clause of the U.S. Constitution and that a conflicting Pennsylvania law was invalid. Justice Story, the same justice who wrote the Court's opinion in *Amistad*, reasoned that the Fugitive Slave Clause created "an unqualified, positive right on the part of the slaveholder, which no state law or regulation can in any way qualify, regulate, control, or restrain."

The case involved professional slave-catcher Edward Prigg, who tracked down former slave Margaret Morgan and returned her to her Maryland owner, John Ashmore. Morgan had left Maryland and married Jerry Morgan, a free African American man from Pennsylvania. Pennsylvania authorities charged Prigg with kidnapping. Pennsylvania law had made it a crime to capture "any negro or mulatto" for the purpose of taking him or her into slavery unless a Pennsylvania court issued a certificate for the action. Pennsylvania authorities had refused to grant Prigg a certificate, but Prigg went ahead and took Margaret Morgan to Maryland.

Who was the Court's sole dissenter in the *Prigg* case?

Justice John McLean of Ohio was the Court's only dissenter. He reasoned that the prosecution of Prigg in Pennsylvania did not conflict with federal law and that a slave is a human being, not mere property.

In what infamous decision did the U.S. Supreme Court regard African Americans as slaves and as property?

The Court infamously ruled 7–2 that African Americans had little to no rights in the decision *Dred Scott v. Sandford* (1857). The Court ruled that former slave Dred Scott was not free even when he resided in a free territory. Chief Justice Roger Brooke Taney,

In one of the Court's most conspicuously poor decisions, a 7–2 majority of justices ruled that former slaves like Dred Scott (pictured here) remained enslaved even in slavery-free states, explicitly citing racial inferiority as justification.

who wrote the Court's majority opinion, referred to African Americans as "that unfortunate race" who were "so far inferior, that they had no rights which the white man was bound to respect." Some historians have cited the Court's decision in the *Dred Scott* case as a key catalyst for the U.S. Civil War.

Sadly, the opinion received much popular support at the time. A. Leon Higginbotham Jr., in his book *Shades of Freedom*, writes: "Chief Justice Roger Brooke Taney's opinion in the *Dred Scott* case did not reflect a unique perspective about African Americans in that era."

Who was Dred Scott?

Dred Scott was a slave owned by Peter Blow in Alabama. Scott moved with Blow to Missouri, another slave state. After Blow died, his executor sold Scott to Dr. John Emerson, a St. Louis–based Army doctor. Emerson then moved his family—and Scott—to Illinois, a free state that did not allow slavery. Emerson later moved back to St. Louis and passed away. Scott and his wife

Harriett filed a lawsuit in Missouri court, arguing that they were freed when Emerson moved to the free state of Illinois. Emerson's widow and her brother, John Sanford (a court clerk misspelled his name as Sandford), contested Scott's lawsuit, leading to *Dred Scott v. Sandford.*

Which two justices dissented in the *Dred Scott* case?

Justice McLean and Justice Benjamin Robbins Curtis were the Court's two dissenters. Both believed that the majority ignored the reality that African Americans were free men in many states of the country and that Dred Scott was free after living in Illinois for several years.

Justice Curtis was so upset by the Court's decision in the *Dred Scott* case that he resigned from the Court shortly thereafter. Justice Curtis returned to his private law practice in Boston after he left the Court. He argued several cases before the U.S. Supreme Court and later served as chief counsel for President Andrew Johnson during his impeachment trial in the Senate.

What case arose after a massacre of African Americans in Louisiana?

The Court's decision in *U.S. v. Cruikshank* (1876) arose from an election dispute in Colfax, Louisiana, that erupted into violence when a group of angry white men stormed a local courthouse that was being protected by a local sheriff and many black Republicans. On Easter Sunday in 1973, the band of whites murdered at least 50 black people, though some estimates rank the number of victims as much higher.

Federal investigators charged more than 90 white men, including William Cruikshank, with a violation of the Ku Klux Klan

Act of 1870. That law made it illegal to "injure, oppress, threaten, or intimidate any citizen with intent to prevent or hinder his free exercise and enjoyment of any right or privilege granted or secured to him by the constitution or laws of the United States, or because of his having exercised the same."

Cruikshank was accused of terrorizing and killing African Americans Levi Nelson and Alexander Tillman and not allowing them to exercise their free-assembly rights. The Court reasoned that Cruikshank and others could not be prosecuted for his acts against Nelson and Tillman because only state authorities could prosecute them for murder (which they did not do).

In what decision did the Court strike down the Civil Rights Act of 1875?

The Court struck down the Civil Rights Act of 1875 in a series of cases that was consolidated and called *The Civil Rights Cases* (1883). Congress had passed the Civil Rights Act of 1875 to address the pervasive problem of discrimination in the private sector. Yes, Congress had passed three amendments—called the "Reconstruction Amendments"—to address massive discrimination against African Americans, but those amendments largely dealt with governmental, not private, discrimination.

The Civil Rights Act of 1875 extended protection to African Americans from private wrongs. For example, the Act outlawed racial discrimination in places of public accommodation, such as hotels, movie theaters, and railroads. Congress believed that the Civil Rights Act of 1875 would help enforce recently enacted constitutional amendments, most notably the 13th Amendment, which outlawed slavery, and the 14th Amendment, which attempted to give former slaves the same general rights as white citizens.

However, the Court struck down the law by a vote of 8–1, reasoning that Congress exceeded its powers in trying to eradicate private wrongs. "It would be running the slavery argument into the ground to make it apply to every act of discrimination," Justice Joseph P. Bradley wrote for the majority. He added that at some point, African Americans "cease to be the special favorites of the law."

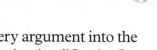

What were the collection of cases that came to be known as *The Civil Rights Cases*?

The cases came from five states: Kansas, California, Missouri, New York, and Tennessee. The case from Kansas, *United States v. Stanley*, involved an inn owner named Murray Stanley who denied a meal to African American Bird Gee. The case from California, *United States v. Ryan*, involved a man named Mitchell Ryan who denied African American George Tyler the opportunity to view a theater show in San Francisco. The Missouri case, *United States v. Nichols*, involved an inn owner named Samuel Nichols who denied lodging to African American W. H. R. Agee. In the New York case, *United States v. Singleton*, Mr. Singleton denied

A lone voice of reason in a dark age for civil rights, Justice John Marshall Harlan I—ironically, a former slaveowner—was known as "The Great Dissenter" for issuing opinions contrary to the Court's prevailing racially motivated rulings known as the Civil Rights Cases.

DID YOU KNOW?

Who was the Court's lone dissenter in *The Civil Rights Cases*?

Justice John Marshall Harlan I, a former slaveowner from Kentucky, established his reputation as "The Great Dissenter" with his solo dissent in *The Civil Rights Cases*. He wrote that "the substance and spirit of the recent amendments of the Constitution have been sacrificed by a subtle and ingenious verbal criticism."

Justice Harlan also noted that the state had a role in providing its citizens protection in places of public accommodation, writing: "In every material sense applicable to the practical enforcement of the Fourteenth Amendment, railroad corporations, keepers of inns, and managers of places of public accommodation are agents or instrumentalities of the State, because they are charged with duties to the public, and are amenable, in respect of their duties and functions, to governmental regulation."

entry to an African American at the Grand Opera House. Finally, in the Tennessee case, *Robinson v. Memphis & Charleston Railroad Company*, the railroad company refused to allow African American Sallie J. Robinson to sit in the first-class section of the railway simply because of her race. In all five cases, the Supreme Court ruled in favor of racism.

Why were the decisions in *The Civil Rights Cases* so devastating in terms of their impact on race?

The Civil Rights Cases represented the U.S. Supreme Court failing to protect the spirit of the intent behind the 39th Congress

passing the 13th and 14th Amendments in order to protect those who had been enslaved. The 39th Congress—composed of the so-called Radical Republicans—were the members who had passed much Reconstruction legislation, including the so-called Reconstruction Amendments: the 13th Amendment, which ended slavery; the 14th Amendment, which made slaves citizens; and the 15th Amendment, which prohibited the denial of the right to vote based on race.

But the 39th Congress did much more than push through these three amendments. They also passed a series of civil rights laws designed to protect former slaves. Many states also passed antidiscrimination laws right after the Civil War during Reconstruction.

Sadly, the efforts of the 39th Congress were met with great resistance in parts of the country. This was helped by a U.S. Supreme Court in the 1880s and 1890s that decided *The Civil Rights Cases* (1883) and then *Plessy v. Ferguson* in 1896.

Who was the Court's lone dissenter in *Plessy v. Ferguson*?

Once again, Justice John Marshall Harlan I was the only justice to dissent in an early race case, and it is mainly because of this famous dissent that he bears the nickname "The Great Dissenter." Justice Harlan wrote that "our Constitution is color-blind and neither knows nor tolerates classes among citizens." He warned his colleagues that their decision would be "as pernicious as the decision" in *Dred Scott.*

His dissent contains some of the most profound language ever written by a U.S. Supreme Court jurist:

> But in view of the constitution, in the eye of the law, there is in this country no superior, dominant, ruling class of citizens. There is no caste here. Our constitution is color-

DID YOU KNOW?

In what infamous decision did the U.S. Supreme Court uphold the "separate but equal" doctrine?

The Court upheld the "separate but equal" doctrine in *Plessy v. Ferguson* (1896), upholding an 1890 Louisiana law providing for separate railway accommodations for different races. Homer Plessy, who was one-eighth black, or an "octoroon," was arrested in 1892 for boarding a whites-only coach. Rodolphe Desdunes, the leader of the New Orleans American Citizens' Equal Rights Association, had recruited his friend Plessy for the purpose of challenging the law. Plessy and Desdunes took the case all the way to the U.S. Supreme Court.

The Court, in an opinion by Justice Henry Billings Brown, reasoned that the law did not violate the 14th Amendment's Equal Protection Clause because the law provided separate but equal facilities for different races. Separate facilities, according to Justice Brown, "do not necessarily imply the inferiority of either race to the other."

blind, and neither knows nor tolerates classes among citizens. In respect of civil rights, all citizens are equal before the law. The humblest is the peer of the most powerful. The law regards man as man, and takes no account of his surroundings or of his color when his civil rights as guaranteed by the supreme law of the land are involved. It is therefore to be regretted that this high tribunal, the final expositor of the fundamental law of the land, has reached the conclusion that it is competent for a state to regulate the enjoyment by citizens of their civil rights solely upon the basis of race.

DISCRIMINATION RELATED TO JURY SERVICE

In what late 19th-century decision did the U.S. Supreme Court protect the rights of African Americans to serve on a jury?

The U.S. Supreme Court ruled in *Strauder v. West Virginia* (1879) that a state law limiting jury service to whites violated the Equal Protection Clause of the 14th Amendment. The law limited jury service to "all white male persons." Tyler Strauder, an African American defendant who was convicted of murder by an all-white jury, contended that he should have a new trial because his constitutional rights were violated by a system that ensured that he was not tried by a jury of his peers.

The Court determined that the Equal Protection Clause was designed "to protect an emancipated race and to strike down all possible legal discriminations' against African Americans."

In what decision did the Court not invalidate the conviction of an African American defendant who was tried by an all-white jury?

The Court had the opportunity to reinforce its ruling in *Strauder v. West Virginia* but failed to do so in the case *Virginia v. Rives* (1880). In this case, Lee Reynolds, an African American man, was convicted of murdering a white man in Patrick County, Virginia, before an all-white jury. Virginia law was different from the West Virginia law that was invalidated in the *Strauder* case. The Virginia law did not explicitly limit jury service to white males. Instead, Patrick County, Virginia, officials by custom only summoned white people to serve on the jury.

Appointed to the U.S. District Court for the Western District of Virginia in 1871 by President Ulysses S. Grant, Alexander Rives was another judge swimming upstream against postbellum discriminatory practices.

Federal judge Alexander Rives ruled that Reynolds's conviction must be reversed because the custom in Patrick County had been to exclude African Americans from jury service. However, the U.S. Supreme Court reversed its opinion, finding that the fact that no African Americans served on Reynolds's jury trial was not sufficient evidence of impermissible discrimination.

This decision meant that defendants were not able to effectively challenge racial discrimination in jury selection as long as the state or governmental entity did not have an explicit policy sanctioning such discrimination.

In what other 19th-century decision did the U.S. Supreme Court speak about the exclusion of African Americans from jury service?

The U.S. Supreme Court ruled in *Ex Parte Virginia* (1879) that Virginia judge J. D. Coles could be punished for refusing to allow African Americans to serve on juries in the Pittsylvania

County Courthouse in Chatham, Virginia. The Civil Rights Act of 1875—which was not invalidated until 1883—made discrimination in selecting jurors a federal crime.

The state of Virginia argued that no problem existed because Judge Coles was not the state government, and thus, the Equal Protection Clause of the 14th Amendment did not apply. Justice William Strong rejected that argument, writing that the "state acts by its legislative, its executive, or its judicial authorities." He added: "We do not perceive who holding an office under a State, and claiming to act for the State, can relieve the holder from obligation to obey the Constitution of the United States, or take away power of Congress to punish his disobedience."

When did the U.S. Supreme Court expand the rights of criminal defendants to a jury process free from racial discrimination?

The U.S. Supreme Court ruled in *Batson v. Kentucky* (1986) that a criminal defendant could establish "purposeful discrimination ... solely on evidence concerning the prosecutor's exercise of peremptory challenges at the defendant's trial." Jury selection consists of two types of challenges: (1) for-cause challenges and (2) peremptory challenges. For-cause challenges are for when a prospective juror is clearly biased or partial. On the other hand, peremptory challenges generally allow an attorney to strike a prospective juror for any reason.

However, the Court in *Batson* ruled that prosecutors may not exercise peremptory challenges in a racially discriminatory manner. In the burglary trial of defendant James Batson, the prosecutor used his peremptory challenges to strike all four African Americans in the jury pool. Batson, an African American, argued that the prosecutor's selective use of peremptory challenges to strike African Americans violated Batson's constitutional rights under the Sixth and 14th Amendments.

Remarkably, it was not until the late 20th century—in *Batson v. Kentucky* (1986) for criminal cases and *Edmonson v. Leesville Concrete Co.* (1991) for civil matters—that the Supreme Court moved to ensure that selection of jurors should not be racially motivated.

A jury had convicted Batson and rejected his constitutional challenges. The Kentucky Supreme Court affirmed his conviction. On appeal, the U.S. Supreme Court reversed its opinion, finding that the trial judge should have made the prosecutor offer a race-neutral explanation for his striking of the four African American jury pool members. The Court established that if a defendant establishes a basic inference or showing of discrimination, the prosecutor must rebut that inference with a race-neutral explanation for his actions. A possible race-neutral explanation might be that the prospective juror who was struck failed to make eye contact with the prosecutor. If the prosecutor articulates a race-neutral reason for his or her actions, the defendant must then show that the prosecutor's allegedly race-neutral reason was pretextual or false.

When did the U.S. Supreme Court rule that a defendant was entitled to a new trial because of a systemic pattern of exclusion of Mexican Americans from jury service?

The Court ruled in *Hernandez v. Texas* (1954) that a Latino defendant was entitled to a new trial because prosecutors had engaged in a systemic pattern of exclusion against Mexican Americans for jury service. The defendant presented evidence that no Mexican American had served on a jury for the past 25 years. The Court reasoned that this type of pattern smacked of discrimination.

The Court did not say that Mr. Hernandez was entitled to proportional representation of a people of Mexican descent necessarily on his particular jury but reasoned that the Constitution required that a jurisdiction not systemically exclude people of a particular race or ethnicity.

When did the U.S. Supreme Court explain that a defendant could not show purposeful discrimination in jury selection based on prosecutorial conduct in his or her specific case?

The U.S. Supreme Court ruled in *Swain v. Alabama* (1965) that a criminal defendant can only establish an Equal Protection violation by presenting proof that prosecutors struck, or dismissed, jurors on the basis of race as a pattern in case after case. According to the Court, the African American defendant in *Swain* had failed to establish a clear pattern in "case after case" of discriminatory jury strikes. "Undoubtedly the selection of prospective jurors was somewhat haphazard and little effort was made to ensure that all groups in the community were fully represented," the Court wrote. "But an imperfect system is not equivalent to purposeful discrimination based on race."

When did the Court extend the rule in *Batson* to civil cases?

The Court extended the *Batson* rule to civil cases in *Edmonson v. Leesville Concrete Co.* (1991). Thaddeus Donald Edmonson,

a construction worker, had sued Leesville Concrete Co. for negligence after he suffered injuries on a job site in Louisiana. Edmonson, an African American, alleged that attorneys for the concrete company had dismissed several African American jurors because of their race.

The Court recognized that the *Batson* rule should be extended to cover civil cases. "If peremptory challenges based on race were permitted, persons could be required by summons to be put at risk of open and public discrimination as a condition of their participation in the justice system," Justice Anthony Kennedy wrote for the Court. "The injury to excluded jurors would be the direct result of governmental delegation and participation."

How did the Court extend *Batson* in criminal cases?

The Court extended *Batson* in *Powers v. Ohio* (1990) and *Georgia v. McCollum* (1992). *Powers* involved a white defendant who alleged discrimination because the prosecution dismissed several African American jurors. The Court in *Powers* reasoned that prosecutors may not exclude jurors based on race even when the race of the jurors is different from the race of the defendant.

McCollum involved a white defendant who was charged with assaulting two African American victims. The defense attorney sought to use his peremptory challenges in order to remove African Americans from the jury, but the Court reasoned that "the Constitution prohibits a criminal defendant from engaging in purposeful discrimination on the ground of race in the exercise of peremptory challenges."

RACIAL DISCRIMINATION IN VOTING

Who was Dr. L. A. Nixon?

Dr. Lawrence A. Nixon was an African American physician located in El Paso, Texas, who challenged the Democratic Party of Texas's denial of his ability to vote in the Democratic Party primary. Dr. Nixon was a charter member of the El Paso branch of the NAACP, which he helped to establish. The U.S. Supreme Court initially ruled in his favor in *Nixon v. Herndon* (1927), reasoning that Texas violated the 14th Amendment's Equal Protection Clause by prohibiting Dr. Nixon from voting in the Democratic primary. Writing for a unanimous Court, Justice Oliver Wendell Holmes Jr. reasoned that "it seems to us hard to imagine a more direct and obvious infringement of the Fourteenth Amendment."

However, Texas still sought to prohibit Dr. Nixon from voting and made a change to its voting law. The new law provided that every political party would henceforth "in its own way determine who shall be qualified to vote or otherwise participate in such political party." In other words, the primary discriminating party was no longer the state of Texas but the Democratic Party in Texas. However, the U.S. Supreme Court still ruled in Nixon's favor in *Nixon v. Condon* (1932) by a 5–4 vote.

When did the U.S. Supreme Court formally repudiate all-white party primaries?

The U.S. Supreme Court repudiated the concept of an all-white political primary election in *Smith v. Allright* (1944). The Democratic Party in Texas argued that as a voluntary association, it could freely choose who could and could not associate and participate in its activities.

However, the U.S. Supreme Court reasoned that the party primary was still intertwined with the state enough that the net ef-

Harlan Stone, who joined the majority opinion in *Smith v. Allwright* (1944), was appointed chief justice by President Franklin Roosevelt in 1941 after serving as a Coolidge-appointed associate justice for 16 years.

fect was that the state of Texas was impermissibly sanctioning rank discrimination based on race. "We think that this statutory system for the selection of party nominees for inclusion on the general election ballot makes the party which is required to follow these legislative directions an agency of the state in so far as it determines the participants in a primary election," the Court wrote.

In what decision did the Court uphold the Voting Rights Act of 1965?

The U.S. Supreme Court unanimously upheld the Voting Rights Act in *South Carolina v. Katzenbach* (1966). The act suspended the use of literacy tests, which were designed to keep African Americans from voting. The act also provided for the placement of federal examiners to ensure that states did not engage in voting discrimination.

Several states gave alternative tests to illiterate whites to ensure their right to vote. South Carolina—supported by Alabama,

DID YOU KNOW?

What was unusual about the *South Carolina v. Katzenbach* decision?

The case was unusual because it was one of the relatively few cases in which the U.S. Supreme Court exercised original jurisdiction. This means that the U.S. Supreme Court was the only court to hear the case; no lower-court decisions occurred. The U.S. Supreme Court had original jurisdiction under the Constitution (specifically Article III, Section 2) because the case involved a controversy between a state suing a citizen of another state, in this case the attorney general of the United States.

Georgia, Louisiana, Mississippi, and Virginia—had challenged the constitutionality of various provisions of the Voting Rights Act. The Court, in an opinion written by Chief Justice Earl Warren, found that Congress had the power under Section 2 of the 15th Amendment, which protects the right to vote, to pass laws prohibiting voting discrimination.

In 2013, how did the Court limit the Voting Rights Act of 1965?

The U.S. Supreme Court limited the reach of the Voting Rights Act of 1965 in *Shelby County v. Holder* (2013) by striking down a part of the law that used a particular formula to determine which jurisdictions needed to get prior approval (called "preclearance") from the U.S. attorney general or a federal court before they could make changes to their voting laws or policies.

A section of the Voting Rights Act provided that those jurisdictions that had a history of discrimination were subject to the preclearance requirement. Shelby County—a county in Ala-

bama—was a jurisdiction with a history of voting discrimination and, thus, was subject to the preclearance requirement. Shelby County challenged provisions of the Voting Rights Act in federal court. They challenged both the preclearance requirement itself and the provision providing for the preclearance formula.

The U.S. Supreme Court invalidated the part of the Voting Rights Act that established the preclearance formula in a 5–4 decision. The majority reasoned that the preclearance formula was created decades earlier and was now outdated, as outright forms of racial discrimination in voting were a relic of the past. In his majority opinion, Chief Justice John G. Roberts Jr. noted that the Voting Rights Act imposed burdens on the traditional notion that states control elections. "The Voting Rights Act sharply departs from these basic principles," he wrote. "It suspends all changes to state election law—however innocuous—until they have been precleared by federal authorities in Washington, D.C."

Justice Ruth Bader Ginsburg authored a dissenting opinion. She reasoned that the preclearance formula was still necessary and vital to ensuring that jurisdictions did not engage in racial discrimination. She emphasized that "the Constitution vests broad power in Congress to protect the right to vote, and in particular to combat racial discrimination in voting." Then, in one of her most memorable passages in her 27-year career on the Court, she colorfully added: "Throwing out preclearance when it has worked and is continuing to work to stop discriminatory changes is like throwing away your umbrella in a rainstorm because you are not getting wet."

STRIKING DOWN SEGREGATION

What was the first major desegregation U.S. Supreme Court decision won by the NAACP?

The NAACP's first major school desegregation case before the Court was *Missouri ex. Rel. Gaines v. Canada* (1938). The

Tate Hall, which housed the University of Missouri Law School in the 1930s, tried to keep Lloyd L. Gaines out of the building until the student got the Supreme Court on his side in 1938. Three months after the ruling, Gaines disappeared.

Court ruled that the state of Missouri violated the equal-protection rights of Lloyd Gaines, who had applied to enter law school at the all-white University of Missouri. The state had argued that it complied with the constitutional requirement of equal protection by offering to pay Gaines to attend a law school for blacks in a neighboring state. The state of Missouri at that time did not have a law school for blacks that offered law classes. Gaines, who had obtained his undergraduate degree from the all-black Lincoln University, now sought a law degree.

Chief Justice Charles Evans Hughes, writing for the Court, determined that Missouri could not evade its legal responsibilities by saying that it would eventually offer a law school for black students. Chief Justice Hughes wrote that "it cannot be said that a mere declaration of purpose, still unfilled, is enough." He also reasoned that Missouri could not rely on paying Gaines's tuition at an out-of-state school, writing: "It is an obligation the burden of which cannot be cast by one State upon another." Legal scholars consider the decision to be the first major victory of the NAACP in its fight to integrate schools.

Who represented Lloyd Gaines?

Charles Hamilton Houston (1895–1950), the special counsel for the NAACP and Justice Thurgood Marshall's mentor, argued the case for Lloyd Gaines before the U.S. Supreme Court. Houston had graduated from Harvard Law School, where he had become the first black editor of the *Harvard Law Review*. He later became the dean of Howard Law School.

What happened to Lloyd Gaines?

Nobody really knows what happened to Lloyd Gaines. He mysteriously disappeared after the Court's ruling and before the NAACP could continue its challenge of *Missouri* before the lower courts on remand from the High Court. The website of the Gaines/Oldham Black Cultural Center at the University of Missouri provides the following information: "Gaines was last seen at his fraternity house in Chicago. One evening around March 19, 1939, he told the housekeeper that he was going to buy some stamps and he was never seen or heard from again."

Some believe that Gaines was murdered. Others believe that he accepted money to leave the state and never returned.

In what decision did the U.S. Supreme Court strike down segregation in K–12 public schools?

The U.S. Supreme Court invalidated segregated public schools in *Brown v. Board of Education* (1954). It is considered one of the most important decisions, if not the most important, in Court history. The decision was a consolidation of challenges to segregated public schools in Kansas, Delaware, South Carolina,

In one of the most iconic images from the civil rights era, young Ruby Bridges is escorted by U.S. Marshals at her new formerly all-white school. *Brown v. Board of Education* opened the door to desegregating schools and to many future advances in civil rights.

and Virginia. *Brown v. Board of Education* was a dispute in Kansas. The other cases were *Gebhart v. Belton* (Delaware), *Briggs v. Elliott* (South Carolina), and *Davis v. County School Board of Prince Edward County* (Virginia).

A group of African American parents, represented by the National Association for the Advancement of Colored People (NAACP), mounted a challenge to the segregated school systems, arguing that it violated the Equal Protection Clause of the 14th Amendment. They not only alleged that the schools their children attended were inferior to the schools attended by white children, but they also alleged that maintaining separate schools based on race was unconstitutional on its face.

The Court unanimously agreed with the parents and the NAACP that segregated schools were "inherently unequal." The Court wrote: "We conclude that, in the field of public education, the doctrine of 'separate but equal' has no place. Separate educational facilities are inherently unequal."

How was Chief Justice Warren crucial to the outcome of the *Brown* decision?

Chief Justice Warren was crucial not only because he wrote the Court's unanimous decision but also because he was important behind closed doors in ensuring that the decision was unanimous. The case initially came up to the Court for argument in 1952 before Chief Justice Warren was on the Court. The justices heard the argument in the case and were divided. They ordered re-argument in the case.

Then, in September 1953, Chief Justice Fred M. Vinson died unexpectedly of a heart attack. President Dwight D. Eisenhower appointed Chief Justice Warren as the new chief justice. Chief Justice Warren persuaded his colleagues that the importance of the decision required a single, unified voice from the Court. Chief Justice Warren wrote a short, 10-page opinion that was understandable to both lawyers and laypeople.

Historians speculate that without Chief Justice Warren's effective leadership, the U.S. Supreme Court may not have been able to speak with a unified voice. The Court was badly fractured before Chief Justice Warren joined the Court. For example, Justice Felix Frankfurter was displeased with Chief Justice Vinson. He allegedly told two law clerks upon hearing of Chief Justice Vinson's death that "this is the first indication that I have ever had that there is a God." Justice Frankfurter did not even attend Chief Justice Vinson's funeral.

What decision did *Brown v. Board of Education* overrule?

The Court in *Brown* overruled *Plessy v. Ferguson* (1896), the decision that upheld an 1890 Louisiana law that mandated separate railway accommodations on the basis of race. The majority in *Plessy* had sanctioned the concept of "separate but equal," a concept that the Court had invalidated in *Brown*.

What attorney in the *Brown* case later became a member of the Warren Court?

Justice Thurgood Marshall, the director of the NAACP's Legal Defense and Education Fund, argued before the U.S. Supreme Court in *Brown v. Board of Education* along with several other prominent African American attorneys, including Robert Carter (1917–2012) and Spottswood William Robinson III (1916–1998). Justice Marshall argued so many cases before the U.S. Supreme Court that he was dubbed "Mr. Civil Rights." In 1967, President Lyndon Baines Johnson nominated Justice Marshall to the U.S. Supreme Court. Justice Marshall was confirmed and became the first African American to ever serve on the High Court.

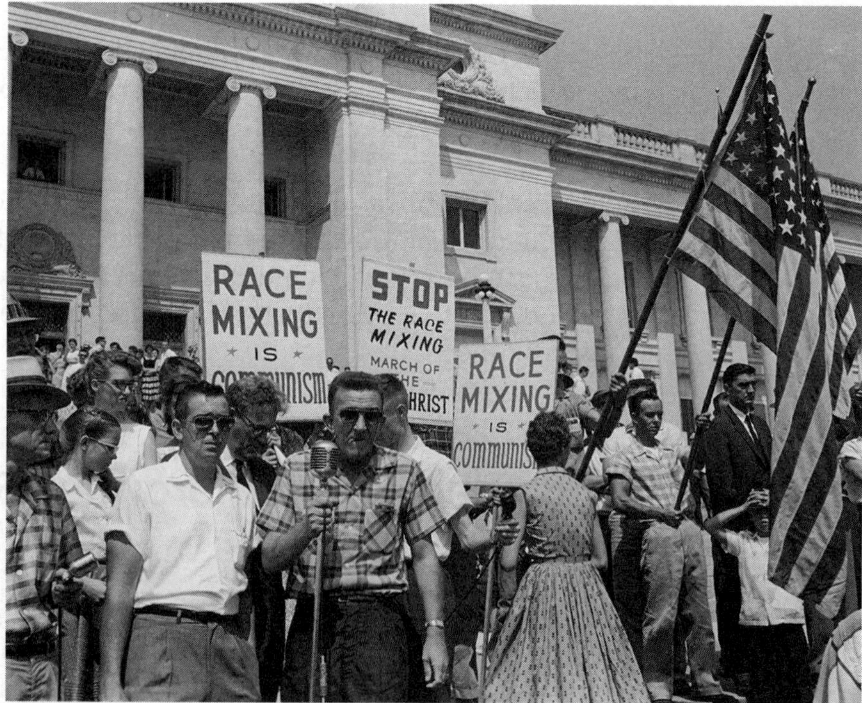

Despite the support of the Supreme Court's *Cooper v. Aaron* ruling and President Eisenhower's Executive Order 10730, integration was not met with open arms by the mayor and white population of Little Rock.

DID YOU KNOW?

What was *Brown II*?

A second *Brown* decision was made by the Court in 1955. In its original decision, the Court had ruled that segregated public schools were unequal but did not decide the remedy or proper course of action to fix the situation. They ordered another argument on this. In *Brown v. Board of Education II* (1955), the Court instructed trial court judges to monitor cases before them in order to ensure that public schools were integrated "with all deliberate speed." In some jurisdictions, local officials focused more on "deliberate" than "speed," which meant that public schools were not desegregated until the 1970s.

How did the Court respond to arguments that a state governor was not bound to obey its decision in *Brown v. Board of Education*?

The U.S. Supreme Court unanimously held in *Cooper v. Aaron* (1958) that state governors and legislators are bound under the U.S. Constitution—and its Supremacy Clause in Article VI—to obey decisions made by the U.S. Supreme Court. Quoting the old judicial review case of *Marbury v. Madison* (1803), the Court wrote that "it is emphatically the province and duty of the judicial department to say what the law is."

Arkansas governor Orval Faubus had created the controversy by ordering the Arkansas National Guard to prevent the integration of Little Rock's Central High School in defiance of a federal court order. Nine African American students—known as "the Little Rock Nine"—had sought to enroll and attend the previously all-white school.

Faubus's actions led to President Dwight D. Eisenhower sending in federal troops to ensure the protection of the students and the integration of the school. The U.S. Supreme Court emphasized: "No state legislator or judicial officer can war against the Constitution without violating his undertaking to support it."

In what decision did the Court invalidate restrictive covenants?

The U.S. Supreme Court ruled in *Shelley v. Kraemer* (1948) that judicial enforcement of racially discriminatory restrictive covenants violated the Equal Protection Clause of the 14th Amendment. Restrictive covenants refer to land use: contractual provisions that limit how a homeowner can sell or lease his or her property. Many areas of the country had restrictive covenants that prohibited individuals from selling their homes to African Americans. These restrictive covenants contributed mightily to housing segregation in this country.

Shelley v. Kraemer began when a Mr. Fitzgerald sold his house to J. D. Shelley, an African American man. Louis Kraemer, a white neighbor, brought suit to void the sale of the home to Shelley. Kraemer cited a restrictive covenant signed in 1911 by 30 of the 39 surrounding homeowners that prohibited the sale of homes to anyone who was not Caucasian. Kraemer asserted that the covenants did not violate the Constitution in part because they involved only private action, not state action.

The U.S. Supreme Court ruled that the restrictive covenant itself was a form of private discrimination beyond the reach of the 14th Amendment's Equal Protection Clause. However, the Court also ruled that the enforcement of a restrictive covenant by a court amounted to state action: "State action, as that phrase is understood for the purposes of the Fourteenth Amendment, refers to exertions of state power in all forms." In his opinion for the Court, Chief Justice Vinson declared: "We hold that in granting judicial enforcement of the restrictive agreements in these cases, the States have denied [Shelley] the equal protection of the laws."

When did the U.S. Supreme Court invalidate a ban on interracial marriages?

The U.S. Supreme Court unanimously ruled in *Loving v. Virginia* (1967) that a Virginia law banning interracial marriages violated the Equal Protection and Due Process clauses of the 14th Amendment. At the time of the Court's decision, 16 states had laws banning interracial marriages.

The *Loving* case arose when Richard Loving, a white man, and Mildred Jeter, a black woman, married in Washington, D.C., and then moved back to their home state of Virginia. Virginia authorities charged the two with violating the so-called anti-miscegenation law. The trial judge imposed a sentence of 25 years but suspended the sentence on the condition that the Lovings leave the state. The trial judge infamously wrote: "Almighty God created the races white, black, yellow, malay and red, and he placed them on separate continents. And but for the interference with his arrangement there would be no cause for such marriages. The fact that he separated the races shows that he did not intend for the races to mix."

The Lovings challenged the constitutionality of the law, leading eventually to a U.S. Supreme Court victory. The Court rea-

State laws prohibiting interracial couples from marrying were officially banned by the Supreme Court in 1967 with the *Loving v. Virginia* case.

soned that the Virginia law violated "the central meaning" of the 14th Amendment by attempting to perpetuate white supremacy.

In what decisions did the Court uphold the Civil Rights Act of 1964?

The U.S. Supreme Court ruled in *Heart of Atlanta Motel v. United States* (1965) and *Katzenbach v. McClung* (1965) that Congress had the power to pass the Civil Rights Act of 1964, the most important civil rights legislation of the 20th century, under the Commerce Clause. Recall that back in *The Civil Rights Cases* (1883), the U.S. Supreme Court had invalidated the Civil Rights Act of 1875, saying that the Constitution did not apply to purely personal acts of discrimination. Congress had attempted to justify the Civil Rights Act of 1875 under its powers in the Reconstruction Amendments.

This ruling was devastating to those who were challenging racial segregation laws, but Congress chose a different tack when it passed the Civil Rights Act of 1964. Here, Congress said that acts of racial discrimination substantially harm the free flow of interstate commerce. For example, the many hotels that refused to accommodate African Americans made it much more difficult for these individuals to travel across the country. The Court agreed with Congress, writing that "overwhelming evidence that discrimination by hotels and motels impedes interstate travel" existed. The motel owner in the *Heart of Atlanta Motel* case argued that Congress had overstepped its bounds by regulating the rights of private business owners.

The Court disagreed, finding that discrimination in public accommodations harmed interstate commerce: "In framing [the civil rights law] Congress was also dealing with what it considered a moral problem. But that fact does not detract from the overwhelming evidence of the disruptive effect that racial discrimination has had on commercial intercourse."

The second case, *Katzenbach v. McClung*, involved Ollie's Barbecue, a privately owned restaurant in Birmingham, Alabama, that limited African Americans to take-out service in the back of the restaurant while providing seating to white patrons in the dining area. The Court reasoned that Congress had a rational basis for concluding that "refusals of service to Negroes have imposed burdens both upon the interstate flow of food and upon the movement of products generally."

RACE AND AFFIRMATIVE ACTION

In what decision did the Court strike down a university's affirmative action program as an impermissible quota?

The U.S. Supreme Court narrowly invalidated the affirmative action program of the University of California at Davis's medical school in *Regents of University of California v. Bakke* (1978). The UC Davis medical school had a policy that reserved 16 of its 100 seats for minority applicants. Allan Bakke, a white male who was rejected by the school in 1973 and 1974, sued the school. Bakke claimed that the school violated his rights under Title VII of the Civil Rights Act of 1964 and the Equal Protection Clause of the 14th Amendment. Bakke's grade point average and MCAT (medical school admissions test) score were significantly higher than many minority candidates' scores. The Court ruled 5–4 that the school's policy amounted to an impermissible quota. The Court determined that the school could not carry its burden of proving that Bakke would have been denied entrance without its "unlawful special admissions program."

In what turned out to be the controlling opinion, Justice Lewis F. Powell Jr. wrote: "The guarantee of equal protection cannot mean one thing when applied to one individual and something else when applied to a person of another color. If both are not accorded the same protection, it is not equal." Justice Powell added that "[p]referring members of any one group for no reason other

DID YOU KNOW?

In its decision, did the Court say that a university could not consider race in its admissions policy?

No; the Court also ruled 5–4 that a university has a compelling interest in achieving a diverse class and that race can be an important factor in reaching that goal. Justice Powell wrote that diversity "clearly is a constitutionally permissible goal for an institution of higher learning." He explained that a university constitutionally can institute an admissions policy where "race or ethnic background is simply one element in the selection process."

than race or ethic origin is discrimination for its own sake. This the Constitution forbids."

What happened to Allen Bakke?

After prevailing in the U.S. Supreme Court, UC Davis admitted Bakke to its medical school program. He graduated from medical school in 1982. He then practiced as an anesthesiologist in Minnesota.

How did the Court address affirmative action 25 years after *Bakke*?

The U.S. Supreme Court once again addressed the subject of affirmative action in education in a pair of decisions challenging affirmative action policies for the University of Michigan's undergraduate program in *Gratz v. Bollinger* (2003) and its affirmative action program in Michigan's law school in *Grutter v. Bollinger* (2003).

The Court invalidated the undergraduate policy in *Gratz*, reasoning that the undergrad policy was close to an invalid racial quota program. Under this policy, minority applicants were given an extra 20 points in the admissions scale. The majority reasoned that this policy of adding points automatically to certain students failed to give sufficient individualized consideration of prospective students.

However, the Court narrowly approved of the law school policy in *Grutter*. Writing for the majority, Justice Sandra Day O'Connor reasoned that the law school's policy, which sought to achieve a "critical mass" of minority students but not a specific numerical quota, furthered the compelling state interest of achieving a diverse student body. She wrote that the law school's policy allowed for an individualized review of each applicant. She added: "We expect 25 years from now, the use of racial preferences will no longer be necessary to further the interest approved today."

How did the U.S. Supreme Court rule with respect to busing in the desegregation of schools?

Several U.S. Supreme Court decisions in the Burger Court era dealt with how far and by what methods a school system must go in order to achieve desegregation in its public schools. In *Swann v. Charlotte-Mecklenberg Board of Education* (1971), the Burger Court unanimously ruled that public school systems could use busing as a means of achieving the goal of desegregating public schools. "We find no basis for holding that the local school authorities may not be required to employ bus transporation as one tool of school desegregation," the Court wrote. "Desegregation plans cannot be limited to the walk-in school."

Some southern school districts contended that children should simply attend their neighborhood schools. Moreover, the Court recognized that given the realities of segregated housing patterns, remaining in those schools might never lead to any real desegregation of the schools. Chief Justice Warren E. Burger wrote

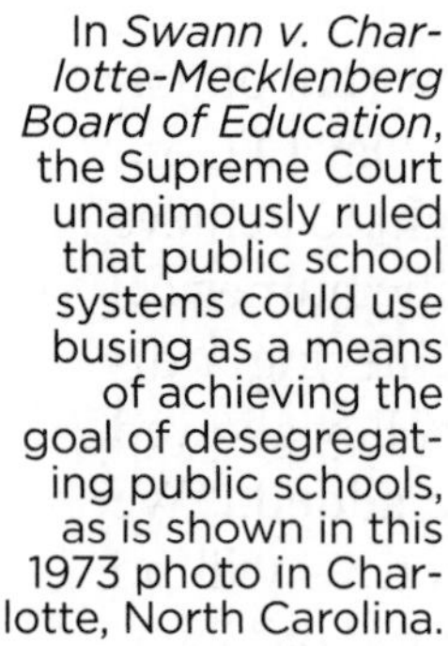

In *Swann v. Charlotte-Mecklenberg Board of Education*, the Supreme Court unanimously ruled that public school systems could use busing as a means of achieving the goal of desegregating public schools, as is shown in this 1973 photo in Charlotte, North Carolina.

in *Swann*: "All things being equal, with no history of discrimination, it might well be desirable to assign pupils to schools nearest their homes. But all things are not equal in a system that has been deliberately constructed and maintained to enforce racial segregation. The remedy for such segregation may be administratively awkward, inconvenient, and even bizarre in some situations and may impose burdens on some; but all awkwardness and inconvenience cannot be avoided in the interim period when remedial adjustments are being made to eliminate the dual school system."

In *Swann*, the Burger Court said that school authorities and district court judges should make sure that school constructions and closings do not operate in a way that reestablishes a dual school system. The goal in the school desegregation cases was for school systems to achieve unitary status.

The Court in *Swann* also noted that schools do not have to achieve the precise ratio of students by race found districtwide in the school system. However, the Court said that it was within the equitable powers of district court judges to rely on "mathematical ratios."

Chief Justice Burger cautioned in his opinion that remedies must not exceed the Court's equitable powers and that such remedial powers could be exercised "only on the basis of a constitutional violation."

To many school desegregation advocates, the *Swann* decision represented the high point of the Court's desegregation cases. The Court cut back on some of these rulings in later decisions, most notably *Milliken v. Bradley* (1974).

How did *Milliken v. Bradley* change the Court's direction on school desegregation?

The *Swann* decision had involved the desegregation of one school district in Charlotte, North Carolina. In the *Milliken* case, a federal district court overseeing the case had approved of plans to desegregate the Detroit school system by imposing a multidistrict remedy. The plan would call for many suburban students to be moved to Detroit city schools and vice versa. The federal district court had implemented the plan, which would affect several school districts that had not participated in so-called de jure segregation (segregation by statute or law). Supporters of the plan argued that it was necessary to involve the suburban school districts in order to achieve real desegregation to counter the effects of "white flight," a phenomenon where many whites move from cities to surrounding suburbs.

The U.S. Supreme Court ruled 5–4 in *Milliken v. Bradley* that the desegregation plan was invalid because it imposed burdens on school districts that were operating as unitary school systems and engaging in no racial segregation. Chief Justice Burger wrote that "without an interdistrict violation and interdistrict effect, there is no constitutional wrong calling for an interdistrict remedy." The ruling meant that many children in the suburbs did not have to be bused to the Detroit city schools and vice versa.

DID YOU KNOW?

What did Justice Thurgood Marshall write in his dissent in *Milliken v. Bradley*?

Justice Marshall, the architect of the NAACP's attack on school segregation, decried the majority opinion in *Milliken* and warned that it would undo efforts to achieve real integration. He warned: "Under such a plan, white and Negro students will not go to school together. Instead, Negro children will continue to attend all-Negro schools. The very evil that *Brown* was aimed at will not be cured but will be perpetuated."

How did the Roberts Court address race in school choice plans?

The Roberts Court ruled 5–4 in *Parents Involved in Community Schools v. Seattle School District* (2007) that school choice plans in Seattle, Washington, and Louisville, Kentucky, that considered race as a key factor were unconstitutional and violative of the Equal Protection Clause.

In assigning slots in schools, the Seattle system assigned students as "white" or "non-white." The Jefferson County, Kentucky, system classified students as "black" or "other." Parents whose kids were not assigned to certain schools alleged that their children were not given those assignments based on race and that such a system violated the Equal Protection Clause.

The Court agreed narrowly. "Before *Brown*, schoolchildren were told where they could and could not go to school based on color of their skin. The school districts in these cases have not carried the heavy burden of demonstrating that we should allow this once again—even for very different reasons," Chief Justice John G. Roberts Jr. wrote in his plurality opinion.

Chief Justice Roberts explained that racial classifications, even those designed to address past discrimination or segregationist practices, are evaluated under strict scrutiny: the highest form of judicial review.

Strict scrutiny requires the government to show that its plan furthers a compelling, or very strong, interest in a very narrowly tailored way. The school districts identified two compelling interests in these cases: (1) addressing the effects of prior discrimination and (2) achieving diversity in the student body.

Chief Justice Roberts reasoned that the first interest—addressing past discrimination—was not relevant because both school districts no longer practiced segregation or were under desegregation decrees issued by a district court. In other words, once a school district was no longer under judicial supervision or a formal desegregation plan, it achieved so-called "unitary" status and eliminated the need to remedy past effects of segregation.

Chief Justice Roberts questioned the school district's definitions of diversity, writing: "Even when it comes to race, the plans here employ only a limited notion of diversity, viewing race exclusively in white/nonwhite terms in Seattle and black/other terms in Jefferson County."

Ultimately, Chief Justice Roberts concluded that the school districts themselves were committing a form of racial discrimination by focusing so much on race. He concluded: "The way to stop discriminating on the basis of race is to stop discriminating on the basis of race."

Justice Stephen Breyer and Justice John Paul Stevens both authored dissenting opinions. Justice Breyer reasoned that the plurality's decision "undermines *Brown*'s promise of integrated primary and secondary education that local communities have sought to make a reality" and that such a thing "cannot be justified in the name of the Equal Protection Clause."

Meanwhile, Justice Stevens criticized Chief Justice Roberts's invocation of the *Brown* decision in order to justify efforts to stop school districts' attempts to achieve greater integration. He wrote:

> There is a cruel irony in The Chief Justice's reliance on our decision in *Brown v. Board of Education.* The first sentence in the concluding paragraph of his opinion states: "Before *Brown*, schoolchildren were told where they could and could not go to school based on the color of their skin." This sentence reminds me of Anatole France's observation: "[T]he majestic equality of the la[w], forbid[s] rich and poor alike to sleep under bridges, to beg in the streets, and to steal their bread." The Chief Justice fails to note that it was only black schoolchildren who were so ordered; indeed, the history books do not tell stories of white children struggling to attend black schools. In this and other ways, The Chief Justice rewrites the history of one of this Court's most important decisions.

GERRYMANDERING

What has the U.S. Supreme Court held about gerrymandering done for racial purposes?

The U.S. Supreme Court recognized that parties could present a cognizable claim of unconstitutional redrawing of voting district lines (a form of so-called "gerrymandering") if such redrawing were done with a clear purpose to discriminate against voters on the basis of race. The Court recognized that this type of claim could have validity in *Gomillion v. Lightfoot* (1960). The evidence in the case showed that city officials sought to carve out nearly every African American voter from voting in the city of Tuskegee's elections.

Writing for the Court, Justice Frankfurter explained: "These allegations, if proven, would abundantly establish that Act 140 was not an ordinary geographic redistricting measure even within familiar abuses of gerrymandering. If these allegations upon a trial remained uncontradicted or unqualified, the conclusion would be

Gerrymandering, a practice by ruling parties of redrawing voting districts to favor their future electoral success, is a portmanteau term coined after an 1812 editorial cartoon called out Massachusetts Governor Elbridge Gerry for creating a district resembling a salamander: the monstrous Gerry-mander.

irresistible, tantamount for all practical purposes to a mathematical demonstration, that the legislation is solely concerned with segregating white and colored voters by fencing Negro citizens out of town so as to deprive them of their pre-existing municipal vote."

Decades later, the Court established in *Shaw v. Reno* (1993) that an Equal Protection Clause claim could be brought if plaintiffs were able to show that the redrawing of political districting lines was done with a clear intent to discriminate on the basis of race. Under *Shaw v. Reno*, a redistricting plan has to meet strict scrutiny if it clearly discriminates on the basis of race. Two years later, the Court ruled in *Miller v. Johnson* (1995) that the redrawing of district lines in North Carolina were drawn so bizarrely that they appeared to be done for racially discriminatory purposes. They involved attempts to actually benefit minority voters—to create minority–majority districts—and thereby increase minority representation in the political bodies. But the U.S. Supreme Court has indicated that whatever the reason, pure racial gerrymandering is likely to be unconstitutional and can only be constitutional if it passes strict scrutiny, the highest form of judicial review.

However, the Court has also ruled in a series of cases—such as *Vieth v. Jubeliler* (2004) and *Rucho v. Common Cause* (2019)—that basic partisan gerrymandering is a political question beyond the ability of the courts to resolve. The question becomes whether

partisan gerrymandering could be used as a guise for racially discriminatory gerrymandering. Only time will tell whether the Court will continue its recent trend of trying to stay out of gerrymandering cases altogether.

Abortion

Who was Norma McCorvey?

Norma McCorvey was the "Roe" of one of the most famous U.S. Supreme Court decisions of all time, *Roe v. Wade*: the case that legalized abortion. McCorvey became pregnant after being gang-raped while returning to her motel on a side road outside of Augusta, Georgia. McCorvey at the time was a 21-year-old carnival worker. The carnival headed to Texas, which is where McCorvey found out that she was pregnant after the rape.

She later explained: "No legitimate doctor in Texas would touch me. I found one doctor who offered to abort me for $500. Only he didn't have a license, and I was scared to turn my body over to him. So there I was—pregnant, unmarried, unemployed, alone and stuck."

She later wrote a book entitled *I Am Roe: My Life, Roe v. Wade, and Freedom of Choice* in which she described her role in the lawsuit. Ironically, in the late 1990s, Roe switched sides and became a vocal

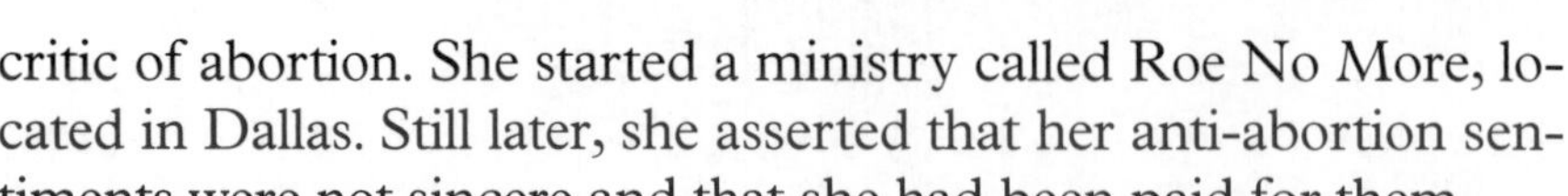

critic of abortion. She started a ministry called Roe No More, located in Dallas. Still later, she asserted that her anti-abortion sentiments were not sincere and that she had been paid for them.

What did the Court decide in *Roe v. Wade*?

The Burger Court ruled 7–2 in *Roe v. Wade* that the "Fourteenth Amendment's concept of personal liberty ... is broad enough to encompass a woman's decision whether or not to terminate her pregnancy." The Court determined that the 14th Amendment's Due Process Clause and its liberty interest included a woman's right of personal privacy to have an abortion. The Court did not rule that women have an unfettered constitutional right to decide whether to have an abortion. Rather, Justice Harry A. Blackmun's opinion balanced the women's interest in personal privacy against the state's interest in protecting future life. Justice Blackmun's opinion divided the pregnancy term into three periods, or trimesters. During the first trimester, women have an unqualified right to have an abortion. During the second trimester, the state can regulate abortions "in ways that are reasonably related to maternal health." During the last trimester—when the

The human face behind *Roe v. Wade*, Norma McCorvey led a complicated and intriguing life before and after the court's ruling, often changing her story to suit her circumstances right up through her so-called deathbed confession in 2017.

fetus becomes viable, or able to live outside of the mother's womb—the state can regulate and even prohibit abortions. The Court also determined that a fetus was not a person within the meaning of the 14th Amendment.

The Court's decision invalidated a Texas law that criminalized abortions except when the abortion was necessary to save the life of the mother.

Who wrote the Court's opinion in *Roe v. Wade*?

Justice Blackmun, who formerly served as counsel to the prestigious Mayo Clinic, wrote the Court's decision in *Roe v. Wade*. Justice Blackmun received countless letters over the years, praising and excoriating him for his historic opinion. At the news conference on his retirement, Justice Blackmun reflected on the decision: "I think it was right in 1973, and I think it was right today. It's a step that had to be taken as we go down the road toward the full emancipation of women."

Which two justices dissented in *Roe v. Wade*?

The two dissenting justices were Justice Byron White and Justice William H. Rehnquist. Justice White criticized the majority for an "improvident and extravagant exercise of the power of judicial review." Chief Justice Rehnquist wrote that he had "difficulty in concluding, as the Court does, that the right of privacy is involved in this case."

Justice White explained:

> I find nothing in the language or history of the Constitution to support the Court's judgment. The Court

DID YOU KNOW?

Who was "Wade" in *Roe v. Wade*?

Dallas District Attorney Henry Wade (far left) is shown here in Dallas, Texas, after the assassination of President Kennedy in 1963. A decade later, he was again in the spotlight as the main defense attorney in *Roe v. Wade.*

Henry Wade was the district attorney for Dallas County, Texas. *Roe* named him as the lead defendant because he was the public official responsible for enforcing the abortion statute. Wade held the district attorney job for more than 35 years. He achieved acclaim for successfully prosecuting Jack Ruby, the man convicted of killing John F. Kennedy assassin Lee Harvey Oswald. Wade died in 2001 at the age of 86.

simply fashions and announces a new constitutional right for pregnant mothers and, with scarcely any reason or authority for its action, invests that right with sufficient substance to override most existing state abortion statutes. The upshot is that the people and the legislatures of the 50 states are constitutionally disentitled to weigh the relative importance of the continued existence and development of the fetus, on the one hand, against a spectrum of possible impacts on the mother, on the other hand. As an exercise of raw judicial power, the Court perhaps has authority to do what it does today; but in my view its judgment is an improvident and extravagant exercise of the power of judicial review that the Constitution extends to this Court.

Who argued the case for *Roe* before the U.S. Supreme Court?

Sarah Weddington (1945–2021) was the attorney who argued the case for *Roe* before the U.S. Supreme Court. Actually, Weddington argued the case twice, as the U.S. Supreme Court first heard the oral argument in 1971 but then ordered a re-argument in 1972 so that the two newest justices on the Court—Justice Lewis F. Powell Jr. and Chief Justice Rehnquist—also could participate in the case. Otherwise, the decision would have been decided by only seven justices.

Weddington argued that women had a constitutional right to make pregnancy decisions. She argued: "We are here to advocate that the decision as to whether or not a particular woman will continue to carry or will terminate a pregnancy is a decision that should be made by that individual; that, in fact, she has a constitutional right to make that decision for herself; and that the State has shown no interest in interfering with that decision."

Weddington was only 26 years old at the time she argued the case for the first time before the U.S. Supreme Court. A graduate of the University of Texas Law School, she later went into politics, serving in the Texas House of Representatives and in the Carter administration as the White House director of political affairs. She later wrote a book about her experiences with *Roe v. Wade* entitled *A Question of Choice*.

Why was the decision in *Roe v. Wade* not the leading story in many newspapers on the date of its decision?

The Court's decision in *Roe v. Wade* was not front-page news because on the day that it was decided—January 22, 1973—former U.S. president Lyndon Baines Johnson died.

What other abortion case did the Court decide on the same day as *Roe v. Wade*?

The Court's other abortion decision decided on January 22, 1973, was *Doe v. Bolton*. The decision involved a constitutional challenge to Georgia's abortion statute. Georgia's statute prohibited abortions unless the pregnancy would endanger the health of the mother, would lead to a damaged fetus, or resulted from a rape. The Court's decision in *Roe* established that the Georgia statute was also unconstitutional, but the Georgia statute also had several procedural requirements for abortions that the Court addressed in a separate opinion. These requirements included limiting abortions to residents of Georgia, requiring abortions to be done in licensed hospitals, and requiring advance approval by an abortion committee of three members of the hospital staff. The Court invalidated these procedural requirements as unduly restricting a woman's right to obtain an abortion.

What did the Court do in the *Planned Parenthood v. Casey* decision?

To the consternation of many conservatives, the Burger Court's 1973 opinion in *Roe v. Wade* remained arguably the most

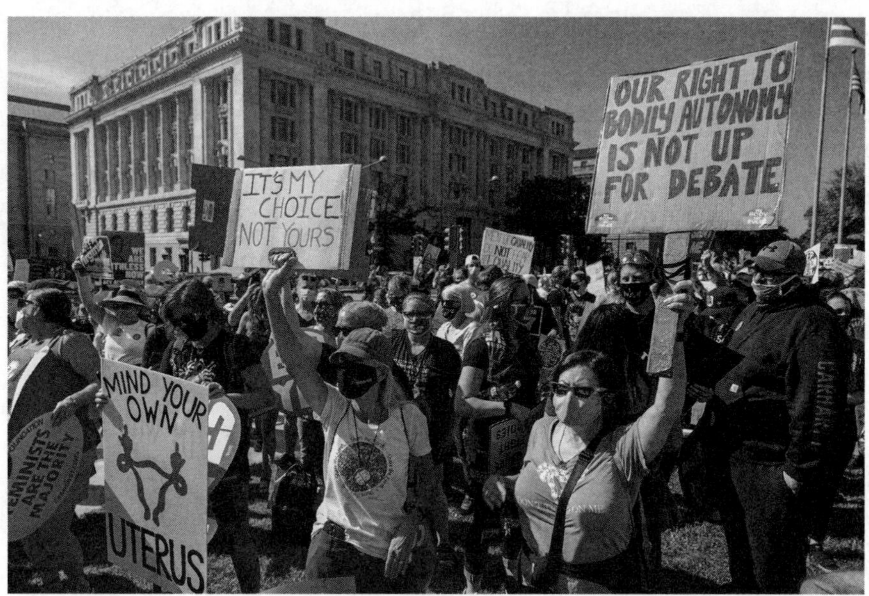

Pro-choice protesters rally in Washington, D.C., during the 2021 Women's March. Many women already—and correctly—feared by then that the Supreme Court would reverse *Roe*.

controversial decision of the past 30–35 years and was not overruled in all that time, though the Rehnquist Court did issue several rulings that limited it to a certain extent. For example, in the 1989 decision *Webster v. Reproductive Health Services*, the Court upheld a Missouri law that declared that life began at conception and forbade the use of public funds for abortions. In her concurring opinion, Justice Sandra Day O'Connor urged the Court to follow the "undue burden" standard: a regulation impacting abortion law does not violate the Constitution unless it unduly burdens a woman's right to receive an abortion.

In 1992, many believed that the Court would overrule *Roe v. Wade* outright with the additions of Justice Clarence Thomas and Justice David Souter to the Court. These two justices were replacing the consistent liberal votes of Justice Thurgood Marshall and Justice William J. Brennan Jr., respectively. However, the Court surprised many observers with its 1992 decision in *Planned Parenthood v. Casey*, which upheld many aspects of Pennsylvania law dealing with abortions, including an informed consent requirement and a 24-hour waiting period. The Court did invalidate a provision that required a woman to tell her husband before obtaining an abortion. The Court also rejected *Roe v. Wade*'s trimester formulation. However, in their plurality opinion, Justice O'Connor, Justice Souter, and Justice Anthony Kennedy refused to flatly overrule *Roe v. Wade*. While they acknowledged that the undue burden standard would replace strict scrutiny as the legal standard, they also reaffirmed "the central holding of *Roe v. Wade*": "The woman's right to terminate her pregnancy before viability is the most central principle of *Roe v. Wade*. It is a rule of law and a component of liberty we cannot renounce."

Justice O'Connor, Justice Kennedy, and Justice Souter were concerned that a decision overturning *Roe v. Wade* would politicize the Court, threaten stare decisis, and lead to the questioning of the Court's legitimacy. Justice Antonin Scalia authored a scathing dissent, calling the plurality opinion "outrageous" and comparing it to the *Dred Scott* decision.

The Court continued to issue decisions in the abortion area. In its 2000 decision *Stenberg v. Carhart*, the Court, by a narrow 5–4 vote, invalidated a Nebraska law prohibiting partial-birth abortions. The majority noted that the law failed to include a health exception for women who needed partial-birth abortions in order to save their own health.

Justice Scalia once again dissented in strong language: "I am optimistic enough to believe that, one day, *Stenberg v. Carhart* will be assigned its rightful place in the history of this Court's jurisprudence beside *Korematsu* and *Dred Scott*."

In what decision did the Court uphold a ban on partial-birth abortions?

In one of its most highly anticipated decisions, a sharply divided U.S. Supreme Court ruled 5–4 in *Gonzales v. Carhart* in favor of a federal law known as the Partial-Birth Abortion Ban Act of 2003, which outlawed a particular type of abortion procedure during the second trimester of pregnancy. In this particular procedure—called intact dilation and extraction—the physician pulls the fetus partially outside the cervix before terminating the fetus, often by crushing the skull. It is called partial birth because the physician initiates delivery and then aborts the fetus's life. The law flatly banned the procedure, and critics pointed out that the law did not even contain a health exception to allow use of the procedure if medically necessary for the woman's health.

The majority of the Court, in an opinion by Justice Kennedy, distinguished the federal law from the Nebraska law that was invalidated by the Rehnquist Court in *Stenberg v. Carhart* (in both cases, Nebraska physician LeRoy Carhart was one of the challengers to the restrictions on abortion), noting that the federal law "is more specific concerning the instances to which it applies and in this respect more precise in its coverage."

Cynics said that the decision is more about the changed composition of the Court since 2000, noting that Justice Samuel A. Alito Jr. replacing Justice O'Connor may have accounted for the different ruling.

Both proponents and opponents of the decision recognize its importance, calling it one of the most significant rulings in the area since *Roe v. Wade.*

In what decision did the Court overrule *Roe v. Wade* and *Planned Parenthood v. Casey*?

The Court overruled *Roe v. Wade* and *Planned Parenthood v. Casey* in *Dobbs v. Jackson Women's Health Organization* (2022). The case concerned a Mississippi law, called the Mississippi Gestational Age Act, that generally barred abortions after 15 weeks of pregnancy.

The Mississippi law in question provided: "Except in a medical emergency or in the case of a severe fetal abnormality, a person shall not intentionally or knowingly perform … or induce an abortion of an unborn human being if the probable gestational age

Associate Justice Samuel Alito, who wrote the majority opinion for the Supreme Court in the controversial *Dobbs v. Jackson Women's Health Organization* decision, was appointed by President George W. Bush in 2006.

of the unborn human being has been determined to be greater than fifteen (15) weeks."

"We hold that *Roe* and *Casey* must be overruled," wrote Justice Alito in his majority opinion. "The Constitution makes no reference to abortion, and no such right is implicitly protected by any constitutional provision, including the one on which the defenders of *Roe* and *Casey* now chiefly rely—the Due Process Clause of the Fourteenth Amendment."

Justice Alito reasoned that the right to an abortion is not a right rooted in history and tradition but rather a judicial creation in the latter part of the 20th century.

Why, according to Justice Alito, was *Roe* such a bad decision?

Justice Alito reasoned that *Roe* was a bad decision because it was not based on the Constitution's language. "*Roe*, however, was remarkably loose in its treatment of the constitutional text," Justice Alito explained. "It held that the abortion right, which is not men-

tioned in the Constitution, is part of a right to privacy, which is also not mentioned."

Justice Alito noted that *Roe* identified three ways the Constitution protected the right to an abortion: (1) the Ninth Amendment's "reservation of rights" language; (2) some combination of privacy from the First, Fourth, and Fifth Amendments, which were extended to the states by the Due Process Clause of the 14th Amendment; and (3) the right to an abortion is directly part of "liberty" within the meaning of the Due Process Clause, which prohibits states from infringing on "life, liberty, or property" interest without due process of law.

Justice Alito addressed the third part first: whether the right to an abortion is a fundamental right that is part of "liberty" under the Due Process Clause. He wrote that to find a fundamental right in the Constitution and its Bill of Rights, one must look to whether the right is rooted in history and tradition or essential to the nation's scheme of "ordered liberty." This inquiry is more difficult, says Justice Alito, when the right is not explicitly spelled out in the Constitution. For example, the Court found that the Second Amendment's right to keep and bear arms is a fundamental right, but that language—"keep and bear arms"—is directly in the Constitution. The right to an abortion is not in the Constitution. The question is whether it falls under the term "liberty."

Justice Alito focused on the lack of history and tradition of recognizing the right to an abortion. "Until the latter part of the 20th century, there was no support in American law for a constitutional right to obtain an abortion," he explained. "No state constitutional provision had recognized such a right. Until a few years before Roe was handed down, no federal or state court had recognized such a right. Nor had any scholarly treatise of which we are aware."

In fact, Justice Alito reasoned that under the common law and then under a variety of state laws, abortion was a crime, at least when done after the 16th to 18th week of pregnancy. "In this country during the 19th century, the vast majority of the States enacted statutes criminalizing abortion at all stages of pregnancy," Justice Alito wrote. "By

1868, the year when the Fourteenth Amendment was ratified, three quarters of the States, 28 out of 37, had enacted statutes making abortion a crime even if it was performed before quickening."

Up until the day of the *Roe* decision, 30 states still had laws that criminalized abortions unless the procedure was done to save the life of the mother. "The inescapable conclusion is that a right to abortion is not deeply rooted in the Nation's history and traditions," Justice Alito writes. "On the contrary, an unbroken tradition of prohibiting abortion on pain of criminal punishment persisted from the earliest days of the common law until 1973."

Justice Alito also rejected the idea that the right to an abortion is part of liberty in and of itself. He distinguished a line of other constitutional right decisions, such as those determining the scope of the right to marry and the right to engage in private acts of sexual conduct as fundamentally different because abortion involves the destruction of "potential life."

What did Justice Alito say about *stare decisis,* the idea that courts should respect prior decisions?

Supporters of *Roe* and *Casey* argued that the Court should respect the concept of *stare decisis*, a Latin term meaning "let the decision stand." The idea is that overruling *Roe* and *Casey* would upset decades of existing precedent and have many bad consequences.

Justice Alito recognized that *stare decisis* is an important feature that lends to stability in the law; however, he quoted the famous phrase that "*stare decisis* is not an inexorable command." He wrote that when it comes to interpreting the Constitution, it is more important that a key constitutional question be "settled right" than merely settled. He later explained on precedent: "Precedents should be respected, but sometimes the Court errs, and occasionally the Court issues an important decision that is egregiously wrong. When that happens, stare decisis is not a straitjacket."

He cited the example of the Court in *Brown v. Board of Education* (1954), which overruled the separate but equal doctrine and segregation in general from *Plessy v. Ferguson* (1896). He also cited two other examples: when the Court upheld a minimum-wage law in *West Coast Hotel Co. v. Parrish* (1937), overruling *Adkins v. Children's Hospital of D.C.* (1923), and the flag-salute decisions when the Court invalidated such a law in *West Virginia Board of Education v. Barnette* (1943) when it previously had upheld one in *Minersville School District v. Gobitis* (1940).

What five factors did Justice Alito identify that justified overruling *Roe*?

Justice Alito identified five factors: (1) the nature of the Court's error; (2) the quality of their reasoning; (3) the "workability" of the rules they imposed on the country; (4) their disruptive effect on other areas of the law; and (5) the absence of concrete reliance.

Regarding the nature of the error, Justice Alito wrote that *Roe* was "egregiously wrong and deeply damaging." He reasoned that the constitutional analysis was far outside the bounds of a reasonable interpretation of the Constitution.

Regarding the quality of reasoning, Justice Alito reasoned that "*Roe* found that the Constitution implicitly conferred a right to obtain an abortion, but it failed to ground its decision in text, history, or precedent" and "relied on an erroneous historical narrative."

Regarding workability of rules, Justice Alito focused on the test created by the U.S. Supreme Court in the *Casey* case: the so-called "undue burden" standard. Recall that in *Casey*, the U.S. Supreme Court retained the essential holding of *Roe*. The determination of whether a burden is due or undue is standardless, according to Justice Alito, adding that ambiguities in the application of this undue burden standard "have caused confusion and disagreement."

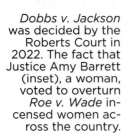

Dobbs v. Jackson was decided by the Roberts Court in 2022. The fact that Justice Amy Barrett (inset), a woman, voted to overturn *Roe v. Wade* incensed women across the country.

Regarding the impact on other areas of the law, Justice Alito wrote that "*Roe* and *Casey* have led to the distortion of many important but unrelated legal doctrines, and that effect provides further support for overruling those decisions." He explained that the abortion decisions have caused the Court to erode standards in First Amendment cases (that involve anti-abortion speakers) and also the rules for determining whether a law is facially too broad.

Regarding reliance, Justice Alito acknowledged that each side in the case posited different opinions on how the Court's decision would impact women but emphasized that each side could petition their legislators on the issue of abortion. He explained: "Our decision returns the issue of abortion to those legislative bodies, and it allows women on both sides of the abortion issue to seek to affect the legislative process by influencing public opinion, lobbying legislators, voting, and running for office."

Ultimately, what does the Court's decision in *Dobbs* mean for abortion?

It means that state legislatures will decide when and under what circumstances abortion is legal and illegal. Justice Alito ex-

DID YOU KNOW?

How did the majority address the concern that overruling *Roe* would cause the public to lose respect for the U.S. Supreme Court as an institution?

Justice Alito responded that the Court has an obligation to explain its decision but that the justices "cannot exceed the scope of our authority under the Constitution, and we cannot allow our decisions to be affected by any extraneous influences such as concern about the public's reaction to our work." He cited the Court's decisions in the school desegregation decision in *Brown v. Board of Education* (1954) and the flag burning as protected speech decision in *Texas v. Johnson* (1989) as key examples. Both *Brown* and *Johnson* were unpopular decisions, at least in certain segments of society, but the Court did what it thought was right in both decisions.

plained the core holding of the Court's decision: "We therefore hold that the Constitution does not confer a right to abortion. *Roe* and *Casey* must be overruled, and the authority to regulate abortion must be returned to the people and their elected representatives."

What standard did the Court say would apply to challenges to abortion laws?

The Court explained that rational basis would be the governing standard when a litigant challenges an abortion law. Previously, the Court had applied the undue burden standard from *Casey*, but the Court overruled *Casey* as well as *Roe* in *Dobbs*. This means that a state defending an abortion law generally must show only that it had a legitimate interest in passing the law and that the law is not arbitrary or irrational.

The Court identified several legitimate interests that a state may have in a law regulating abortions. These include "respect for and preservation of prenatal life at all stages of development; the protection of maternal health and safety; the elimination of particularly gruesome or barbaric medical procedures; the preservation of the integrity of the medical profession; the mitigation of fetal pain; and the prevention of discrimination on the basis of race, sex, or disability."

The Court identified several of these legitimate interests, particularly the protection of prenatal life and the elimination of gruesome or barbaric procedures, to uphold the Mississippi law regulating abortions.

Does the Court's decision in *Dobbs* impact other Court decisions, such as the Court's decision on same-sex marriage?

In his majority opinion, Justice Alito stressed that this decision concerns only abortion and no other issue. He wrote: "[N]othing in this opinion should be understood to cast doubt on precedents that do not concern abortion." The difference between decisions involving private sexual matters and same-sex marriage do not involve what abortion does: the right to potential life.

What did Justice Thomas reason in his concurring opinion?

Justice Thomas agreed with the result of the Court's decision and wrote a separate concurring opinion to stress that the Due Process Clause only prohibits the government from passing laws that violate procedural due process rather than substantive due process. Procedural due process refers to the process the govern-

ment must follow before passing a law that negatively impacts a life, liberty, or property issue. Substantive due process, on the other hand, refers to the underlying substance of a law. Justice Thomas believes that substantive due process impermissibly allows judges to impose their personal predilections and views into law. He warned that substantive due process "involves policymaking rather than neutral legal analysis."

What did Justice Brett M. Kavanaugh say in his concurring opinion?

Justice Kavanaugh explained that the right to an abortion is found nowhere in the text of the Constitution. He described the Constitution as neutral toward the subject of abortion. He explains: "On the question of abortion, the Constitution is therefore neither pro-life nor pro-choice. The Constitution is neutral and leaves the issue for the people and their elected representatives to resolve through the democratic process in the States or Congress—like the numerous other difficult questions of American social and economic policy that the Constitution does not address."

Justice Kavanaugh continued: "In sum, the Constitution is neutral on the issue of abortion and allows the people and their elected representatives to address the issue through the democratic process. In my respectful view, the Court in *Roe* therefore erred by taking sides on the issue of abortion."

What did Chief Justice John G. Roberts Jr. write in his separate opinion?

Chief Justice Roberts wrote an opinion concurring in the judgment. He believed that the Court could uphold the Mississippi law limiting abortions on one hand but not overrule *Roe* and *Casey* completely. He felt that the Court did not need to go that far.

He took a middle-ground position between the majority and the dissent. Chief Justice Roberts reasoned that the Mississippi law in question was constitutional because the state could legitimately reason that prohibiting abortions after 15 weeks was a reasonable way to address the issue. However, Chief Justice Roberts disagreed with the Court's overruling of both *Roe* and *Casey*.

"The Court's opinion is thoughtful and thorough, but those virtues cannot compensate for the fact that its dramatic and consequential ruling is unnecessary to decide the case before us," wrote Chief Justice Roberts.

What did the dissenting justices write?

The dissenting justices—Justice Stephen Breyer, Justice Sonia Sotomayor, and Justice Elena Kagan—wrote a joint opinion. They emphasized that the majority opinion did not respect the rights of women. They explained: "Whatever the exact scope of the coming laws, one result of today's decision is certain: the curtailment of women's rights, and of their status as free and equal citizens."

Chief Justice John Roberts (left) was nominated by President George W. Bush in 2005 after the death of William Rehnquist.

The dissenting justices fundamentally disagreed with the majority that *Roe* and *Casey* were aberrations that came out of nowhere. Instead, the dissenting justices reasoned that *Roe* and *Casey* were part of a general pattern of the Court protecting individuals and individual freedom. They wrote that "*Roe* and *Casey* fit neatly into a long line of decisions protecting from government intrusion a wealth of private choices about family matters, child rearing, intimate relationships, and procreation."

Gun Rights

Why is interpreting the Second Amendment more of a challenge, perhaps, than other amendments in the Bill of Rights?

The Second Amendment is an oddly worded provision. It reads: "A well-regulated militia, being necessary to the security of a free state, the right to keep and bear arms shall not be infringed." Some claim that the Second Amendment is more about the right of the states to have a militia free from control by the federal government. Others emphasize that the Second Amendment is primarily about the individual's right to keep and bear arms.

In what decision did the Court reject a Second Amendment challenge to carrying sawed-off shotguns?

The U.S. Supreme Court ruled in *United States v. Miller* (1939) that a prohibition on unregistered shotguns under the National Firearms Act of 1934 did not violate the Second Amendment. Federal authorities charged Jack Miller and Frank Layton with feloniously transporting a double-barrel shotgun with a barrel of less than 18 inches in length from Oklahoma to Arkansas.

The Court rejected Miller and Layton's Second Amendment challenge, writing: "In the absence of any evidence tending to show that possession or use of a 'shotgun having a barrel of less than eighteen inches in length' at this time has some reasonable relationship to the preservation or efficiency of a well-regulated militia, we cannot say that the Second Amendment guarantees the right to keep and bear such an instrument. Certainly it is not within judicial notice that this weapon is any part of the ordinary military equipment or that its use could contribute to the common defense."

Many interpreted the *Miller* decision as meaning that the Second Amendment protected only a collective right to bearing arms under the militia, not an individual's right to keep and bear arms.

When did the Court first find that the Second Amendment protected an individual's right to keep and bear arms?

For most of American history, the courts found that the Second Amendment only protected the right of the militia, not an individual's right to keep and bear arms. However, in 2008, the U.S. Supreme Court ruled 5–4 in *District of Columbia v. Heller* (2008) that the Second Amendment protected an individual's right to keep and bear arms. Justice Antonin Scalia, in his majority opinion, divided the Second Amendment into a prefatory clause (the militia clause) and an operative clause (the right to keep and bear arms). This phrasing was once again adept, as Justice Scalia elevated the right to keep and bear arms over the militia clause.

Justice Scalia relied heavily on the fact that the Second Amendment mentions "the right of the people." Justice Scalia

Widely familiar as the center of the U.S. federal government, the District of Columbia is neither a state nor part of any state, making the district a logical testing ground for a constitutional issue without complication of states' rights.

noted that the Bill of Rights contains three other mentions of the right of the people—(1) the right of the people to peaceably assemble in the First Amendment; (2) the right of the people to be free from unreasonable searches and seizures in the Fourth Amendment; and (3) the Ninth Amendment, which uses similar language—"retained by the people." Justice Scalia explained: "All three of these instances unambiguously refer to individual rights, not collective rights, or rights that may be exercised only through participation in some corporate body."

Justice Scalia then turned his attention to the language of the operative clause: "the right of the people to keep and bear arms." He reasoned that the phrase "keep arms" meant to have weapons in one's home. The right to keep arms means that an individual has the right to store firearms in his or her house for self-defense purposes. Justice Scalia also determined that the word "bear arms" referred to the right of individual people to carry weapons outside of organized militia service. He wrote that the right to bear arms was "unambigiously used to refer to the carrying of weapons outside of an organized militia."

Justice Scalia concluded that handgun violence presented a serious problem in society and said that the District of Columbia had other tools to address this. However, he continued: "But the enshrinement of constitutional rights necessarily takes certain policy choices off the table. These include the absolute prohibition of handguns held and used for self-defense in the home."

To Justice Scalia, what was the importance of state constitutional provisions regarding keeping and bearing arms?

Justice Scalia analyzed those state constitutions that had provisions similar to the Second Amendment. He found nine state constitutional provisions and noted that seven of them had a clear provision for an individual's right to keep and bear arms. He noted that four states—Kentucky, Ohio, Indiana, and Missouri—used language that talked about an individual's right to "bear arms in defence of themselves and the State." Three states—Mississippi, Connecticut, and Alabama—used language that even more clearly reflected an intent to protect an individual right: each citizen has the "right to bear arms in defence of himself and the State." Finally, two states—Massachusetts and Tennessee—used the language about "common defence," which does suggest more of a right to a militia than an individual citizen. However, the bulk of the state provisions clearly reflected an intent to protect an individual right, reasoned Justice Scalia.

"That of the nine state constitutional protections for the right to bear arms enacted immediately after 1789 at least seven unequivocally protected an individual citizen's right to self-defense is strong evidence that that is how the founding generation conceived of the right," Justice Scalia concluded.

Did Justice Scalia in *Heller* believe that the Second Amendment was unlimited?

The Court in *Heller* emphasized that the Second Amendment right was not unlimited. Justice Scalia wrote that "nothing in our opinion should be taken to cast doubt on longstanding prohibitions on the possession of firearms by felons and the mentally ill, or laws forbidding the carrying of firearms in sensitive places

DID YOU KNOW?

What did Justice Scalia say about rational basis review for gun laws?

Justice Scalia questioned the use of the rational basis standard to review constitutional challenges to gun laws. He wrote in a footnote: "If all that was required to overcome the right to keep and bear arms was a rational basis, the Second Amendment would be redundant with the separate constitutional prohibitions on irrational laws, and have no effect."

such as schools and government buildings, or laws imposing conditions and qualifications on the commercial sale of arms."

What was the ultimate conclusion reached in *Heller*?

The ultimate conclusion reached was that the restrictive handgun ban in the District of Columbia was unconstitutional and violated the Second Amendment right to keep and bear arms. Justice Scalia explained that "[a]ssuming that *Heller* is not disqualified from the exercise of Second Amendment rights, the District must permit him to register his handgun and must issue him a license to carry in the home."

Who was Heller?

Dick Heller provided security at the Thurgood Marshall Judicial Center as a special police officer with the District of Columbia police force. Heller had to carry a gun at this job but could not have an operable firearm at his home, which was directly across from abandoned public housing.

Dick Heller, one of six plaintiffs filing the eponymous *Heller v. DC* Second Amendment case, was a licensed special police officer and resident of the District of Columbia. As a result of the case, D.C.'s Firearms Control Regulations Act of 1975 was declared unconstitutional.

Who was the original lead plaintiff in the challenge to the D.C. gun law at issue in the *Heller* case?

Originally, the first listed plaintiff was Shelly Parker, an African American woman who had challenged drug dealers in her neighborhood. The complaint in the case read: "As a consequence of trying to make her neighborhood a better place to live, Ms. Parker has been threatened by drug dealers." The U.S. Court of Appeals for the D.C. Circuit determined that Parker and the plaintiffs other than Dick Heller lacked standing to pursue the litigation. The appeals court determined that Dick Heller had standing to pursue the litigation because he was the only one of the six plaintiffs who had applied and been denied a license to own a handgun. "The denial of the gun license is significant," the appeals court wrote. "It constitutes an injury independent of the District's prospective enforcement of its gun laws."

Which justices wrote dissenting opinions in *Heller*?

Justice John Paul Stevens and Justice Stephen Breyer both wrote dissenting opinions in *Heller*. Justice Stevens read the history very differently from Justice Scalia. He also viewed the Second Amendment as primarily about the militia. "The Second Amendment was adopted to protect the right of the people of each of the several States to maintain a well-regulated militia," he wrote. "It was a response to concerns raised during the ratification of the Constitution that the power of Congress to disarm the state militias and create a national standing army posed an intolerable threat to the sovereignty of the several States."

He continued: "Until today, it has been understood that legislatures may regulate the civilian use and misuse of firearms so long as they do not interfere with the preservation of a well-regulated militia. The Court's announcement of a new constitutional right to own and use firearms for private purposes upsets that settled understanding, but leaves for future cases the formidable task of defining the scope of permissible regulations."

For his part, Justice Breyer focused on the level of handgun violence in the United States. He viewed the D.C. ordinance banning handguns as "a permissible legislative response to a serious, indeed life-threatening, problem." Justice Breyer emphasized that many cities in the Founding Era limited firearms within city limits. He also quoted quite a few statistics about gun-related violence in the United States, such as "[f]rom 1993 to 1997, there were 180,533 firearm-related deaths in the United States, an average of over 36,000 per year." He added that firearms appear to be a "very popular weapon among criminals."

What was Justice Stevens's view on the language of the militia clause of the Second Amendment?

Justice Stevens emphasized that the militia clause of the Second Amendment explained that the overall purpose of the Second Amendment was to protect the rights of states to have a militia free from federal governmental control. He explained: "The preamble to the Second Amendment makes three important

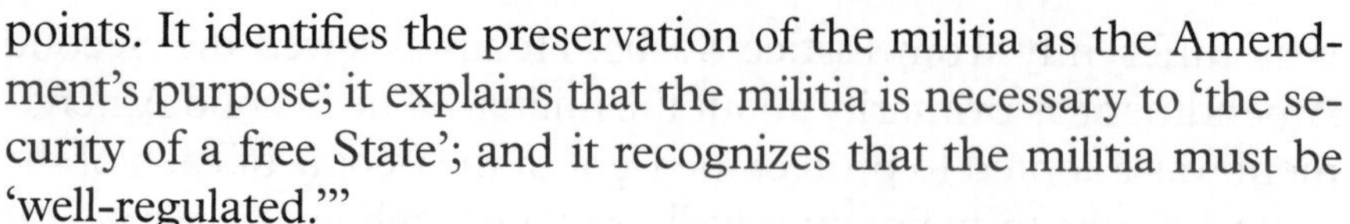

points. It identifies the preservation of the militia as the Amendment's purpose; it explains that the militia is necessary to 'the security of a free State'; and it recognizes that the militia must be 'well-regulated.'"

What was Justice Stevens's response to Justice Scalia's argument about "the right of the people" language in the Second Amendment?

Justice Stevens reasoned that the words "the people" in the Second Amendment refer back to the ultimate purpose of the Second Amendment: that the people have a right to participate in the militia and, more importantly, that "the ultimate purpose of the Amendment was to protect the States' share of the divided sovereignty created by the Constitution."

One point of contention in the interpretation of the Second Amendment is whether the right to bear arms falls to individuals or exists only in the context of a "well-regulated militia." Some point to a vast difference in the level of arms technology now versus during the birth of the nation.

DID YOU KNOW?

What was Justice Stevens's ultimate conclusion on the meaning of the Second Amendment?

Justice Stevens's ultimate conclusion is that the Second Amendment was focused on the militia, not any sort of individual right. He explains: "When each word in the text is given full effect, the Amendment is most naturally read to secure to the people a right to use and possess arms in conjunction with service in a well-regulated militia. So far as appears, no more than that was contemplated by its drafters or is encompassed within its terms."

Why did the U.S. Supreme Court decide that the right to keep and bear arms should be incorporated?

In his majority opinion, Justice Samuel A. Alito Jr. framed the question as whether the right to keep and bear arms was "essential to our scheme of ordered liberty" or "deeply rooted in this Nation's history and tradition."

Justice Alito reasoned that the core concept of the Second Amendment—and why it is so vitally important in a free society—is that it enables individuals to engage in the self-defense of their homes. He reasoned that those who drafted and ratified the Bill of Rights considered the Second Amendment's right to keep and bear arms to be seminally important. The fear of many of the Framers, according to Justice Alito, was that a standing army supported by the federal government would disarm the citizenry and subject them to the whims of the government. Justice Alito added that both the Federalists and the Anti-Federalists, the two major founding political parties at the nation's beginning, both agreed on how fundamental the right to keep and bear arms was.

Justice Alito concluded that "it is clear that the Framers and ratifiers of the Fourteenth Amendment counted the right to keep and bear arms among those fundamental rights necessary to our system of ordered liberty."

What was the significance of the Court's decision in *McDonald v. City of Chicago*?

The Court's decision in *McDonald v. City of Chicago* (2010) was significant because it was this decision that held that the Second Amendment's right to keep and bear arms also applied to state and local governments in addition to the federal government. The city of Chicago had a virtual flat ban on handgun possession. Otis McDonald, an antigang activist in his 70s, was one of several individuals who challenged the ban. McDonald said that he needed a handgun for self-defense because several gang members had threatened him for his antigang activity. Another plaintiff was Colleen Lawson, another Chicago resident, whose home had been burglarized. She, like McDonald, said that she needed a handgun for self-defense purposes.

What New York law did the U.S. Supreme Court strike down on Second Amendment grounds?

The U.S. Supreme Court invalidated a restrictive gun licensing law in *New York State Rifle & Pistol Association v. Bruen* (2022). The law criminalized the possession of "any firearm" without a license, whether inside or outside the home, punishable by up to four years in prison or a $5,000 fine for a felony offense and one year in prison or a $1,000 fine for a misdemeanor.

Under New York law, a license applicant who wants to possess a firearm at home (or in his place of business) must convince a

The Sullivan Act, a 1911 gun control law sponsored by New York state senator Timothy Sullivan (pictured), heavily restricted gun licensing. The law stood for over 100 years before being struck down by the Supreme Court's ruling in *New York State Rifle & Pistol Association v. Bruen.*

"licensing officer"—usually a judge or law-enforcement officer—that, among other things, he is of good moral character, he has no history of crime or mental illness, and "no good cause exists for the denial of the license."

If a person wants to carry a firearm outside his home or place of business for self-defense, the applicant must obtain an unrestricted license to "have and carry" a concealed "pistol or revolver" as per New York penal law §400.00(2)(f). To secure that license, the applicant must prove that "proper cause exists" to issue it.

However, the law did not define "proper cause." New York courts interpreted proper cause to mean that a person has "a special need for self-protection distinguishable from that of the general community." The net effect of this New York law is that it prohibited nearly anyone from carrying a firearm in public.

New York was one of only six states that had such a restrictive gun-carry permission process. Under this law, as Justice Clarence Thomas wrote in the Court's majority opinion, "authorities have discretion to deny concealed-carry licenses even when the applicant satisfies the statutory criteria, usually because the applicant has not demonstrated cause or suitability for the relevant license."

Who challenged the New York law?

New York State Rifle & Pistol Association, Inc., is a public-interest group that was organized to defend the Second Amendment rights of New Yorkers. Brandon Koch and Robert Nash were law-abiding, adult citizens of Rensselaer County, New York. Koch lived in Troy, while Nash lived in Averill Park. Both Koch and Nash were members of the New York State Rifle & Pistol Association.

In 2014, Nash applied for a permit to carry a handgun in public. He contended that he lived in an area where a string of robberies occurred. New York authorities denied his request, saying that he did not have a special need for the carry permit.

Koch also applied for the general carry permit but was denied because he did not show "proper cause." Thus, both Nash and Koch could carry guns to go hunting but could not carry them generally.

How did the Court in the *New York* case change the law in the Second Amendment area?

Previously, a number of lower courts had first analyzed whether a challenged restriction impacts conduct within the scope of the Second Amendment. If it does not, then the restriction is constitutional. In other words, if the gun regulation deals with activity outside the scope of general Second Amendment protection, then the law is constitutional, and that is the end of the Second Amendment analysis.

If the restriction does impact Second Amendment conduct, then the question is whether the weapons in question are (1) in

common usage and (2) in typical usage by law-abiding citizens for lawful purposes, such as for hunting or self-defense. The courts would ask "how close the law comes to the core of the Second Amendment right and the severity of the law's burden on that right." In essence, lower courts evaluated Second Amendment challenges under a version of intermediate scrutiny, asking whether the government had a substantial interest in the gun regulation and whether the law was narrowly drawn.

Justice Thomas changed this standard. He explained: "In keeping with *Heller*, we hold that when the Second Amendment's plain text covers an individual's conduct, the Constitution presumptively protects that conduct. To justify its regulation, the government may not simply posit that the regulation promotes an important interest. Rather, the government must demonstrate that the regulation is consistent with this Nation's historical tradition of firearm regulation. Only if a firearm regulation is consistent with this Nation's historical tradition may a court conclude that the individual's conduct falls outside the Second Amendment's 'unqualified command.'"

Why did the Court invalidate the New York law?

The Court noted that the petitioners were law-abiding citizens who simply wanted to carry a handgun for protection both at home and in public. "Nothing in the Second Amendment's text draws a home/public distinction with respect to the right to keep and bear arms," Justice Thomas explained. "The Second Amendment's plain text thus presumptively guarantees petitioners Koch and Nash a right to 'bear' arms in public for self-defense."

Justice Thomas examined the history of state regulations on the carrying of firearms. Ultimately, he concluded that "[n]one of these historical limitations on the right to bear arms approach New York's proper-cause requirement because none operated to prevent law-abiding citizens with ordinary self-defense needs from carrying arms in public for that purpose."

Justice Thomas noted that "[a]part from a few late 19th-century outlier jurisdictions, American governments simply have not broadly prohibited the public carry of commonly used firearms for personal defense."

Justice Thomas concluded:

> The constitutional right to bear arms in public for self-defense is not "a second-class right, subject to an entirely different body of rules than the other Bill of Rights guarantees." We know of no other constitutional right that an individual may exercise only after demonstrating to government officers some special need. That is not how the First Amendment works when it comes to unpopular speech or the free exercise of religion. It is not how the Sixth Amendment works when it comes to a defendant's right to confront the witnesses against him. And it is not how the Second Amendment works when it comes to public carry for self-defense.
>
> New York's proper-cause requirement violates the Fourteenth Amendment in that it prevents law-abiding citizens with ordinary self-defense needs from exercising their right to keep and bear arms. We therefore reverse the judgment of the Court of Appeals and remand the case for further proceedings consistent with this opinion.

With *New York State Rifle & Pistol Association v. Bruen*, the Supreme Court created a national standard for processing concealed weapons permits on a "shall-issue" basis.

What did Justice Brett M. Kavanaugh highlight in his concurring opinion?

Justice Kavanaugh highlighted the fact that New York's law giving law-enforcement officials special discretion to deny carry permits was one of only six states that have such a law. Most other states have so-called "shall-issue licensing regimes." Under these laws, Justice Kavanaugh explained, a state can still require that an applicant "undergo fingerprinting, a background check, a mental health records check, and training in firearms handling and in laws regarding the use of force, among other possible requirements."

He also highlighted that the Court was not saying that limits on gun regulation do not exist. "Properly interpreted, the Second Amendment allows a 'variety' of gun regulations," Justice Kavanaugh explained, citing Justice Scalia's passage in *Heller* where he had emphasized the same point.

What did Justice Alito explain in his concurring opinion?

Justice Alito, who authored the Court's opinion in *McDonald v. City of Chicago*, emphasized that the case was about the right of self-defense. He also cited examples from amicus briefs in which individuals brandished a firearm in public in order to save someone who was being attacked. He cited examples of a gay man in Arkansas who was being attacked by four gay-bashers. However, a friend of the victim pulled out a pistol and stopped the brutal attack. He also cited the example of a woman in Jefferson City, Tennessee, who was being attacked until a bystander pulled out a firearm and saved the woman.

Justice Alito also wrote to reiterate the following: "All that we decide in this case is that the Second Amendment protects the right of law-abiding people to carry a gun outside the home for self-defense and that the Sullivan Law, which makes that virtually impossible for most New Yorkers, is unconstitutional."

Justice Alito also explained that the means–ends analysis employed by the appeals court in this litigation did not adequately protect Second Amendment values. Under the means–ends analysis, the court assesses a law's burden on the Second Amendment right and the strength of the state's interest in imposing the challenged restriction. Justice Alito explained that this "mode of analysis places no firm limits on the ability of judges to sustain any law restricting the possession or use of a gun."

Justice Alito concluded: "Today, unfortunately, many Americans have good reason to fear that they will be victimized if they are unable to protect themselves. And today, no less than in 1791, the Second Amendment guarantees their right to do so."

What did Justice Amy Coney Barrett highlight in her concurring opinion?

Justice Barrett also wrote a concurring opinion in the case. She emphasized "two methodological points" that the Court did not decide.

First, she noted that the Court did not decide "the manner and circumstances in which postratification practice may bear on the original meaning of the Constitution"—in other words, the exact significance of evidence that takes place after the ratification of the Second Amendment as part of the Bill of Rights.

She also questioned whether courts should rely mainly on the ratification of the Second Amendment in 1791 or the 14th Amendment in 1868. She explained: "Second and relatedly, the Court avoids another 'ongoing scholarly debate on whether courts should primarily rely on the prevailing understanding of an individual right when the Fourteenth Amendment was ratified in 1868' or when the Bill of Rights was ratified in 1791."

Which justice wrote a dissenting opinion?

Justice Breyer—joined by Justice Sonia Sotomayor and Justice Elena Kagan—authored the dissenting opinion. He began his opinion by emphasizing the number of American deaths by firearms, writing: "In 2020, 45,222 Americans were killed by firearms."

Justice Breyer claimed that the majority opinion was based on "several mistakes":

> First, the Court decides this case on the basis of the pleadings, without the benefit of discovery or an evidentiary record. As a result, it may well rest its decision on a mistaken understanding of how New York's law operates in practice. Second, the Court wrongly limits its analysis to focus nearly exclusively on history. It refuses to consider the government interests that justify a challenged gun regulation, regardless of how compelling those interests may be. The Constitution contains no such limitation, and neither do our precedents. Third, the Court itself demonstrates the practical problems with its history-only approach. In applying that approach to New York's law, the Court fails to correctly identify and analyze the relevant historical facts. Only by ignoring an abundance of historical evidence supporting regulations restricting the public carriage of firearms can the Court conclude that New York's law is not "consistent with the Nation's historical tradition of firearm regulation."

Justice Breyer explained that "when courts interpret the Second Amendment, it is constitutionally proper, indeed often necessary, for them to consider the serious dangers and consequences of gun violence that lead States to regulate firearms."

Trivia

Who were the first six justices to serve on the U.S. Supreme Court?

The first six justices to serve on the U.S. Supreme Court were Chief Justice John Jay, Chief Justice John Rutledge, Justice William Cushing, Justice James Wilson, Justice John Blair, and Justice James Iredell. President George Washington initially had nominated Robert H. Harrison, but he declined the nomination due to poor health. In his place, Washington nominated Justice Iredell.

Why did Chief Justice Jay resign from the Court?

Chief Justice Jay, one of the three authors of the Federalist Papers along with Alexander Hamilton and James Madison, resigned from the Court in 1795 in order to become the governor

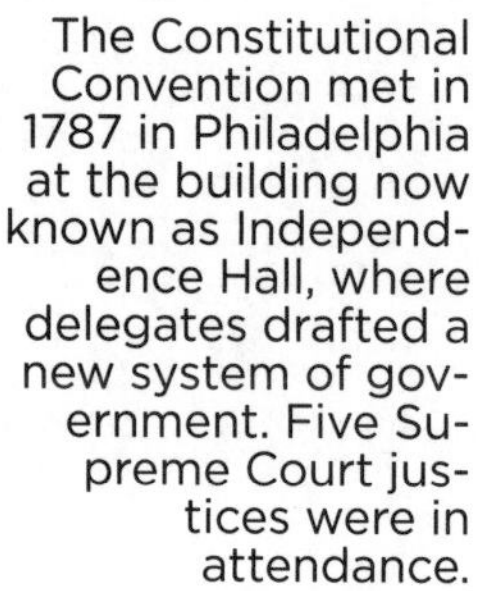

The Constitutional Convention met in 1787 in Philadelphia at the building now known as Independence Hall, where delegates drafted a new system of government. Five Supreme Court justices were in attendance.

of New York. Chief Justice Jay had previously sought the top political position in New York. In 1792, while still a member of the U.S. Supreme Court, he was the Federalist candidate for governor but was defeated by George Clinton. However, Chief Justice Jay rebounded to capture the gubernatorial election in May 1795. He then resigned from the U.S. Supreme Court on June 29, 1795.

Who was the only U.S. Supreme Court justice to have signed the Declaration of Independence?

Justice Wilson (1742–1798) of Pennsylvania, one of the six original U.S. Supreme Court justices, was the only member of the U.S. Supreme Court to have signed the Declaration of Independence. Justice Wilson also served as a delegate to the Constitutional Convention of 1787 in Philadelphia and signed the Constitution in September 1787. Justice Wilson was born in Scotland and moved to the United States in 1766.

Which U.S. Supreme Court justices attended the Constitutional Convention of 1787?

Five U.S. Supreme Court justices attended the Constitutional Convention of 1787. They were Justice Wilson from Pennsylvania, Chief Justice John Rutledge from South Carolina, Chief Justice Oliver Ellsworth from Connecticut, Justice William Paterson from New Jersey, and Justice Blair from Virginia.

CAREERS AWAY FROM THE COURT

How many U.S. Supreme Court justices were former or future state governors?

Ten justices have served as state governors. They are:

- Justice Thomas Johnson, who was governor of Maryland from 1777 to 1779
- Chief Justice John Rutledge, who was governor of South Carolina from 1779 to 1782
- Justice William Paterson, who was governor of New Jersey from 1790 to 1792
- Chief Justice John Jay, who was governor of New York from 1795 to 1801
- Justice Levi Woodbury, who was governor of New Hampshire from 1823 to 1824
- Chief Justice Salmon P. Chase, who was governor of Ohio from 1856 to 1860
- Chief Justice Charles Evans Hughes, who was governor of New York from 1907 to 1910
- Justice Frank Murphy, who was governor of Michigan from 1937 to 1939

- Chief Justice Earl Warren, who was governor of California from 1943 to 1953
- Justice James Francis Byrnes, who was governor of South Carolina from 1951 to 1955

Which U.S. Supreme Court justices formerly served as U.S. solicitor general?

Six U.S. Supreme Court justices formerly served as U.S. solicitor general in their careers before serving on the Court. They are:

- Chief Justice William Howard Taft, who served as solicitor general from 1890 to 1892
- Chief Justice Charles Evans Hughes, who served as solicitor general from 1929 to 1930
- Justice Stanley Reed, who served as solicitor general from 1935 to 1938
- Justice Robert H. Jackson, who served as solicitor general from 1938 to 1940
- Justice Thurgood Marshall, who served as solicitor general from 1965 to 1967
- Justice Elena Kagan, who served as solicitor general from 2009 to 2010

Who was the only U.S. Supreme Court justice to serve as a U.S. senator *after* he left the Court?

Justice David Davis (1815–1886) is the only member of the U.S. Supreme Court to serve as a U.S. senator after leaving the Court. Justice Davis served on the Court from 1862 to 1877. He resigned from the Court to run for the Senate, where he served from 1877 to 1883.

DID YOU KNOW?

Which former justice was a practicing medical doctor?

Justice Samuel Freeman Miller, who served on the Court from 1862 to 1890, graduated from Transylvania University with a degree in medicine. He practiced medicine for 12 years in Knox County, Kentucky, before going into the practice of law. Two other justices had some experience with medical training. Justice Noah Haynes Swayne studied medicine in his youth before turning to law, and Justice Hugo Black attended Birmingham Medical School for one year.

Fourteen other justices served in the U.S. Senate before they ascended to the U.S. Supreme Court, but Justice Davis was the only one to first serve on the Court and then serve in the Senate.

Which former justices were newspaper editors or reporters?

Justice John McLean, who served from 1830 to 1862, published the *Western Star* newspaper in Lebanon, Ohio. Justice Henry Baldwin, who served from 1830 to 1844, published with his law partners a newspaper called *The Tree of Liberty*. Justice Stanley Matthews, who served from 1881 to 1889, edited the weekly *Tennessee Democrat* and later the *Cincinnati Morning Herald*. Chief Justice Melville Fuller, who served as chief justice from 1888 to 1910, was an editor of *The Age*, a daily newspaper. Justice John Hessin Clarke, who served from 1916 to 1922, was publisher of *The Vindicator* in Youngstown, Ohio. Chief Justice William Howard Taft, who served as chief justice from 1921 to 1930, was a reporter for the *Cincinnati Commercial* during his law school days. Justice James Byrnes, who served from 1941 to 1942, was the owner and editor of the *Aiken Journal and Review* in Aiken, South Carolina.

Which U.S. Supreme Court justices previously served as law clerks to U.S. Supreme Court justices?

Justice Byron White clerked for Chief Justice Fred M. Vinson from 1946 to 1947. Chief Justice William H. Rehnquist clerked for Justice Robert H. Jackson from 1951 to 1952. Justice John Paul Stevens clerked for Justice Wiley Blount Rutledge from 1947 to 1948. Justice Stephen Breyer clerked for Justice Arthur Goldberg from 1964 to 1965. Chief Justice John G. Roberts Jr. clerked for Chief Justice Rehnquist from 1980 to 1981. Justice Kagan clerked for Justice Thurgood Marshall from 1987 to 1988. Justice Neil M. Gorsuch clerked for Justice Byron White and Justice Anthony Kennedy from 1993 to 1994. Justice Brett M. Kavanaugh clerked for Justice Kennedy from 1993 to 1994. Justice Amy Coney Barrett clerked for Justice Antonin Scalia from 1998 to 1999. Justice Ketanji Brown Jackson clerked for Justice Breyer from 1999 to 2000.

Which justice left the Court for a term to represent the United States in Nuremberg?

Justice Robert H. Jackson left the U.S. Supreme Court for a term to serve as the United States' chief prosecutor at the Nuremberg Nazi war crimes trials.

What did Justice Lewis F. Powell Jr. say to another justice after Justice Scalia's active questioning at an oral argument in 1986?

Justice Scalia was known as a forceful questioner at oral arguments. He would frequently ask several pointed and direct questions

David Souter, a Rhodes Scholar, was appointed to the Supreme Court by President George H. W. Bush in 1990, serving as an associate justice until his retirement in 2009.

at the attorneys appearing before the High Court. He, in other words, was not bashful. After Justice Scalia's first day of oral arguments in 1986, Justice Powell allegedly whispered to Justice Thurgood Marshall: "Do you think he knows that the rest of us are here?"

Which justice is a former Rhodes Scholar?

Justice David Souter spent two years as a Rhodes Scholar at Magdalen College, Oxford. Interestingly, Justice Breyer was a Marshall Scholar at Magdalen College, Oxford.

What did Justice Felix Frankfurter say upon hearing of the passing of Chief Justice Vinson?

Justice Frankfurter, who was not a fan of Chief Justice Vinson, allegedly said upon hearing of the chief justice's passing: "This is the first indication I have ever had there is a God."

Which justices ultimately succeeded the justices for which they used to clerk?

Chief Justice John G. Roberts Jr. succeeded Chief Justice Rehnquist, for whom he clerked. Justice Ketanji Brown Jackson succeeded Justice Breyer, for whom she clerked.

Which U.S. Supreme Court justices were not born in the United States?

Justice Wilson, who served on the Court from 1789 to 1798, was born in Caskardy, Scotland, in 1742. Justice Iredell, who served from 1790 to 1799, was born in Lewes, England. Justice David Josiah Brewer, who served from 1889 to 1910, was born in Asia Minor (present-day Turkey).

Who is the only U.S. Supreme Court justice to have signed the Declaration of Independence?

Justice Samuel Chase is the only justice to have signed the Declaration of Independence.

Which justice had the most children?

Justice Benjamin Robbins Curtis had 12 children: five with his first wife, Eliza; three with his second wife, Nancy; and four with third wife, Malleville. Justice Robert Trimble, who served from 1826 to 1828, had 11 children with his wife, Nancy. Chief Justice John Marshall had 10 children.

DID YOU KNOW?

Which justice served the longest time on the Court?

Justice William O. Douglas, who served from 1939 to 1975, served the longest of any justice in history: more than 36 years.

Which presidents have appointed the most justices to the U.S. Supreme Court?

George Washington elevated 11 men to the U.S. Supreme Court. Franklin D. Roosevelt appointed nine.

Which president who served two full terms only made one appointment to the U.S. Supreme Court?

James Monroe appointed only Justice Smith Thompson to the bench in 1823.

Which justice served the shortest amount of time?

Justice Byrnes served only 15 months on the U.S. Supreme Court. Henry Abraham, in his book *Justices, Presidents, and Sena-*

tors, writes: "Jimmy Byrnes lasted for little more than a year on the Court: a man of action, a doer and a planner, he was not comfortable as a jurist."

What justice served as a postmaster general in his early career?

Justice Samuel Nelson, who served on the Court from 1845 to 1872, served as postmaster general of Cortland, New York, from 1820 to 1823.

What former justice was a practicing medical doctor?

Justice Samuel Freeman Miller, who served on the Court from 1862 to 1890, graduated from Transylvania University in 1838 with a degree in medicine. He practiced medicine for 12 years in Knox County, Kentucky, before going into the practice of law.

Which chief justices were associate justices before their elevation to the top post?

Chief Justice Edward Douglass White served as an associate justice from 1894 to 1910. President William Howard Taft nominated him for chief justice in 1910, and he served in that capacity until his death in 1921. Chief Justice Charles Evans Hughes served as an associate justice from 1910 to 1916. He resigned to run for president but lost to President Woodrow Wilson. President Herbert Hoover then nominated him for chief justice, a position he served in from 1930 to 1941. Chief Justice Harlan Fiske Stone served as associate judge and then was elevated to chief justice by President Franklin D. Roosevelt

One of the few Supreme Court justices to have served as U.S. solicitor general, and one of the few who formerly worked on a newspaper, William Howard Taft also has the distinction of being the only U.S. president to have also served on the Supreme Court.

in 1941. Chief Justice Rehnquist was appointed as an associate justice by President Richard Nixon in 1972 and then was elevated to chief justice by President Ronald Reagan in 1986.

What former U.S. Supreme Court justice prosecuted ax murderer Lizzie Borden?

Justice William Henry Moody, who served on the Court from 1906 to 1910, prosecuted Lizzie Borden when he was a U.S. attorney in Massachusetts.

What U.S. Supreme Court justice prosecuted the Tarzan Burglar?

Justice Sonia Sotomayor prosecuted Richard Maddicks, better known as "the Tarzan Burglar," when she served as an assistant district attorney under legendary district attorney Robert Morgenthau in New York. The Tarzan Burglar terrorized people in Harlem by swinging from ropes into their apartments and even killed three people.

At her confirmation hearing, Justice Sotomayor spoke of the Tarzan case:

> You asked me a second question about the Tarzan murderer case, and that case brought to life for me in a way that perhaps no other case had fully done before the tragic consequences of needless deaths.
>
> In that case, Mr. Maddicks was dubbed "the Tarzan murderer" by the press because he used acrobatic feats to gain entry into apartments. In one case, he took a rope, placed it on a pipe on top of a roof, put a paint can at the other end, and threw it into a window in a building below and broke the window. He then swung himself into the apartment and, on the other side, shot a person he found.

EDUCATION

What law school boasts the most alumni who ended up being members of the U.S. Supreme Court?

Seventeen justices of the U.S. Supreme Court have graduated from Harvard Law School. They are:

- Justice Harry A. Blackmun
- Justice Louis Brandeis
- Justice William J. Brennan Jr.
- Justice Stephen Breyer
- Justice Harold Hitz Burton

Twenty-one Supreme Court justices attended Harvard Law School—four of whom went on to graduate from other institutions, leaving seventeen Harvard graduates to serve on the Court—making it the school with the highest number of Supreme Court alumni.

- Justice Benjamin Robbins Curtis
- Justice Felix Frankfurter
- Justice Neil M. Gorsuch
- Justice Horace Gray
- Justice Oliver Wendell Holmes Jr.
- Justice Elena Kagan
- Justice Anthony Kennedy
- Justice Lewis F. Powell Jr.
- Chief Justice John G. Roberts Jr.
- Justice Edward Terry Sanford
- Justice Antonin Scalia
- Justice David Souter

Several other justices attended Harvard Law School for a time but either transferred to another school or did not graduate. These include Justice Ruth Bader Ginsburg, who transferred to Columbia Law School; Justice Henry Billings Brown; Chief Justice Fuller; and Justice William Henry Moody.

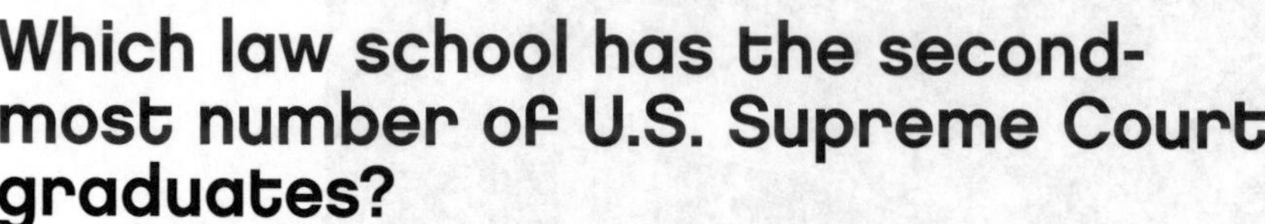

Which law school has the second-most number of U.S. Supreme Court graduates?

Yale Law School boasts nine members of the U.S. Supreme Court as graduates. They are:

- Justice Samuel A. Alito Jr.
- Justice David Davis
- Justice Abe Fortas
- Justice Brett M. Kavanaugh
- Justice Sherman Minton
- Justice Sonia Sotomayor
- Justice Potter Stewart
- Justice Clarence Thomas
- Justice Byron White

Who is the only U.S. Supreme Court justice to have attended the University of Texas Law School?

Justice Tom C. Clark is the only person who sat on the U.S. Supreme Court to have graduated from the University of Texas Law School.

Who is the only U.S. Supreme Court justice to have graduated from the University of Colorado Law School?

Justice Wiley Blount Rutledge, who later had a distinguished academic career before becoming a judge, is the only U.S. Supreme Court justice to have graduated from the University of Colorado.

DID YOU KNOW?

What U.S. Supreme Court justice was tutored by Horatio Alger?

Justice Benjamin N. Cardozo, who graduated from Columbia at the age of 19, had been tutored as a child by the popular novelist and Harvard graduate Horatio Alger.

What U.S. Supreme Court justice was formerly a member of the Ku Klux Klan?

Justice Black, from Alabama, had been a member of the Ku Klux Klan for a period of time in the 1920s. It is ironic because Justice Black later became a defender of civil rights and individual underdogs.

Justice Black himself addressed the reality of his Klan membership with the following words:

> My words and acts are a matter of public record. I believe that my record as a Senator refutes every implication of racial or religious intolerance. It shows that I was of a group of liberal Senators who have consistently fought for civil, economic, and religious rights of all Americans, without regard to race or creed.... I did join the Klan. I later resigned. I never rejoined. I have never considered and I do not now consider the unsolicited card given to me shortly after my nomination to the Senate as a membership of any kind in the Ku Klux Klan. I never used it. I did not even keep it. Before becoming a

Senator I dropped the Klan. I have had nothing to do with it since that time. I abandoned it.

Which U.S. Supreme Court justices were lifelong bachelors?

Five justices never married: Justice James Clark McReynolds, who served on the Court from 1914 to 1941; Justice Clarke, who served on the Court from 1916 to 1922; Justice Cardozo, who served on the Court from 1932 to 1938; Justice Frank Murphy, who served on the Court from 1940 to 1949; and current Justice Souter, who ascended to the bench in 1990.

Which U.S. Supreme Court justice graduated college at the age of 14?

Justice John Archibald Campbell graduated from the University of Georgia at the age of 14. He served on the U.S. Supreme

John Archibald Campbell was appointed to the Supreme Court in 1853 by President Franklin Pierce, serving until his retirement in 1861.

Court from 1853 to 1861. He resigned his Court seat at the start of the Civil War and became the Confederate government's assistant secretary of war.

What former U.S. Supreme Court justices served as law school deans?

Justice Horace Harmon Lurton, who served from 1909 to 1914, was dean of Vanderbilt University School of Law. Chief Justice Stone, who served from 1925 to 946, was dean of Columbia University Law School from 1910 to 1923. Justice Owen Roberts, who served from 1930 to 1945, was dean of the University of Pennsylvania Law School from 1948 to 1951. Justice Wiley Blount Rutledge, who served from 1943 to 1949, was dean of the University of Iowa Law School. Justice Kagan, who began serving on the Court in 2010, was dean of Harvard Law School.

What 20th-century U.S. Supreme Court justice never received a high school diploma?

Amazingly, Justice Charles Evans Whittaker, who served on the Court from 1957 to 1962, never graduated from high school or college. He obtained entrance to Kansas City Law School based on high test scores.

Which U.S. Supreme Court justices share the same birthday?

Justice Lucius Quintus Cincinnatus Lamar II, who served from 1888 to 1893; Chief Justice Warren E. Burger, who served from 1969 to 1986; and Justice David Souter, who served from 1990 to 2009, all were born on September 17. Justice Owen Roberts, who served from 1930 to 1945, and Justice Byrnes, who served from 1941 to 1942, were both born on May 2. Chief Justice Roger Brooke Taney and Justice Pierce Butler were both born on March 17. Justice Davis and Justice Samuel Blatchford were both born on March 9. Justice Thomas Todd and Justice Potter Stewart were both born on January 23.

Which former chief justices never had prior judicial experience before being appointed to the U.S. Supreme Court?

Seven of the nation's 17 chief justices in U.S. history did not have prior judicial experience before being appointed to the U.S. Supreme Court: Chief Justice John Marshall, Chief Justice Taney, Chief Justice Salmon P. Chase, Chief Justice Morrison Waite, Chief Justice Fuller, Chief Justice Earl Warren, and Chief Justice Rehnquist. Chief Justice Rehnquist initially was appointed as associate justice in 1972 and then became chief justice in 1986.

AGE

Which justices lived to be nanogenarians?

The following 10 justices lived to be at least 90 years of age:

- Justice John Paul Stevens (1920–2019): 99
- Justice Stanley Forman Reed (1884–1980): 95
- Justice Oliver Wendell Holmes Jr. (1841–1935): 93
- Justice Sandra Day O'Connor (1930–): 92
- Justice George Shiras Jr. (1832–1924): 92
- Justice Gabriel Duvall (1752–1844): 91
- Justice William J. Brennan Jr. (1906–1997): 91

DID YOU KNOW?

What justice had a famous feud wih Justice Hugo Black?

Justice Jackson wrote to President Truman of his nemesis on the U.S. Supreme Court, Justice Hugo Black, "If war is declared on me, I propose to wage it with the weapons of the open warrior, not those of the stealthy assassin." Justice Jackson and Justice Black feuded mightily during their tenure on the Court together in the 1940s and 1950s. Justice Jackson believed that Justice Black sabotaged his efforts at becoming chief justice of the U.S. Supreme Court.

- Justice Lewis F. Powell Jr. (1907–1998): 90
- Justice Harry A. Blackmun (1908–1999): 90
- Justice James Francis Byrnes (1882–1972): 90

Among these 10 is Justice Sandra Day O'Connor, who is still living at the time of this writing.

What justice was appointed at the age of 40?

Justice Douglas was the second-youngest justice to ever be appointed to the U.S. Supreme Court behind Justice Joseph Story, who was appointed when he was 32.

NICKNAMES

What justice was known as "the Notorious RBG"?

Justice Ginsburg, the second woman to serve on the U.S. Supreme Court, became a virtual rock star in her later years as well

Only the second woman to serve on the Supreme Court, Ruth Bader Ginsburg had spent her legal career advocating for equal gender rights. Once appointed, she solidified her reputation as a champion of individual rights and rose to the status of a cultural icon.

as a pop culture icon. In 2013, New York University law student Shana Knizknick gave Justice Ginsburg the nickname "the Notorious RBG" after reading one of her powerful dissenting opinions. Knizknick's nickname was a play on the moniker of the deceased popular rap musician Biggie Smalls, who was better known as "the Notorious BIG."

Justice Ginsburg actually embraced the pop culture icon status and even the comparison to the Notorious BIG. At a speech at an Ivy League law school, she pointed out that, after all, both she and the Notorious BIG had been born and grown up in Brooklyn, New York.

Which two justices were sometimes called "the Arizona Twins"?

Chief Justice Rehnquist and Justice O'Connor were sometimes called "the Arizona Twins" since both lived and worked as lawyers in that state. The two were law school classmates at Stanford Law School. The two dated in law school, and, according to Renee Knake Jefferson and Hannah Brenner Johnson in their book *Shortlisted: Women in the Shadows of the Supreme Court*, Chief Justice Rehnquist "proposed marriage to her soon after both graduated from Stanford Law School in 1952. They enjoyed a lifelong friendship and served together on the U.S. Supreme Court for many years. In fact, the first time O'Connor ever visited the Supreme Court, she was there to attend Rehnquist's swearing-in ceremony for the Court."

Which two justices were known as "the Minnesota Twins"?

Chief Justice Burger and Justice Blackmun were known as "the Minnesota Twins," as both were from that state. At one time, they were very close friends, with Justice Blackmun even serving as a groomsman at Chief Justice Burger's wedding. During their time together on the Court, they drifted a bit apart, as Justice Blackmun moved more to the left and Chief Justice Burger was more conservative.

Which justices were known as "the Four Horsemen"?

"The Four Horsemen" referred to a group of four older justices who served as a conservative bloc on the Court. They were known for thwarting many parts of President Franklin D. Roosevelt's "New Deal" legislation. They were Justice Butler, Justice Willis Van Devanter, Justice George Sutherland, and Justice McReynolds.

POLITICAL AMBITIONS

Which chief justice sought the presidency in 1868 and 1872?

Chief Justice Salmon P. Chase, who served as the country's sixth chief justice of the U.S. Supreme Court from 1864 to 1873,

DID YOU KNOW?

Which justice was called "the Lone Ranger"?

Chief Justice Rehnquist was dubbed "the Lone Ranger" by his law clerks in the early 1970s because he had a habit of filing solitary dissents. When he was an associate justice on the Burger Court, Chief Justice Rehnquist was often the most conservative member on the Court and, thus, was ideologically alone in several areas of jurisprudence.

sought the Democratic nomination for president in 1868 and the Republican nomination for president in 1872.

Chief Justice Chase was a career politician who served in all three branches of the federal government, as he was not only a U.S. Supreme Court justice but also a former U.S. senator from his home state of Ohio, served as the secretary of the treasury under President Abraham Lincoln, and was the former governor of Ohio.

Which justice resigned from the Court in 1916 to run for president?

Chief Justice Hughes resigned his position as associate justice on the U.S. Supreme Court when he received the Republican nomination for president in 1916. Chief Justice Hughes, a Republican, challenged Democratic incumbent President Woodrow Wilson. Chief Justice Hughes was considered the favorite in the election and carried many of the states in the Northeast, including New York.

However, President Wilson dominated the southern and western parts of the country and won a second term. For his part,

Chief Justice Hughes later served as U.S. secretary of state under President Warren G. Harding. Later in his life in 1930, President Herbert Hoover named Chief Justice Hughes as chief justice of the U.S. Supreme Court.

Which justices helped to decide the presidential election of 1876?

The presidential election between Republican Rutherford B. Hayes and Democrat Samuel Tilden was hotly contested. Tilden actually won the popular vote, but neither candidate captured the required number of electoral votes. Tilden led the electoral vote count 184–165, but 20 electoral votes remained from four states that were disputed. Either candidate needed 185 electoral votes in order to capture the election.

Congress created a 15-member Electoral Commission to determine who won the election. Five members came from the Sen-

Charles E. Hughes was appointed associate justice of the Supreme Court in 1910 by President Taft, but he resigned in 1916 to campaign against incumbent President Wilson. He would join the Supreme Court again as Chief Justice in 1930, appointed by President Hoover, and serve until his retirement in 1941.

ate, five members from the House, and five members from the U.S. Supreme Court for the total of 15 members. The majority party got three, and the minority party in each House got two. Because the Republicans controlled the Senate, they had three members to the Democrats' two members. Because the Democrats were the majority party in the House, they got three members and the Republicans two. Four Court seats were set by two Republicans, Justice Miller and Justice William Strong, and two Democrats, Justice Nathan Clifford and Justice Stephen Johnson Field. The fifth U.S. Supreme Court member was to be Justice Davis, who was considered an independent. However, he resigned from the Commission after he left the Court to become a U.S. senator in Illinois. The fifth seat went to Justice Joseph P. Bradley, a Republican.

The Committee was thus composed of eight Republicans and seven Democrats. The Commission voted 8–7 in favor of giving the disputed 20 electoral votes to Republican Rutherford B. Hayes. Thus, Rutherford B. Hayes became president.

What justice served as a key political advisor to President Lyndon Baines Johnson?

Justice Abe Fortas was a key advisor to President Lyndon Baines Johnson even when Justice Fortas served on the Court. David O'Brien writes in his book *Storm Center*: "The President [Johnson] considered Fortas to be in his elite group of foreign policy advisors. Regularly joining White House meetings on the Vietnam War, Fortas attended more cabinet meetings than the man he replaced on the bench, UN Ambassador Arthur Goldberg." O'Brien notes that Justice Fortas also "attended meetings on fiscal policy, labor legislation, election reform, and campaign financing."

RACE

Who was the first African American to be seriously considered for a U.S. Supreme Court appointment?

William Hastie (1904–1976) was the first African American to be seriously considered for the U.S. Supreme Court. Hastie was seriously considered by President John F. Kennedy to replace Justice Charles Evans Whittaker in 1962. However, President Kennedy selected Justice Byron White for the seat.

Hastie graduated first in his class at Amherst University and then obtained a law degree from Harvard. In 1937, President Franklin D. Roosevelt appointed Hastie as a federal district judge for the Virgin Islands, making him the first African American federal judge. More than 10 years later in 1949, President Harry S. Truman elevated Hastie to the U.S. Court of Appeals for the Third Circuit, and he obtained another first: the first African American to be named to a federal appeals court judgeship. Hastie served on the Third Circuit until his passing in 1976.

Who was the first African American justice to be appointed to the U.S. Supreme Court?

Justice Thurgood Marshall—who previously had served as U.S. solicitor general and the U.S. Court of Appeals for the Second Circuit—was the first African American to be appointed to the U.S. Supreme Court. President Lyndon Baines Johnson famously said of his pick on the Court in June 1967: "I believe it is the right thing to do, the right time to do it, the right man and the right place."

Justice Marshall was best known, of course, for his civil rights advocacy on behalf of the NAACP and his many litigating triumphs on the U.S. Supreme Court. He advocated so effectively on behalf of those issues that he was called "Mr. Civil Rights."

Who was the second African American justice to serve on the U.S. Supreme Court?

Justice Clarence Thomas was appointed by President George H.W. Bush in 1991 to replace Justice Thurgood Marshall. Justice Thomas had served briefly as a federal appeals court judge on the U.S. Court of Appeals for the D.C. Circuit before his historic nomination. "Judge Thomas's life is a model for all Americans, and he's earned the right to sit on this nation's highest court," said President Bush.

Justice Thomas survived a tough confirmation process, highlighted by charges of sexual harassment from his former employee, law professor Anita Hill, by a vote of 52–48. He remains on the Court at the time of this writing and is the justice with the most seniority on the current Court.

GENDER

Which female jurist first was considered a potential U.S. Supreme Court nominee?

Judge Florence Allen, who served on both the Ohio Supreme Court and the U.S. Court of Appeals for the Sixth Circuit, was considered as a potential U.S. Supreme Court nominee during the time when President Franklin D. Roosevelt held office. However, President Roosevelt never nominated her. Judge Allen was the first female to serve on a state high court, which she did in Ohio. She also was the first woman to serve on a U.S. federal appeals court

Florence Allen served on the Sixth Circuit from her appointment by FDR in 1934 until her death in 1966. She was considered for the Supreme Court but never nominated.

when President Roosevelt nominated her for the Sixth Circuit post in 1934, where she served until 1966. The Senate unanimously confirmed Judge Allen for the Sixth Circuit post.

Renee Knake Jefferson and Hannah Brenner Johnson, in their book *Shortlisted: Women in the Shadows of the Supreme Court*, refer to Judge Allen as "the first shortlisted woman." People in the Hoover administration considered Judge Allen as a U.S. Supreme Court candidate before his successors, President Roosevelt and President Harry S. Truman, did. Jefferson and Johnson explain: "Allen was revered and respected as a jurist. Her gender did not seem to impact public perception of her competence or qualification."

What female lawyer made the shortlist of U.S. Supreme Court candidates during the Kennedy and Johnson administrations?

Soia Mentschikoff, a distinguished American lawyer and law professor, made the shortlist during both the Kennedy and

DID YOU KNOW?

Who was the first woman of color shortlisted for the U.S. Supreme Court?

Judge Amalya Lyle Kearse was shortlisted for the U.S. Supreme Court by both President Ronald Reagan and President Bill Clinton. Her brilliance and achievements were recognized by politicians on both sides of the political aisle. President Jimmy Carter had appointed her to the U.S. Court of Appeals for the Second Circuit in 1979. Judge Kearse remains a senior judge on the Second Circuit at the time of this writing. She took senior status in 2002. Judge Kearse is also known as a world-class bridge player, having won several national championships in the game.

Johnson administrations. She started college at the age of 15 and earned her law degree at Columbia Law School at the age of 22. She then worked at a Wall Street firm in New York, making partner. She also made history in 1947 when she became the first woman to teach at Harvard Law School. She left Harvard to teach at the University of Chicago. In 1974, she became the dean at Miami Law School, becoming the first female to serve as a law school dean.

What female lawyer made the shortlist during the Nixon administration?

President Richard Nixon seriously considered placing Mildred Little on the U.S. Supreme Court. Little served on the City of Los Angeles Municipal Court, the County of Los Angeles Superior Court, and the California Court of Appeals. Jefferson and Johnson write: "Lillie came the closest any woman had before her to being selected for the Supreme Court. Her presence on President Nixon's publicly revealed shortlist garnered both support and controversy."

What females have served on the U.S. Supreme Court?

Six women have served on the U.S. Supreme Court: Justice O'Connor, Justice Ginsburg, Justice Sotomayor, Justice Kagan, Justice Amy Coney Barrett, and Justice Ketanji Brown Jackson.

RELIGION

Who was the first Catholic justice on the Court?

Chief Justice Taney was the first Catholic jurist on the U.S. Supreme Court. President Andrew Jackson appointed Chief Justice Taney, however, not because of his religious views; Chief Justice Taney had been a close advisor to President Jackson.

Who was the first person of the Jewish faith to be seriously considered for a U.S. Supreme Court position?

Judah Benjamin, a senator from Louisiana, was offered a position to the Court by President Millard Fillmore in 1853, but Benjamin declined the position. Benjamin later served as the secretary of state under President Jefferson Davis of the Confederacy. When the Civil War ended, Benjamin fled the United States to England, where he had a successful career as a barrister.

Who was the first Jewish justice on the Court?

Justice Brandeis, who served on the Court from 1916 to 1939, was the first person of the Jewish faith to serve on the U.S. Supreme Court. Justice Brandeis encountered anti-Semitism during the confirmation process and also while he was justice. Justice McReynolds refused to take part in the Court's annual picture because it meant that he would have to stand next to Justice Brandeis.

What other Jewish people have served on the U.S. Supreme Court?

After Justice Brandeis, other people of the Jewish faith to serve on the U.S. Supreme Court have been Justice Cardozo, Justice Frankfurter, Justice Goldberg, Justice Fortas, Justice Ginsburg, and Justice Breyer.

OTHER FIRSTS

What justice had the first televised confirmation hearings?

Justice O'Connor, the first woman to be nominated to the U.S. Supreme Court, had the first televised confirmation hearings.

Which justice holds the record for the most lone dissents?

Justice Douglas holds the record, with 208 lone dissenting opinions.

Sandra Day O'Connor, shown here being sworn in by Chief Justice Warren Burger, was both the first female Supreme Court justice and the first justice whose confirmation hearings were televised.

FAMOUS PHRASES

Which justice wrote that he couldn't define obscenity, but "I know it when I see it"?

Justice Stewart wrote in a concurring opinion in *Jacobellis v. Ohio* (1964): "I shall not today attempt further to define the kinds of material I understand to be embraced within that shorthand description; and perhaps I could never succeed in intelligibly doing so. But I know it when I see it, and the motion picture involved in this case is not that."

The movie in question was a French drama film entitled *Les Amants* (meaning "The Lovers"), featuring French actress Jeanne Moreau. The phrase became one of the most well-known and oft-cited phrases in modern U.S. Supreme Court history. Justice Stewart later regretted that his phrase became so popular, saying: "I think that's going to be on my tombstone."

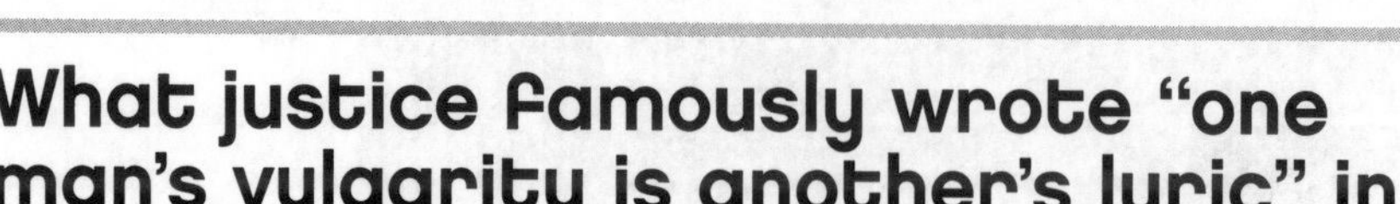

What justice famously wrote "one man's vulgarity is another's lyric" in a First Amendment case?

Justice John Marshall Harlan II wrote these words in his majority opinion in *Cohen v. California* (1971). The Court reversed the breach-of-the-peace conviction imposed on Paul Robert Cohen for wearing a jacket bearing the words "Fuck the Draft" into a Los Angeles County Courthouse. Justice Harlan ruled that Cohen essentially was being punished merely for offensive language and followed up with the classic phrase, "one man's vulgarity is another's lyric."

What justice used the term "the ugly abyss of racism" in a dissenting opinion?

Justice Murphy, who was a consistent defender of individual freedoms, used this evocative phrase in his dissenting opinion in *Korematsu v. United States* (1944). In *Korematsu,* the Court upheld the constitutionality of the internment of Japanese American citizens during the time of World War II. Justice Murphy disagreed vehemently with the decision and, in dissent, criticized the internment program as one that "goes over the very brink of constitutional power and falls into the ugly abyss of racism."

What justice wrote that "our whole constitutional heritage rebels at the thought of giving government the power to control men's minds"?

Justice Thurgood Marshall wrote these powerful words in *Stanley v. Georgia* (1969), a case involving the prosecution of a

man for possessing allegedly obscene materials in his home. While obscenity is not a form of protected speech, Justice Marshall believed that the state of Georgia exceeded its power in punishing a man for the films he watched in his own home.

Which justice wrote these infamous words: "The paramount destiny and mission of women are to fulfill the noble and benign offices of wife and mother"?

Justice Bradley wrote these infamous words in his concurring opinion in *Bradwell v. Illinois* (1873), an early example of the gender iniquity in society. Myra Bradwell had passed the Illinois Bar in 1969 but was denied the right to practice law in the state because she was a woman. She carried her fight to the U.S. Supreme Court, but the Court reasoned that the state of Illinois had the right to determine who practiced law in the state and rejected Bradwell's constitutional claims.

Joseph Philo Bradley was appointed to the Supreme Court in 1870 by President Ulysses S. Grant, serving until his death in 1892.

Justice Bradley wrote a concurring opinion in which he elaborated on the role of women in society: "The natural and proper timidity and delicacy which belongs to the female sex evidently unfits it for many of the occupations of civil life.... The paramount destiny and mission of women are to fulfill the noble and benign offices of wife and mother. This is the law of the Creator."

The Illinois Supreme Court later granted her admission to practice law in 1890, and the U.S. Supreme Court did so as well in 1892.

Further Reading

Asch, Sidney H. *The Supreme Court and Its Great Justices*. New York: Arco, 1971.

Ball, Howard. *Hugo L. Black: Cold Steel Warrior*. New York: Oxford University Press, 1996.

Bass, Jack. *Unlikely Heroes*. Tuscaloosa: University of Alabama Press, 1990.

Bent, Silas. *Justice Oliver Wendell Holmes*. New York: The Vanguard Press, 1932.

Bickel, Alexander M. *The Least Dangerous Branch: The Supreme Court at the Bar of Politics*. 2nd edition. New Haven, CT: Yale University Press, 1986.

Biskupic, Joan. *Sandra Day 0'Connor: How the First Woman on the Supreme Court Became Its Most Influential Justice*. New York: Ecco/HarperCollins, 2005.

———. *American Original: The Life and Constitution of Supreme Court Justice Antonin Scalia*. New York: MacMillian, 2009.

———. *The Chief: The Life and Turbulent Times of Chief Justice John Roberts*. New York, Basic Books, 2019.

Black, Charles L. *The Unfinished Business of the Warren Court*, 46 *Washington Law Review* 3 (1970).

Blasi, Vincent. ed. *The Burger Court: The Counterrevolution That Wasn't*. New Haven, CT: Yale University Press, 1983.

Bobelian, Michael. *Battle for the Marble Palace: Abe Fortas, Earl Warren, Lyndon Johnson, Richard Nixon and the Forging of the Modern Supreme Court*. Tucson, AZ: Schaffner Press, 2019.

Breyer, Stephen G. *Active Liberty: Interpreting Our Democratic Constitution.* New York: Alfred A. Knopf, 2005.

Burns, James MacGregor. *Packing the Courts: The Rise of Judicial Power and the Coming Crisis of the Supreme Court.* New York: Penguin Publishing Group, 2009.

Canellos, Peter S. *The Great Dissenter: The Story of John Marshall Harlan, America's Judicial Hero.* New York: Simon & Schuster, 2021.

Carter, Robert, and Thurgood Marshall. "The Meaning and Significance of the Supreme Court Decree," 24 *Journal of Negro Education* 397 (Summer 1955).

Cox, Archibald. *The Court and the Constitution.* Boston: Houghton Mifflin, 1987.

Cushman, Claire. Ed. *The Supreme Court Justices: Illustrated Biographies, 1789-1995.* 2nd edition. Washington, DC: Congressional Quarterly, 1995.

Davis, Sue. *Justice Rehnquist and the Constitution.* Princeton, NJ: Princeton University Press, 1989.

De Hart, Jane Sherron. *Ruth Bader Ginsburg: A Life.* New York: Alfred A Knopf, 2018.

Douglas, William O. *Points of Rebellion.* New York: Random House, 1970.

———. *Court Years 1939–1975: The Autobiography of William O. Douglas.* New York: Random House, 1980.

Driver, Justin. *The Schoolhouse Gate: Public Education, the Supreme Court, and the American Mind.* New York: Pantheon Books, 2018.

Feldman, Noah. *Scorpions: The Battles and Triumphs of FDR's Great Supreme Court Justices.* New York: Twelve, 2010.

Fisher, Louis. *Supreme Court Expansion of Presidential Power.* Lawrence, KS: University Press of Kansas, 2017.

Foskett, Ken. *Judging Thomas: The Life and Times of Clarence Thomas.* New York: William Morrow, 2004.

Frank, John P. *Historical Bases of the Federal Judicial System*, 13 *Law & Contemporary Problems* 3 (1948).

Frank, John P. *Marble Palace: The Supreme Court in American Life*. New York: Alfred A. Knopf, 1958.

Frank, John P. *Clement Haynesworth, the Senate and the Supreme Court*. Charlottesville, VA: University Press of Virginia, 1991.

Ginsburg, Ruth Bader. *My Own Words*. New York: Simon & Schuster, 2016.

Greenburg, Jan Crawford. *Supreme Conflict: The Inside Story of the Struggle for Control of the United States Supreme Court*. New York: Penguin, 2008.

Greenhouse, Linda. *Becoming Justice Blackmun: Harry Blackmun's Supreme Court Journey*. New York: Times Books, 2006.

Holmes, Oliver Wendell Jr. *The Common Law*. Boston: Little, Brown, 1881.

Hudson, David L. Jr. *The Rehnquist Court: Understanding Its Impact and Legacy*. Westport, CT: Praeger, 2007.

Hughes, Charles Evans. *The Autobiographical Notes of Charles Evans Hughes*. Boston: Harvard University Press, 1973.

Hutchinson, Dennis. *The Man Who Once Was Whizzer White: A Portrait of Byron R. White*. New York: Free Press, 1998.

Irons, Peter. *The Courage of Their Convictions: Sixteen Americans Who Fought Their Way to the Supreme Court*. New York: Free Press, 1988.

———. *Brennan vs. Rehnquist: The Battle for the Constitution*. New York: Alfred A. Knopf, 1994.

———. *A People's History of the Supreme Court*. New York: Viking, 1999.

Jeffries, John C. *Justice Lewis F. Powell, Jr: A Biography*. New York: Fordham University Press, 2001.

Jenkins, John A. *The Partisan: The Life of William Rehnquist*. New York: Public Affairs, 2012.

Kalman, Laura. *Abe Fortas: A Biography*. New Haven: Yale University Press, 1990.

Karlan, Pamela S. *A Constitution for All Times*. The MIT Press, Cambridge, Mass, 2013.

Kaufman, Andrew L. *Cardozo*. Boston: Harvard University Press, 1998.

King, Willard L. *Melville Fuller: Chief Justice of the United States, 1888–1910*. New York: MacMillan, 1950.

Kluger, Richard. *Simple Justice: The History of Brown v. Board of Education and Black America's Struggle for Equality*. New York: Alfred A. Knopf, 1975.

Knight, Alfred H. *The Life of the Law*. New York: Crown Publishers, 1996.

Lazarus, Edward. *Closed Chambers: The First Eyewitness Account of the Epic Struggles Inside the Supreme Court*. New York: Crown, 1998.

Lee, Mike. *Saving Nine: The Fight Against the Left's Audacious Plan to Pack the Supreme Court and Destroy American Liberty*. New York: Center Street, 2022.

Lessig, Lawrence. *Fidelity & Constraint: How the Supreme Court Has Read the American Constitution*. London, Oxford University Press, 2019.

Lewis, Anthony. *Gideon's Trumpet*. New York: Random House, 1964.

———. *Make No Law: The Sullivan Case and the First Amendment*. New York: Random House, 1991.

McCloskey, Robert. *The American Supreme Court*. Chicago: Chicago University Press, 2000.

Murphy, Bruce Allen. *Wild Bill: The Legend and Life of William O. Douglas*. New York: Random House, 2003.

Murphy, Bruce Allen. *Scalia: A Court of One*. New York: Simon & Schuster, 2014.

Newman, Roger K. *Hugo Black: A Biography*. New York, Pantheon Books, 1994.

Newton, Jim. *Justice for All: Earl Warren and the Nation He Made*. New York: Riverhead Books, 2006.

O'Brien, David M. *Storm Center: The Supreme Court in American Politics*. New York: W.W. Norton, 1986.

O'Connor, Sandra Day. *Out of Order*. New York: Random House, 2014.

O'Connor, Sandra Day, and H. Alan Day. *The Majesty of the Law: Reflections of a Supreme Court Justice*. New York: Random House, 2004.

Pack, Michael, and Mark Paoletta. *Created Equal: Clarence Thomas in His Own Words*. Washington, DC: Regnery Publishing, 2022.

Paul, Joel Richard. *Without Precedent: John Marshall and His Times*. New York: Riverhead Books, 2018.

Pearson, Drew. *The Nine Old Men*. Garden City, NY: Doubleday Doran & Co., 1937.

Peltason, J.W. *Fifty-Eight Lonely Men: Southern Federal Judges and School Desegregation*. Champaign, IL: University of Illinois Press, 1971.

Powell, H. Jefferson. *The Original Understanding of Original Intent*. 98 *Harvard Law Review* 885 (1985).

Rodell, Fred. *Nine Men: A Political History of the Supreme Court from 1790 to 1955*. New York: Random House, 1955.

Scalia, Antonin. *A Matter of Interpretation: Federal Courts and the Law*. Princeton, NJ: Princeton University Press, 1997.

Schwartz, Bernard. *Super Chief: Earl Warren and His Supreme Court*. New York: New York University Press, 1983.

———. *A History of the Supreme Court*. New York: Oxford University Press, 1993.

Simon, James F. *Independent Journey: The Life of William O. Douglas*. New York: Harper & Row, 1980.

Smith, Jean Edward. *John Marshall: Definer of a Nation*. New York: Henry Holt, 2006.

Sotomayor, Sonia. *My Beloved World.* New York: Alfred A. Knopf, 2013.

Starr, Kenneth W. *First among Equals: The Supreme Court in American Life*. New York: Warner Books, 2002.

Stern, Seth, and Stephen Wermiel. *Justice Brennan: Liberal Champion.* Boston: Houghton Mifflin, 2010.

Stevens, John Paul. *Five Chiefs: A Supreme Court Memoir.* New York: Little, Brown, 2011.

———. *The Making of a Justice.* New York: Little, Brown, 2018.

Story, Joseph. *Commentaries on the Constitution of the United States.* Boston: Gray & Co., 1833.

Thomas, Clarence. *My Grandfather's Son: A Memoir.* New York: HarperCollins, 2007.

Toobin, Jeffrey. *The Nine: Inside the Secret World of the Supreme Court.* New York: Doubleday, 2012.

Tribe, Laurence. *God Save This Honorable Court.* New York: Random House, 1985.

Tushnet, Mark V. *Making Civil Rights Law: Thurgood Marshall and the Supreme Court.* New York: Oxford University Press, 1996.

Urofsky, Melvin I. *Dissent and the Supreme Court: Its Role in the Court's History and the Nation's Constitutional Dialogue.* New York: Random House, 2015.

Williams, Juan. *Thurgood Marshall: An American Revolutionary.* New York: Crown, 2000.

Woodward, Bob, and Scott Armstrong. *The Brethren.* New York: Simon & Schuster, 1979.

Yarbrough, Tinsley E. *John Marshall Harlan: Great Dissenter of the Warren Court.* New York: Oxford University Press, 1992.

———. *Judicial Enigma: The First Justice Harlan.* New York: Oxford University Press, 1995.

Zelden, Charles L. *Thurgood Marshall: Race, Rights, and the Struggle for a More Perfect Union.* New York: Routledge, 2013.

INDEX

NOTE: (ILL.) INDICATES PHOTOS AND ILLUSTRATIONS

D

G

H

P

S

U

V

Y–Z